THE BOOK OF
JEWISH WISDOM

THE BOOK OF

JEWISH
WISDOM

The Talmud of the
Well-Considered Life

EDITED BY

JACOB NEUSNER

· AND ·

NOAM M. M. NEUSNER

CONTINUUM · NEW YORK

1996

The Continuum Publishing Company
370 Lexington Avenue
New York, NY 10017

Printed in the United States of America

Library of Congress Cataloging-in-Publication Data

Talmud. English. Selections.
    The book of Jewish wisdom : the Talmud of the well-considered life/
edited by Jacob Neusner and Noam M.M. Neusner.
       p.   cm.
    Includes bibliographical references and index.
    ISBN 0-8264-0890-7 (hardcover : alk. paper)
    1. Wisdom—Religious aspects—Judaism—Quotations, maxims, etc.
2. Ethics in rabbinical literature—Quotations, maxims, etc.
3. Conduct of life—Quotations, maxims, etc. I. Neusner, Jacob, 1932– .
II. Neusner, Noam M. M. (Noam Mordecai Menahem) III. Title.

BM499.5.E52N48 1996
296.1'20521—dc20
                                                  95-46768
                                                  CIP

For Andrea Joy Neusner

Contents

Preface

Out of the treasures of the religion set forth by the Torah, the religion the world knows as Judaism, come insights into the human condition, truths for the well-considered life, that everyone may share. Centuries of reflection upon the meaning of everyday events, the outcome of folly, and the reward of wisdom in ordinary affairs have constituted a long period of tradition. Guided by the Torah, the ancient Judaic sages wrote down what they had learned out of the past and observed for themselves, setting forth this wisdom over time.

Here we present principal parts of the Judaic tradition of wisdom, concentrating on the oral part of the Torah, represented by the documents of law and scriptural exegesis, the Talmud of Babylonia and the Midrash-compilations, respectively. The Talmud (encompassing both law and scriptural exegesis, *halakhah* and *aggadah*) is one of the great classical writings of human civilization—enduring, influential, nourishing. It claims its place among the most successful pieces of writing in the history of humanity, along with the Bible, Plato's *Republic*, Aristotle's *Politics*, the Qur'an, and a very few other writings.

What those books have in common is the power to demand attention and compel response for many centuries after their original presentation. The Qur'an, for example, is received by Muslims as God's word, as is the Bible by Christians and the Torah—comprised of the Hebrew Scriptures or Old Testament and the oral traditions ultimately preserved in the Talmud—by the faithful of Judaism. For generations beyond memory, the Talmud exercised the power to impart its ideals of virtue, moral and intellectual, and so shaped generations of Israel into a single intellectual model, one of enormous human refinement. Here is what, for the Torah, it means to be a human being, in God's likeness, after God's model.

Among those great and enduring classics of humanity, the Talmud, like the great Hindu classic, the *Mahabharata*, is distinctive because it is not really a book but a living tradition, a focus for ongoing participation in age upon succeeding age. The anthropologist of Hindu religion, William Saxe, states, "The *Mahabharata* . . . was not a book at all, but rather an oral epic . . . a tradition more than a book . . . not only a book but also a political model, a bedtime story, a tradition of dance, a dramatic spectacle, and much much more." The same is true of the Talmud. It is not so much a book as an intellectual enterprise for eternity. It contains notes on the basis of which we may reconstruct a conversation, insights out of which we may recapitulate experience, above all, wisdom from which we may draw guidance on the path of life. And in these pages we cull out of the Talmud and its associated documents the wisdom that the Torah offers to humanity in the twenty-first century.

The senior editor expresses thanks for ongoing support of research and a life of learning to the University of South Florida, where he holds the position of Distinguished Research Professor of Religious Studies. A full-service university on the urban frontier, USF provides an ideal setting for research bearing both academic value and, as in the case of this anthology, broad public interest.

Further gratitude goes to Bard College, the base of a visiting professorship at the time of the editing of this book, for enriching collegiality in a stellar department and for the opportunity to participate in yet another kind of higher education.

The junior editor expresses thanks to *The Tampa Tribune*, a university of another kind devoted to the examination of the human condition.

JACOB NEUSNER
NOAM MORDECAI MENAHEM NEUSNER

Introduction

These questions did Alexander (the Great) of Macedonia ask the elders of the South.

He said to them, "Who is called wise?"

They said to him, "Who is wise? He who has foresight."

He said to them, "Who is called mighty?"

They said to him, "Who is mighty? He who overcomes his impulses."

He said to them, "Who is called rich?"

They said to him, "Who is rich? He who is satisfied with his portion."

He said to them, "What should a person do to live?"

They said to him, "He should kill his 'self.'" (He should be so humble as to merit eternal life.)

"What should someone do to die?"

"He should resurrect his 'self.'" (He should so indulge himself as to merit eternal death.)

BAVLI TAMID 32A
TRANSLATED BY PETER HAAS

What Is Wisdom?

Wisdom is the formulation, in affecting stories and pithy sayings, of experienced and sound judgment about living a well-considered life—one of proportion, foresight, good sense, and reflection. Wisdom records what humanity has learned from experience. Wisdom discerns out of many, comparable events a governing truth and formulates that truth in rules to guide the formation of character and conduct and conscience. The opposite of the wisdom is foolishness. For while the fool learns nothing from what happens and so repeats the same mistake, the wise person draws conclusions from mistakes and acts upon them. The difference between the one and the other is never the first, but always the second, act of stupidity, which only the fool commits.

How does wisdom take place? If in the everyday world we see repeated both the same act and the same result and draw the conclusion
that, if we do such an act, then the result will be thus and so, that process of observation, reflection, analysis, and critical judgment yields wisdom. Then, cast in the form of a compelling, exemplary story or a
well-crafted saying, wisdom takes on a life of its own. It goes on its
journey, from one life to another, from one social order to the next.

Because the insights of wisdom see deep into the universal givens
of the human condition, in the premise that, differ though we may, a
certain reason and order prevail across boundaries of ethnic origin, national language and loyalty, class and culture, wisdom means to speak
universal truths. Christians may learn from wisdom nurtured in the
setting of Judaism, and vice versa; Buddhists can teach the West, and
Muslims teach East and West alike. People who do not believe in God
may share their insight with people who do. For the human condition
of birth, growth to maturity, love, marriage, home and family, sickness,
suffering, old age and death, virtue and vice, foolishness and intelligence—that human condition defines the issues on which, in one way
or another, all of us everywhere reflect.

Wisdom encompasses common sense, but transcends it. For wisdom
recapitulates not the obvious but the paradoxical. Wisdom does its work
through the contrast of opposites. Take for instance the following saying:

> R.[1] Simeon b. Eleazar says, "(1) Do not try to make amends with
> your fellow when he[2] is angry, or (2) comfort him when the corpse
> of his beloved is lying before him, or (3) seek to find absolution
> for him at the moment at which he takes vow, or (4) attempt to see
> him when he is humiliated."
>
> TRACTATE ABOT 4:18

Here, common conduct leads to quick apology, shallow words of comfort, easy grace, and overbearing sympathy, shading over into conde-
scension. But wisdom's best sense counsels not to intrude in another

---

1. R. stands for Rabbi, a title of honor, best rendered as "my lord." It is not
particular to Classical Judaism, but was used in the Aramaic speaking world in
which many peoples lived as a term of respect. Where the sources give that
title—and they generally do—it is rendered in the translation.

2. Translations render the gender-usages of the texts. Hebrew uses "Adam"
to refer to both male and female, and it ordinarily uses "he" in a nonexclusionary
way, to speak of "he or she." Where that is not the case, the original text is
explicit. It would misrepresent the character of the sources presented here to
translate contemporary gender-usages into writings with their own rules for referring to both sexes in a single pronoun.

person's anger, grief, fit of temper, or moment of embarrassment. Making too-quick amends, bringing ill-timed comfort, relieving the burden of a vow taken in a fit of wrath, or confronting one who wants privacy—these are foolish actions, taken for a good motive. To mean well, therefore, is not necessarily to do the right thing, and good intention may mask self-indulgence. Timing matters too—and that is where wisdom takes over. The fool rushes in, the wise person possesses a certain delicacy and tact. Wisdom may stand for common sense, but more commonly, it represents an uncommon insight, a different way of seeing things, as in the counsel of Simeon b. Eleazar.

But each religious tradition, ethnic community, nation and language, culture and literature preserves its own special view of matters. A small group living by itself will see the social order differently from a small group living among other, hostile groups. A large and commanding nation will formulate discerning principles of conduct in indifference to matters deeply affecting weak and dependent ones. So while the human condition exhibits points of constancy, it also is mediated through circumstance and context, and these prove special. But the power of wisdom—the capacity to see the rule in the case—transcends these. Indeed, sages—wise men and women—must address the challenge of speaking across the ages and beyond the limits of place. That we can entertain the wisdom contained in Simeon b. Eleazar's statement and the colloquy of Alexander and the Judaic sages shows how the Judaic sages, nearly two millennia ago, transcended time and condition.

Reflecting deeply upon the particulars of a given circumstance, wisdom translates what is distinctive to a given place or time into generalizations of broad intelligibility. That is not because wisdom overcomes lines of difference. Rather, by its very nature, its focus upon the human condition, wisdom moves from the case to the principle and so by nature treats what appears different as representative of what may turn out quite universal, the distinctive as indicative of humanity in general. The specificities of a given religion will then define the setting and dictate the idiom of thought. But the power of wisdom to translate the specific into the human, therefore the universal, condition—observations, reflection, critical analysis—also endows wisdom with the strength to overcome difference. That is why, when we hear a saying formulated in terms of the specific, we may identify its main point with our own condition, however that may differ from the circumstance in which the saying is formulated.

Take for instance the following, which speaks of the case of holy Israel (that is, the religious community, not to be confused with today's State of Israel, a political entity) in particular, but addresses sensibility in general:

> Hillel says, "Do not walk out on the community. And do not have confidence in yourself until the day you die. And do not judge your companion until you are in his place. And do not say anything which cannot be heard, for in the end it will be heard. And do not say: When I have time, I shall study, for you may never have time."
>
> TRACTATE ABOT 2:4

Hillel's saying stresses an activity quite distinctive to the world of Judaism, which is study of the Torah, in the setting of truths that transcend frontiers. Responsibility to the community, humility down to death, forbearance in judgment, discretion—these virtues of soul and society alike apply universally. And practicing their opposites will bring downfall in any social order, not only the Israelite one to which Hillel speaks. But Hillel brings us to a very particular source of humanity's heritage of universal wisdom, the Judaic one.

The Wisdom of the Torah

This collection does not rely on fables or aphorisms, but on arguments and discussions. The wisdom here makes its case in a unique manner, and its creators tended to assume that their readers would understand. But that is not always so. To make this wisdom accessible, we recognize that it is not enough to simply state that it transcends time and place—it also has a unique character. So while we have just told you that the wisdom of Judaism moves beyond the boundaries of context and culture, it emanates from them all the same.

We impose an even stricter vision of Judaism's wisdom: not Jewish in the ethnic and cultural sense, but the wisdom derived from and defined by the Torah, which creates a supernatural community that calls itself the people Israel,[3] the holy people. We offer, in particular,

---

3. "Israel" referring to the supernatural community, heirs and continuators of the saints Abraham and Sarah and so onward, is not to be confused with the new nation begun in 1948. In the history of Judaism, from Scripture to the present day, "Israel" refers not to a particular place but to the holy people formed in response to the revelation of the Torah at Sinai. "He who keepeth Israel slumbereth not nor sleeps" (Ps. 121:2) refers not to the radar operators of the Israeli Air Force but to God, and the "Israel"of the Psalmist is the people

the teachings of the Talmud and related writings concerning the well-considered life. To situate the Talmud and related writings within Judaism, we have to explain what Judaism means by "the Torah" and how the Talmud and related writings fit into the Torah. That situation concerns not trivialities of history—where, when, why a given document was written or compiled—but religion: the place, within the narrative of a faith, that a given piece of writing wins for itself.

The word *Torah* stands for "the Teaching," meaning God's revelation to Moses at Sinai. That act of self-manifestation cannot be construed as a single moment in historical time, for Judaism receives the Torah as God's eternal will, God's instruction to holy Israel for all time, for every circumstance. That instruction takes form in writing first of all. "The Torah" refers in the first instance to the Pentateuch, the Five Books of Moses, Genesis, Exodus, Leviticus, Numbers, and Deuteronomy. These writings occupy a privileged position, but do not exhaust the contents of the Torah. For the Torah, as the word is understood by Judaism, encompasses the remainder of the Hebrew Scriptures of ancient Israel, divided into the Prophets (Joshua, Judges, Samuel, Kings, Isaiah, Jeremiah, Ezekiel, and the Twelve Minor Prophets), and the Writings (Psalms, Proverbs, Job, Song of Songs, Ruth, Lamentations, Ecclesiastes, Esther, Daniel, Ezra, Nehemiah, and Chronicles). All of the Hebrew Scriptures form a necessary component of the definition of the Torah—but they are not sufficient to complete that definition.

In this anthology we afford access to the wisdom not of the Hebrew Scriptures, which many know and read, but to another critical component of the Torah, one that, outside of circles of the learned, even within the Jewish community, is not well known. For by "the Torah" Judaism has meant not only the Hebrew Scriptures of ancient Israel ("the Old Testament" of Christianity), but also another set of documents as well, which are deemed to fit together with the Hebrew Scriptures and to form "the one whole Torah of Moses, our rabbi." These other documents are known, collectively, as "the Torah that is memorized," or the oral Torah: the components of the timeless revelation of God to Moses that are formulated orally and transmitted orally, through a chain of tradition.

---

chosen by God, from Abraham onward, for service. In the liturgy of the synagogue, "Israel" likewise refers to the supernatural community, not to a merely this-worldly, political, or ethnic entity. That "Israel" is, then, a religious—not an ethnic or a national—social group, comparable to the Church as "the mystical body of Christ" or "the Abode of Islam" as distinct from the specific nations that are Muslim, whether Malaysia or Libya.

This brings us back to the narrative of the faith that calls itself "the Torah," and that the world knows as "Judaism." According to the account of the revelation of Sinai that Judaic writings set forth, it was in two media that at Sinai God revealed the Torah to Moses, who is called "our rabbi," or "our lord." One is the familiar, written medium, and the other, the medium of memory. From Sinai forward this other part of the one whole Torah revealed by God to Moses at Sinai was handed on from master to disciple, as claimed in the opening sentence of a key component of the Torah, tractate Abot ("the fathers," or "the founders"). That sentence states:

> Moses received Torah at Sinai and handed it on to Joshua, Joshua to elders, and elders to prophets. And prophets handed it on to the men of the great assembly.
> They said three things: (1) "Be prudent in judgment. (2) "Raise up many disciples. (3) "Make a fence for the Torah."

Tractate Abot 1:1

Two things are important in this statement; first, the conviction that an oral tradition came forth from Sinai through a long, unbroken chain of learning; and, second, the first specific teaching beyond what is known in the written Torah. The statement assigned to the men of the great assembly does not quote the written part of the Torah, or Scripture, but stands on its own ground.

The importance of that fact for our definition of Judaism and its wisdom is simple. The masters listed in the remainder of tractate Abot, firmly situated in the chain of tradition of Sinai, between God and Moses, and end up as important figures in the Torah, even as they live in the first and second centuries of the Common Era. These same sages take prominent parts in the formation of the first document of normative Judaism beyond the Hebrew Scriptures, which is the Mishnah, a philosophical law-code completed at about 200 C.E. (= A.D.). And the Mishnah stands at the beginning of the writing down of the revealed tradition of Sinai, originally formulated orally and transmitted through memory, that accompanies, and imparts sense and significance to, the written part of the Torah. In a moment I shall identify the other principal parts of the oral Torah.

How, exactly, is the process of oral formulation and oral transmission recorded? Returning once more to the narrative account of the faith, we find this picture of the formulation and transmission of the Mishnah. These sages vastly preferred oral to written tradition, formulating the Mishnah to make it easy to remember, assuming the tradition was going to be memorized. That preference did not merely accommodate the limited technology of the day—with no such thing as a printing press, anything published had to be copied over and over again. It formed a strong preference, a matter of (for our sages) theology, replicating in their own day the way in which God handed to Moses the oral part of the Torah at Sinai. Here is how the publication of the Mishnah is portrayed, with God standing at the head of the chain of tradition:

> Our rabbis have taught on Tannaite authority:
> What is the order of Mishnah teaching? Moses learned it from the mouth of the All-Powerful.
> Aaron came in, and Moses repeated his chapter to him, and Aaron went forth and sat at the left hand of Moses. His sons came in, and Moses repeated their chapter to them, and his sons went forth. Eleazar sat at the right of Moses, and Itamar at the left of Aaron.
> R. Judah says, "At all times Aaron was at the right hand of Moses."
> Then the elders entered, and Moses repeated for them their Mishnah chapter. The elders went out. Then the whole people came in, and Moses repeated for them their Mishnah chapter. So it came about that Aaron repeated the lesson four times, his sons three times, the elders two times, and all the people once.
> Then Moses went out, and Aaron repeated his chapter for them. Aaron went out. His sons repeated their chapter. His sons went out. The elders repeated their chapter. So it turned out that everybody repeated the same chapter four times.
> On this basis said R. Eliezer, "A person is liable to repeat the lesson for his disciple four times. And it is an argument *a fortiori*: If Aaron, who studied from Moses himself, and Moses from the Almighty —so in the case of a common person who is studying with a common person, all the more so!"
> R. Aqiba says, "How on the basis of Scripture do we know that a person is obligated to repeat a lesson for his disciple until he learns it (however many times that takes)? As it is said, 'And you teach it to the children of Israel' (Deut. 31:19). And how do we know that that is until it will be well ordered in their mouth? 'Put it in their mouths' (Deut. 31:19). And how on the basis of Scripture do we know that he is liable to explain the various aspects of the matter? 'Now these are the ordinances which you shall put before them' (Exod. 31:1)."
>
> BAVLI ERUBIN 54B

The premise of this picture emerges clearly: the document is orally formulated and orally transmitted, without resorting to the medium of writing at all. And that means, so far as the presentation of the Mishnah is concerned, its authors assumed a public process of declamation.

The concept of a tradition concerning a scripture in addition to Scripture will not surprise the other principal religions of the West: Christianity and Islam. In insisting that the Hebrew Scriptures (in this case, "written Torah") take on sense and meaning only in dialogue with some other, authoritative tradition ("the oral Torah"), classical Judaism takes a position that Christians and Moslems can understand out of the resources of their own faith. They too possess or affirm the Scriptures of ancient Israel and also a necessary complement. Judaism is not the only religion to deem the Hebrew Scriptures as God-given but also incomplete. All Christians receive the Gospels, the Letters of Paul, and certain other writings as "the New Testament," which, together with "the Old Testament" (those same Hebrew Scriptures of ancient Israel), constitutes the Bible. The Old Testament then is read in light of the New; the Letter to the Hebrews shows how this takes place. Islam, likewise, values the Bible and respects both Judaism and Christianity, but finds the fullness of knowledge of God only in the seal of prophecy, in the Prophet and in the God-dictated Qu'ran. Nor do we have to leave our own country for another time and place for an important analogue. Another instance out of contemporary religious life in which the Bible is deemed holy and authoritative, but insufficient and incomplete, is the Mormon Church, which deems the Bible sacred but also sets forth the Book of Mormon as a further, essential component of God's revelation. It follows that diverse, important heirs of the revealed Scriptures of ancient Israel deem those Scriptures necessary but not sufficient accounts of God's self-manifestation to mankind.

To state matters simply: Just as Christianity reads the Old Testament through the prism of the New, so Judaism reads the written Torah in dialogue with the oral Torah. This topical anthology culls the teachings of wisdom that the oral part of the Torah sets forth. In the introduction, we define the specific documents that embody that oral part of the Torah. Here is a selection of what "our sages of blessed memory," as the sages of the oral Torah are called, have to teach all who search in, among other places, the other part of the Torah that is Judaism for the wisdom to live a well-ordered, well-considered life. Since wisdom, by definition, addresses not holy Israel in particular but the human condition in general, teaching the laws of life to whom it may concern, we expect that there will be many who come in quest. We are confident they will find rewards in these teachings of "our sages of blessed memory."

What Is Jewish Wisdom?

Now that the standing of the documents that contribute our repertoire of the wisdom of Judaism is clear, let us turn to the particular character of that wisdom, which means at once to speak out of the experience of holy Israel and to address all those who seek to live the well-considered life. Let us take a single case, which gives us a foretaste of what we should expect. Here is an explicit statement of what our sages of blessed memory mean by "wisdom," the sort of action and attitude that, in their view, exemplify wisdom, in so many words. The Talmud does not identify the speaker or the audience, which means the Talmud itself is speaking, and you and we are the audience: a conversation that takes place in an eternity, unbound by context or circumstance, limited only by insight and truth:

> There is the following story.
>
> There was a Jerusalemite who went to a town, where he was received by a friend. He spent some time there. The time came for him (to die), and he entrusted his property into the hands of his friend by whom he had been received.
>
> He said to him, "If my son comes to you and wants this property, if he does not carry out three acts of wisdom, do not give him this property."
>
> The people had agreed that none of them would show the house of his father's friend to a stranger (who might ask for it).
>
> The son heard and went to that place, and he knew the name of the man. He came and sat at the gate of the town. He saw someone carrying a load of twigs. He said to him, "Will you sell those twigs?"
>
> He said to him, "Yes."
>
> He said to him, "Take the price and go, carry the wood to So-and-so."
>
> He followed him until he came to the house of that man.
>
> He called to them, "Take away this load."
>
> He said, "Who ordered it?"
>
> He said to him, "You did not tell me, but they belong to the man who is following me." (This is the first clever act of the son, in finding the house.)
>
> He came down and greeted him, saying to him, "Who are you?"
>
> He said to him, "I am the son of that Jerusalemite, who died here with you."
>
> He took him in and made a meal for him.
>
> Now that man had a wife and two sons and two daughters. They sat down to eat, and he set before them five chickens.
>
> He said to him, "Take and divide it up (among us)."

He said to him "That is not mine to do, for I am a guest."

He said to him, "Please me."

He took one bird and gave it to the master of the house and his wife, the next and set it for his two sons, and the third and set it before the two daughters, and took the remaining two for himself. (This is the second clever act of the son.)

He said to him, "How is that for a division?"

He said to him, "But did I not say to you that I am a guest, and the honor is not mine? Nonetheless, I divided matters up quite properly. You and your wife and one chicken are three; your two sons and a chicken are three; and your two daughters and a chicken are three; and I and the two chickens are three."

The next day he made a meal for him and brought before them one chicken. He said to the guest, "Take and divide it up."

He said to him "That is not mine to do, for I am a guest."

He said to him, "Please me."

He took the head and set it before the master of the house, the entrails and set them before the wife, the thighs for the sons, the wings for the daughters, and the body for himself.

He said to him, "How is that for a division?"

He said to him, "But did I not say to you that I am a guest, and the honor is not mine? Nonetheless, I divided matters up quite properly.

"I gave you the head, because you are the head of the house, the entrails to your wife, because children issue from the womb, the thighs to your sons, the pillar of the house, the wings for your two daughters, because they are going to fly away from your house and go to their husbands.

"And I took for myself the (body which is shaped like a) boat, because in a boat I came.

"So now give me the inheritance left by my father, so that I may go along."

So he went and give him his inheritance and he went along.

LAMENTATIONS RABBATI XXXV:VII.3

The sole point at which a distinctively Judaic component comes to the surface is the reference to the man's origin, Jerusalem. That suffices. But through the pages of this book, we shall find the formulation of wisdom exceedingly particular to the Judaic setting.

How to Study the Oral Torah

What makes the stories and sayings of wisdom difficult is a very particular trait, one that does not occur in the foregoing but is quite common. That trait is the constant reference to the written Torah, that is,

Scripture. It is uncommon for a wise saying or story to omit all reference to a precedent out of ancient Israel's holy life, or to cite a fact embodied in a verse of Scripture, or otherwise to invoke the presence of holy Israel as portrayed in Scripture. The reason, as I shall explain, is that Scripture embodied a permanent, eternal paradigm, a reality in which holy Israel made its life. Citing verses of Scripture invoked facts of life, as much as observations about right conduct or stories about wit and problem-solving (the Jerusalemite for instance) portrayed facts of life. Those familiar with the Passover Seder will recognize the format, since the reading of the Haggadah—or Seder manual—involves a recitation of verse about the Exodus, followed by rabbinical extrapolation of the meaning of those verses, followed by new conclusions about the story.

Another instance, helpful to us in the present setting because it defines the wise person and the fool, shows us how Scripture forms a constant presence throughout the formulation of those universally valid rules of wise conduct and intelligent attitude that our sages proposed to offer to whom it may concern. In this example, we use three typefaces to underscore the sources of what is said: Scripture in italics, first of all, then the basic document, tractate Abot, the Fathers, in bold-face type; and finally, in ordinary type, the amplification of that document's statements in the companion-talmud to tractate Abot, called in Hebrew Abot deRabbi Nathan, and, in English, The Fathers According to Rabbi Nathan. We give the basic teaching in bold-face type, then the amplification in regular type:

> **There are seven traits that characterize an unformed clod, and seven a sage. (1) A sage does not speak before someone greater than he in wisdom. (2) And he does not interrupt his fellow. (3) And he is not at a loss for an answer. (4) He asks a relevant question and answers properly. (5) And he addresses each matter in its proper sequence, first, then second. (6) And concerning something he has not heard, he says, "I have not heard the answer." (7) And he concedes the truth (when the other party demonstrates it). And the opposite of these traits apply to a clod.**
>
> TRACTATE ABOT 5:7
>
> **A sage does not speak before someone greater than he in wisdom.**
>
> This refers to Moses, for it is said, *And Aaron spoke all the words which the Lord has spoken to Moses and did the signs in the sight of the people* (Exod. 4:30).
>
> Now who was the more worthy to speak, Moses or Aaron?
>
> One has to say it was Moses.
>
> For Moses had heard the message from the mouth of the

Almighty, while Aaron heard it from Moses.

But this is what Moses said: "Is it possible for me to speak in a situation in which my elder brother is standing?

Therefore he said to Aaron, "Speak."

Thus it is said, *And Aaron spoke all the words which the Lord had spoken to Moses* (Exod. 4:30).

And he does not interrupt his fellow

This refers to Aaron.

For it is said, *Then Aaron spoke . . . Behold, this day have they offered their sin-offering and their burnt offering . . . and such things as these have happened to me* (Lev. 10:19).

He kept silence until Moses had finished speaking and did not say to him, "Cut it short."

But afterward he said to Moses, Then Aaron spoke . . . Behold, this day have they offered their sin-offering and their burnt offering . . . and such things as these have happened to me .

"And we are in mourning."

Some say that Aaron drew Moses apart from the group and said to him, "My brother, if of tithes, which are of lesser sanctity, it is forbidden for one who has yet to bury his deceased to eat, a sin offering, of greater sanctity, all the more so should be forbidden as a meal to a person who has yet to bury his deceased."

Moses immediately agreed with him, as it is said, *And when Moses heard it, it was well-pleasing in his sight* (Lev. 10:20),

and in the view of the Almighty as well.

He does not answer hastily.

This is exemplified by Elihu ben Barachel the Buzite.

For it is said, *I am young and you are very old, which is why I held back and did not tell you my opinion. I said, Days should speak, and the multitude of years should teach wisdom* (Job 32:6).

This teaches that they remained seated in silence before Job. When he stood up, they stood up. When he sat down, they sat down. When he ate, they ate. When he drank, they drank. Then he took permission from them and cursed his day:

After this Job opened his mouth and cursed his day and said, Let the day perish when I was born, and the night in which it was said, A man-child is brought forth (Job 3:1).

Let the day perish on which my father came to my mother and she said to him, "I am pregnant."

And how do we know that they answered not out of turn? Then Job answered and said (Job 3:2). Then answered Eliphaz the Temanite and said (Job 4:1). Then answered Bildad the Shuhite and said (Job 8:1). Then answered Zophar the Naamathite and said (Job 11:10). Then Elihu the son of Barachel the Buzite answered and said (Job 32:1).

Scripture arranged them one by one so as to let everyone in the world know that a sage does not speak before someone greater than he is wisdom. And he does not interrupt his fellow. And he does not answer hastily.

He asks a relevant question and answers properly:

This is exemplified by Judah, who said, *I will be surety for him* (Gen. 43:9).

Not asking a relevant question is exemplified by Reuben, as it is said, *And Reuben said to his father, You shall slay my two sons* (Gen. 42:37).

And he addresses each matter in its proper sequence, first, (then second):

This is exemplified by Jacob.

And some say, this is exemplified by Sarah.

then second:

This is exemplified by the men of Haran.

And he concedes the truth:

This is exemplified by Moses: *And the Lord said to me, They have said well that which they have spoken* (Deut. 18:17).

It is further exemplified by the Holy One, blessed be he: *The Lord spoke to Moses, saying, The daughters of Zelophehad speak right* (Num. 27:6).

THE FATHERS ACCORDING TO RABBI NATHAN XXXVIII:XI-XVII

The basic teaching is given in its own terms. It is freestanding. Then the talmud to the tractate wishes to supply cases and examples, facts that clarify what is meant. This it does both in its own narrative and also in its citations of cases from Scripture.

Let us now broaden the scope of the discussion, to place into proper context the constant presence of Scripture in the oral Torah. For we shall understand nothing of the wisdom of Judaism until we can define the context and circumstance in which wisdom takes place. Judaic wisdom speaks out of eternity to all times, addresses no place in particular because it is utopian in the most profound sense, and deems the specificities of history and time of no consequential dimensions of human existence. So we must ask not about Scripture, but about conceptions of history and eternity that govern in such a way as to encompass, also, the life of ancient Israel recorded in Scripture.

In the Judaism set forth by principal documents that record the oral part of the dual Torah, particularly those that reached closure from ca. 200 to ca. 600 C.E., concepts of history, coming to expression in the categories of time and change, along with distinctions between past, present, and future utterly give way to a conception of recording and explaining the social order different from that of history. It is one that sets aside time and change in favor of enduring paradigms recapitulated in each succeeding age. The concept of history as we know it, and as Scripture knows it, surrenders to an altogether different way of conceiving time and change as well as the course of noteworthy, even memorable social events. The past takes place in the present. The present embodies the past. And there is no indeterminate future over the horizon, only a clear and present path to be chosen if people will it. With distinctions between past, present, and future time found to make no difference, and in their stead, different categories of meaning and social order deemed self-evident, the Judaism of the dual Torah transforms ancient Israel's history into the categorical structure of eternal Israel's society, so that past, present, and future meet in the here and now.

In that construction of thought, history finds no place, nor do time or change. The movement of events toward a purposive goal has no relevance, and a different exegesis of happenings supplants the conception of history. When the written Torah takes a place in the discussion, it is because its saints—Moses, Aaron, in the passage before us—endure even now. There is no then, no now, but only a single undifferentiated time, in which past and present meet. And, it must follow, no part of the oral Torah accommodates the notions of change and time, unique events and history, particular lives and biography. All things are transformed by this way of thinking, that is other than the historical one that Scripture uses to organize the facts of the social existence of Israel.

When people recapitulate the past in the present, and when they deem the present to be no different from a remote long ago, they organize and interpret experience in an other-than-historical framework, one that substitutes enduring permanence for historical change. Instead of history, thought proceeds through the explanation of unique patterns, which we call paradigms, the likenesses or unlikenesses of things to an original pattern. The familiar modes of classifying noteworthy events, the long-ago and the here-and-now, lose currency. Memory as the medium of interpretation of the social order falls away, and historical thinking ceases to serve. Universal paradigms govern, against which all things—now, then, anytime—are compared, and events lose all specificity and particularity. The characterization of this Judaism as a historical religion and of the medium of that religion as memory in no way conforms to the facts of the Judaism being studied here.

In this Judaism, with the past very present, the present is an exercise in recapitulation of an enduring pattern, laid out in the sources before us. Memory is null, containing nothing, forming no source of meaning. So, with the loss of the experience of memory in favor of a different kind of encounter with time past, present, and future, time as a conception in the measurement of things ceases to serve. Time is neither linear nor cyclical; it simply is not a consideration in thinking about what happens and what counts. Instead, paradigms for the formation of the social order of transcendence and permanence govern, so that what was now is, and what will be is what was and is.

Let us now reflect on the traits of that world of the Torah, Judaism, out of which the wisdom we have collected emerges. What we shall see is that, for the Torah, history—unique events, formed into a pattern, distinguished from the present in past time—plays no part. For Judaism no distinctions separate past from present. The past is always a presence. The present participates in the past as well. And that helps us make sense of the dominant trait of the wisdom-writings of the oral Torah, the constant allusion to Scripture. That is not because Scripture provided illustrations out of the past or authoritative precedents out of the past to dictate the course of everyday life. It is because Scripture in narrative form conveyed an immediate, an acutely contemporary reality, a presence as real and palpable as the present-tense life people knew at any given point in time. The conventional understanding of scriptural homilies—Moses did it this way, so, therefore should we—evaporates.

The sages identified in the written part of the Torah the governing models of Israel's enduring existence, whether past or future. When we speak of the presence of the past, we describe the consciousness of people who could open Scripture and find themselves right there, in its record—not only Lamentations, but also prophecy, and, especially, in the books of the Torah. Since, then, sages did not see themselves as removed in time and space from the generative events to which they referred the experience of the here and now; they also had no need to make the past contemporary.

If, therefore, we wish to understand the Torah as formulated by Judaism, we shall have to set aside the forms of historical consciousness we today find self-evident—"That was then, this is now"—and explore those other forms that defined perception for the sages—"That was then and now and always." In the oral part of the Torah, a historical way of thinking about past, present, and future, time and eternity, the here-and-now in relationship to the ages,—that is, Scripture's way of thinking—gave way to another mode of thought altogether. It was one that replaced history with a different model for the organization of experience: things that happen and their meaning.

This other model we call a paradigm, because it imposed meaning and order on things that happened. Paradigmatic modes of thought took the place of historical ones. Thinking through paradigms, with a conception of time that elides past and present, removes all barriers between them. That way of reading Scripture—the paradigmatic and, also ahistorical, way—proves ideally suited to the labor of wisdom, with its power to overcome the specificities of time, space, and circumstance. Hence the paramount trait of the wisdom-writings we shall examine— the ubiquitous presence of Scripture—proves remarkably appropriate to the task of wisdom itself, that labor of discovering the laws of life, which govern always and everywhere.

The Character of Jewish Wisdom

Before we consider one by one the documents that record the oral Torah, let us therefore consider the one that stands for all of them. The Talmud is made up of a philosophical law code, the Mishnah, and an equally philosophical analysis and commentary upon the Mishnah. The former is constructed as an essay in natural history, using the methods of hierarchical classification formulated by classical philosophy in the analysis of the data of everyday life. The commentary, called the Gemara, is constructed in accord with the rules of argument and demonstration called dialectical. Important traits of classical dialectics of Socrates, Plato, and Aristotle, are replicated in the Gemara's argument. That commentary extends to the laws and the principles of the laws contained in the Mishnah. It is intellectually ambitious but not wordy: a few questions recur throughout. That briefly describes the document.

But that definition misses the key to the document and what makes it open-ended, a writing to which every generation makes its contribution. The Talmud is open-ended and invites the disciple to join in its discussion. The main trait of the Talmud is its argumentative character, its dialectical argument, question–answer, back-and-forth. Once we have not only a proposition but the reason for it, then we may evaluate the reason, criticize it, or produce a contrary proposition based on a better reason and argument. And since the Talmud shows its hand at every point, its framers indicate that they want us to join in. And we do, and that is why so many generations of Jews in quest of learning have found in Talmud study the substance of a worthwhile life: Talmud study, shaping the perspective of the learning Jew, his or her way of seeing many things in one rational, reasonable manner.

When the Talmud's Gemara (also known simply as "the Talmud") analyzes the Mishnah, it is through a dialectical inquiry made up of questions and answers, yielding propositions and counterarguments. A closer look still shows that what the Talmud gives us is not a finished statement but notes toward the main points of an argument. These notes permit us to reconstruct the issues and the questions, the facts and the use made of those facts, with the result that when we grasp the document, we also enter into its discipline and join in its argument. Few documents invite readers to join the writers, and none with the success of this one.

For, through the centuries from the formal closure of the Talmud, in about 600 C.E., the Talmud formed the single authoritative writing of Judaism, the source of the theology and the law that defined the faith and the community of holy Israel, God's first love, wherever they might be located. Enriched by commentaries, responsa, and law codes over the centuries, the Talmud described the practical affairs of the community of Judaism. But because of its particular character, as the script for a sustained analytical argument, the Talmud further shaped the minds of those who mastered its modes of thought and, because of its profound sensibility, the document further imparted to those who responded to its teachings a character of intellectual refinement and personal responsibility, an alertness to the meaning of word and deed alike. No wonder, then, that the master of Talmudic learning, the disciple of sages in its native category, has defined the virtuous life for Judaic faithful, down to our own time. Because of its power to impart form and structure to the mind of holy Israel, its capacity to define the good and holy way of life for those who wished to be Israel, God's people, the Talmud enjoyed complete success in that various world to which its compilers or authors entrusted their work. Not many books can compete.

The most important question about the Talmud concerns not what it says but how it works, meaning, why the Talmud has exercised the amazing power that it has wielded over the life of holy Israel, God's people, for the whole of its history. After all, how many documents compare? Here is a piece of writing that faced a particular group of people and from its appearance to our own time defined for that group everything that really mattered: questions of order, questions of truth, questions of meaning, questions of purpose. Individuals devoted their lives to the study of this writing, but more important, the entire society of Judaism—that is, the community formed by the Torah—found in the Talmud those modes of thought and inquiry, those media of order and value, that guided the formation of public affairs and private life as well. The Talmud is a public, political, anonymous, collective, social statement; its compilers intended to define the life of the public polity by forming the kingdom of God in the here-and-now that the Torah, beginning with the Pentateuch, had recorded as God's will for Israel, the holy people.

The Logic of the Talmud

The Talmud is not merely an encyclopaedia of information, but a sustained, remarkably protracted, uniform inquiry into the logical traits of passages of the Mishnah or of Scripture. It is not disorganized, nor is it overall just a compilation of this, that, and the other thing. Quite to the contrary, an outline of the Talmud, beginning to end, shows that the Talmud moves from main points to subsidiary ones, follows a coherent program of argument, presents information in a generally coherent way for a clear, propositional purpose, and, in all, can be followed in the same way we follow other writings.

The Talmud as a whole is cogent, doing some few things over and over again; it conforms to a few simple rules of rhetoric, including choice of languages for discrete purposes, and that fact attests to the coherent viewpoint of the authorship at the end—the people who put it all together as we have it—because it speaks, overall, in a single way, in a uniform voice. So how does it do its work, and why does it work? If the compilers put together two stories, what message have they made? If they have take as self-evident the coherence of a given set of propositions, what has instructed them?

And in discerning the answers to those questions, we shall also discern how they see the world. What people find self-evident defines the source of truth and meaning that governs for them. And the Talmud will express that profound principle when it perceives an incongruity and says, "Now, who ever mentioned that?" or, "What does subject A have to do with subject Z?" The point of disharmony requires attention, and in the harmonization of incongruity we shall witness a much newer truth.

And there is a deeper dimension still. A piece of writing holds together because of a logic of coherence, which the writer and the reader share, and which the writer uses to show the reader why one thing follows from another, and how two things hold together. In a composite such as the Talmud, the issue of coherence surfaces everywhere. In following the unfolding of an argument, knowing precisely where we stand, understanding how one thing follows from some other and leads us to a further conclusion—these are precisely the elements that generate the power of the document. If you are ever studying a passage of the Talmud and ask yourself what one thing has to do with another, you may take comfort in the fact that you have asked the one question that you must ask—and must answer if you are to make sense of things.

The Talmud does some few things, and does them over and over again in the same order. Most of the Talmud deals with the explanation and amplification of the Mishnah's rules or of passages of Scripture. That is to say, every sustained discussion begins with a passage of the Mishnah, which will be read with great sensitivity. The rules of reading the Mishnah are few and strong. We will be told the meanings of words and phrases, but more than information, we will be asked to participate in the sustained inquiry into the foundations of the written Torah, which are received as oral Torah in the Mishnah's view. We further will be told that the implicit governing principle of a rule before us intersects with the inferred governing principle of some other, on a different subject, and these have to be compared, contrasted, harmonized, or differentiated. All of this is exhilarating and empowers us to join in the analysis and argument. And from that process, we argue, a unique brand of wisdom emerges: the wisdom not only of stating a concluding thought, but getting there.

True, the Talmud is made up of diverse materials. Its compilers used ready-made writing as well as making up their own compositions. But once we outline some pages, from the very beginning to the very end of the discussion of a given paragraph of the Mishnah, we can see what was essential to the purpose of the Talmud's compilers, and for instance, what served a subsidiary purpose of just giving us information on a topic at hand. So we will find a proposition, demonstrated at some length, followed by an appendix of topically interesting material, which is not party to the argument but which is useful and illuminating. Once we understand how things are put together and why a given passage is included, we see the document as coherent, purposeful, and quite reasonable in its inclusions and juxtapositions—anything but that mess that people tell us it is.

We are able to identify the types of compositions and large-scale composites of which the Talmud's framers made use, which allow us systematically to study the classifications of those types, e.g., Mishnah-commentary, other-than-Mishnah-commentary, to take the two most obvious classifications of all. Not by a repertoire of examples but by a complete catalogue of all items, therefore, we know precisely what types of materials are used, in what proportions, in what contexts, for what purposes, and the like. Generalizations, accompanied by reasonably accurate statements of the numbers and proportions of exemplary data, take a probative role in all study of the character and definition of the Talmud.

Now, why is all this necessary? Talmudists share the conviction that they study the record of God's revelation, that is, God's self-manifestation. In that world view, therefore, the study of Talmud affords them the chance to learn the logic of God, how God thinks and those patterns of reason that govern in the creation of the world. From the wording of the Torah, they work our way back to the processes of thought, the rules of coherent analysis, that yielded that wording. The premise behind oral Torah, laid out in Abot and explained earlier in this introduction, thus comes full circle: the sages regard themselves as inheritors of a magnificent and divine legacy of not only content, but of intellectual process.

The Talmud throughout speaks in a single, uniform voice, and that voice is unique in the context of rabbinic compilations of late antiquity. Now there can be no further argument on that point; the evidence of the uniformity of discourse is spread out in stupefying detail. Why does it matter, and what is at stake in this-worldly terms? In fact, the difference it makes is fundamental: Is the Talmud organized or disorganized, purposive or random, systematic or chaotic? Many accounts of the character of the Talmud as a piece of writing describe the document as unsystematic. Some describe the document as disorganized, others as exhibiting no well-established program that accounts for why a given passage appears where it does and not somewhere else. We take the view that it is coherent, purposive, and organized. And those qualities, overlooked by many perhaps, is what makes the Talmud's wisdom wise.

The Structure of the Talmud

The oral Torah is divided into two parts, one devoted to norms of conduct or laws, the other focused upon the amplification of Scripture. The former begins with a law code and continues with a supplementary compilation and two huge commentaries to the law code, aimed at setting forth norms of conduct; the latter is made up of twelve compilations of verses of Scripture and commentaries thereon, aimed at formulated authoritative theology. The half of the oral Torah devoted to law comprises the Mishnah, Tosefta, and two Talmuds; the half devoted to Scripture, lore, and theology, is made up of Midrash compilations (*Midrash* meaning "exegesis of Scripture").

Norms of Behavior

THE MISHNAH: The authoritative documents that preserve in writing the originally oral Torah of Sinai begin with the Mishnah, a philosophical law-code that came to closure in ca. 200 C.E. in the land of Israel (a.k.a., "Palestine"). The Mishnah, organized in six divisions, covering laws of (1) agriculture, (2) time, (3) the family, (4) the civil order, (5) the cult, and (6) purity, is subdivided into sixty-three tractates, all but two of them devoted to specific topics. These tractates break down into more than 550 chapters. The document is therefore enormous. The Mishnah is formulated to facilitate memorization, that is, in mnemonic patterns. It is the only document of the oral Torah that systematically exhibits such traits; though, it is often claimed, many sayings were formulated and transmitted orally—that is, through memory—no other entire document can be shown to have conformed to the narrative of orality in the way that the Mishnah does.

THE TOSEFTA: Organized in accord with the structure of the Mishnah's tractates, the Tosefta collects sayings that are assigned to the same authorities who appear in the Mishnah but that are not collected there. These sayings are set forth in three groupings, as a given tractate requires: (1) sayings that cite those of the Mishnah and gloss them (in the pattern of The Fathers According to Rabbi Nathan, as we noticed above); (2) sayings that cover matters treated in the Mishnah and complement them; (3) sayings that stand separate from those of the Mishnah and supplement them, by giving further rules on a given topic, but not by amplifying a rule set forth in the Mishnah itself. The Tosefta is approximately four times larger than the Mishnah.

THE TALMUD OF THE LAND OF ISRAEL: Taking up the first four of the Mishnah's six divisions, the Talmud is in two parts, the Mishnah itself, and the Gemara, which is a clause-by-clause commentary on the chosen thirty-nine tractates of the Mishnah. It is generally assumed that this Talmud reached closure in ca. 400 C.E.

THE TALMUD OF BABYLONIA: The second Talmud takes up the second, third, fourth, and fifth divisions of the Mishnah. It too cites the Mishnah and then gives a clause-by-clause commentary. In addition, its Gemara contains large-scale topical compilations, which treat the subject matter of the Mishnah but do not analyze the Mishnah's propositions on that subject matter. Further, its Gemara devotes substantial attention to the systematic exegesis of Scripture, on the one side, and to the amplification of stories about Scriptural saints and events, on the other. The Talmud of Babylonia (then a province in the Iranian Empire, covering present-day Iraq) reached closure in ca. 600 C.E., just before the Moslem conquest of Iran (and most of the Middle East). In volume, its thirty-seven tractates vastly exceed the earlier Talmud. Because of its extensive coverage of both the oral Torah presented in the Mishnah and also the written Torah, the second Talmud became normative and formed the complete and final statement of the whole Torah, originally oral as much as written. It defined the law and theology of Judaism from ancient times to our own day.

Norms of Belief

The earliest compilations of Midrash-exegeses of Scripture set forth verse-by-verse comments; since at some points they cite the Mishnah and the Tosefta verbatim, these derive from the third and possibly the fourth centuries C.E. They are Mekhilta Attributed to R. Ishmael, on Exodus; Sifra, on Leviticus; Sifré, on Numbers, and another Sifré, on Deuteronomy. A later set of compilations move from the narrow limits of verse-by-verse exegesis to the exploration of problems and the presentation of propositions through extensive analysis of diverse verses of Scripture and events set forth in Scripture. They are Genesis Rabbah, covering the book of Genesis; Leviticus Rabbah, a set of highly propositional formulations in exegetical style; Pesiqta de Rab Kahana, covering much of the holy season of Judaism through propositional disquisitions in the manner of Leviticus Rabbah; and Pesiqta Rabbati, a companion to the foregoing, dealing with holidays not treated there. These compilations are generally assigned to the fifth and early sixth centuries. The final set of compilations in late antiquity are Lamentations Rabbati, on the book of Lamentations; Song of Songs Rabbah; Esther Rabbah I; and Ruth Rabbah. These too are read in the synagogue. They are organized around verses of Scripture but possess traits distinctive to themselves as well. The greatest theological statement of the Torah as set forth by our sages of blessed memory is Song of Songs Rabbah. These Midrash-compilations are generally assigned to the fifth and sixth centuries.

Tractate Abot is generally presented along with the Mishnah, though it probably reached closure only a half-century or so after the Mishnah, in ca. 250 C.E. It differs from the Mishnah in form and program, concerning itself with matters of sagacity and wisdom, norms of life for the sages and their disciples. It bears its own talmud, as we have already seen, in the Fathers According to Rabbi Nathan, of indeterminate date but probably belonging to the period in which the second Talmud reached closure.

In terms of the life-setting of the various documents, the norms of behavior form the focus for study among sages in the schoolhouse and court session, and the norms of belief occupy learning in the synagogue. The same sages appear in both types of writings.

Conclusion

Why the wisdom of Judaism in particular? And what is the special message of this corpus of insight into the human condition in general?

Every great religion sets forth stores of human experience and knowledge in the form of precious jewels of wisdom. In the realm of wisdom, religions compete on equal terms, all of them proposing to afford enlightenment to humanity in general. But the holy community called "Israel," in the setting of religion, guiding its life through the Torah and aiming to know, serve, and love God as God knows and loves us, through its wisdom shares with the rest of humanity a quite special treasure.

In these pages that distinctive wisdom that comes from an enduring encounter with failure and disappointment is what Judaism contributes to the common good. For the situation of holy Israel in Talmudic times and for long afterward afforded little occasion for pride, but much for humility. The Talmud and related writings that set forth the Torah as Judaism receives it came to formulation and closure at the very moment at which two great religions, also heirs of the Hebrew Scriptures of ancient Israel, took shape: Christianity in the first century A.D., Islam in the seventh century A.D. (for Islam, the first century A.H., after the Hegira, that is, the Prophet Muhammed's move). Both religions conquered the world, Christianity that of Rome, and Islam, much of that of Christianity. Each claimed to supersede the prior one, Christianity taking the place of "Israel after the flesh," and Islam through the Prophet forming the seal and end of the revelation of God to humanity. The Israel that found its being in the revealed Torah of Sinai as explained by our sages of blessed memory could not derive hope from the triumph of either of these world-conquering faiths, but only disappointment from both.

So in the Torah as our sages portray it, we read the message to the losers, those with little to celebrate, the ones buried in the onrush of history. And the particular wisdom of holy Israel as set forth in these pages means to speak not to the surface of the water but to the depths, the view from the bottom of the sea, the perspective of those too low to gain vistas of perspective on great things.

Here, then, is the wisdom of the Judaism of the dual Torah, oral and written. It means, in the details of homely situations, to teach the Jews the lesson that their subordinated position itself gave probative evidence of the holy community's true standing: the low would be raised up, the humble placed into authority, the proud reduced, the world made right. Many of the sayings we consider make just this point: What appears on top in fact is lowly, but humility is a mark of power. But the wisdom of Judaism did more than react, reassure, and encourage. It acted upon and determined the shape of matters. That Judaism for a long time defined the politics and policy of the community. It instructed Israel, the Jewish people, on the rules for the formation of the appropriate world and it laid forth the design for those attitudes and actions that would yield an Israel both subordinate and tolerated, on the one side, but also proud and hopeful, on the other. The wisdom of Judaism began in the encounter with a successful Christianity and persisted in the face of a still more successful Islam.

For holy Israel, the religious community formed by the Jewish people, such Judaism not only reacted to, but also shaped, Israel's condition in the world. Making a virtue of a policy of subordination that was not always necessary or even wise, the wisdom of Judaism defined the Jews' condition and set the limits to its circumstance. The religion of a small, weak group, Judaism more than held its own against the challenge of triumphant Christendom and world-conquering Islam. The reason for the success of the wisdom of Judaism was that that system answered the question of why God's people, in exile, held a subordinated, but tolerated position within the world framed by the sibling-rivals, Ishmael of Isaac, Esau of Jacob. The appeal to exile accounted for the dissonance of present unimportance and promised future greatness: "today if only you will . . . ." Therefore the question was urgent, the answer self-evidently true, in its appeal to the holy way of life explained by the received world view addressed to the Israel consisting of the believers throughout the world. Here was the family of Abraham, Isaac, and Jacob: Israel. Now tolerated, sometimes oppressed, in exile, in time to come the family will come home to its own land. The road back fully mapped out, people had now to remember who they were, where they were going, and what they had to do—or not to do—in order to get from here to there.

The wisdom before us comes from a Judaism that explained for Israel its subordinated but tolerated condition, indeed made that condition into God's will, and the acceptance of that condition in the heart as much as in the mind into the definition of virtue. The world beyond works out its affairs to accommodate God's will for Israel, and Israel's relationship to that larger world remains wholly within the control and subject to the power of Israel—but in a paradoxical way. For what Israel must do is accept, submit, accommodate, receive with humility the will and word of God in the Torah. The power to govern the fate of the nation rested with the nation, but only so far as the nation accorded that power to God alone. Were people perplexed on who is Israel? The Torah answered the question: God's people, living out, here and now, the holy life prescribed by God. Did people wonder how long that people had to endure the government of gentiles? The Torah addressed that issue: so long as God willed. The very God who had created the heavens and the earth dictated the fate of Israel—but also cared what each Jew ate for breakfast and responded to the conduct of every collectivity of Israel, each pool of the sacred formed by even a handful of Jews. The Judaism of the dual Torah in its distinctive idiom recapitulated the principle of the Judaism of the Torah of "Moses." The system laid emphasis upon the everyday as a sequence of acts of sanctification. It promised remission and resolution—salvation—in consequence of the correct and faithful performance of those acts of sanctification. The subordinate position of Israel therefore served to attest to the true status of Israel, small and inconsequential now, but holy even now and destined for great reward at the end of time.

The power of Judaism, embodied in concrete terms by its wisdom, therefore lay in its remarkable capacity to define and create the world of Israel, the Jewish people. Israel understood that the nation that had ceased to be a nation on its own land and once more regained that condition could and would once more reenact that paradigm. Faced by enormous challenges from successful, kindred religions from the first century in Christendom, and from the seventh in Islam, Judaism therefore enjoyed remarkable success in that very world that it both created and also selected for itself, the world of Israel, the Jewish people. Both Islam and Christendom presented a single challenge: the situation of subordination along with toleration.

The power of Judaism lay in its capacity to do two things. First, Judaism in its classical statement, shaped in the fourth-century Talmud of the Land of Israel and then fully articulated by the sixth-century Talmud of Babylonia, presented doctrines both to explain and to draw renewal from the condition of subordination and toleration, so that the facts of everyday life served to reenforce the claims of the system. Second, that same Judaism taught an enduring doctrine of the virtues of the heart that did more than make Israel's situation acceptable. And here is that core of wisdom that these pages portray.

That same doctrine so shaped the inner life of Israel as to define virtue in the very terms imposed by politics. Israel within recreated, in age after age, that exact condition of acceptance of humility and accommodation that the people's political circumstance imposed from without. Consequently, the enduring doctrine of virtue not only made it possible for Israel to accept its condition; it recreated in the psychological structure of Israel's inner life that same condition, so bringing into exact correspondence political facts and psychological fantasies.

It was the feminization of rabbinic Judaism that accounts for its success: that is, its holding in the balance deeply masculine and profoundly feminine traits. Judaism triumphed in Christendom and Islam because of its power to bring into union both heart and mind, inner life and outer circumstance, psychology and politics. The Judaism of the dual Torah not only matched the situation of Israel the conquered but (ordinarily) tolerated people. That Judaism created, within the psychological heritage of Israel, that same condition, that is to say, the condition of acceptance of a subordinated, but tolerated position, while awaiting the superior one.

Let us not at the end lose sight of the remarkable power of this religion of humility, for, after all, it is a religion that endures not in long-ago books of a faraway time and place, but in the lives of nearly everybody who today practices Judaism. It is a religion of mind and heart, but also family and community, one that asks entire devotion to God, not only the parts of life God can command, the life of the people together in community, but especially the secret places of existence not subject to God's will but only one's own. In these pages we have spoken of ideas and systems, the social order and its parts and how they are integrated into a theory of the whole. But beyond the objective facts of evidence and analysis of theories of the social order and their unfolding, we should not miss the defining fact. It lies not with the theory of refined intellects but the hard, coarse reality that, for the whole of their history from the formation of this Judaism to the present moment, wherever they lived, whatever their circumstances, the people, Israel, drew nourishment from these ideas and found in this system the power to endure.

Now the world did not make life easy, affording to the faith of Israel no honor, and to the Israelite no respect by reason of loyalty to that vocation. But both Islam and Christianity through conversion, which is to say, apostasy, offered Israel easy access to an honored place. At the sacrifice of home and property, even at the price of life itself, Israel resisted them and reaffirmed its eternal calling. For whatever the choice of private persons, that social order formed by Israel endured, above it all, against it all, despite it all, through all time and change. And, in the lifetime of many who read these very pages, even beyond the gates of hell, the surviving remnants determined to be Israel. They chose once more to form, in a precise sense to embody, the social order of that one whole Torah that God taught to Our Rabbi, Moses, at Sinai, that publicly revealed Torah that rests on the private, personal, and profoundly wise virtue, portrayed in numerous, diverse ways, in these pages.

Whether in Poland or Algeria, whether in Morocco or Iraq and Iran, whether in the land called the Land of Israel or in distant corners of the exile: north, south, west, or east, Israel kept the faith, abided by the covenant, was guided by wisdom such as that portrayed in these pages; that same Israel lived in stout hope and perfect trust in God. That fact defines the power of this Judaism, this dual Torah. The act of defiance of fate in the certainty of faith in God's ultimate act of grace is the one thing God cannot have commanded at Sinai. Wisdom gives the power to do what none can coerce, to give what even God must request but cannot demand.

God can have said, and many times in the Torah did say, "Serve me," but God could only beseech, "And trust me too." For even God cannot coerce trust. To give or withhold trust is left up to us. Only Israel could give what God could only ask, but not compel: the gifts of the heart, love and trust, for which the loving God yearns, which only the much-loved Israel can yield freely, of its own volition. And that is what Israel, in response to Sinai, willingly gave, and by its loyal persistence in its life as Israel, whether in the Land or in the patient exile, freely gives today. Then the time has come to discover, in that same dual Torah, the God who speaks and so is made manifest. And when God speaks, what we are to hear, to begin with, is the way in which to conduct our everyday lives in quest, service, and above all, love of God, wherein lies the truest wisdom of all.

If people want to know why eternal Israel found the will to endure, why confronted with alternatives promising honor and esteem, every generation repeated the stubborn affirmation of the first—"We shall do and we shall obey"—here is the place to begin.

How to Read This Book

This is a collection of wisdom, and as such, we expect the reader to dive directly to an area of personal interest or need. We have tried to make each section's wisdom self-evident for exactly that reason. The Talmud and related writings of the ancient sages of the holy people, Israel, God's first love, from which the passages are drawn, need not be studied from beginning to end to be understood, and it is part of its character that you can start nearly anywhere, or any page, to begin a lifetime's journey seeking knowledge. So feel free to begin anywhere, and let curiosity guide you.

Nevertheless, we offer a word of caution and advice. The Talmud is a unique document with a special perspective. Although we argue that wisdom is self-evident, we also warn the reader that the special character of Jewish wisdom is its structure, its context, and its logic. Moreover, we do not intend to merely offer an encyclopaedia of aphorisms or Talmudic stories. We invite the reader to focus not only on one particular lesson, but on the entire character of a unique and religious text.

After all, while the Talmud invites the reader to begin at any point, it also discourages the capricious. In presenting wisdom topically, we hope that the reader will find joy not only from the passages, but in the manner in which they are presented. But that manner is itself a mystery to many, and requires some explanation. The senior editor of this collection has made a career trying to bring that wisdom closer to explanation and translation; many others have devoted themselves to the same task. So, as a road map, we offer an introduction that not only defines Jewish wisdom, but also explains how that wisdom emerged, what it serves, and why, after all, we consider it wise. In the end the test of wisdom takes place in the life of humanity, and the wisdom of Judaism, we shall see, sustained and ennobled a people that throughout history has confronted trying times.

Arrogance

Whence [in Scripture] do we derive an admonition against the arrogant?

Said Raba said Zeiri, "'Listen and give ear, do not be proud' (Jer. 13:15)."

R. Nahman bar Isaac said, "From the following: 'Your heart will be lifted up, and you will forget the Lord your God' (Deut. 8:14).

"And it is written, 'Beware, lest you forget the Lord your God' (Deut. 8:11)."

R. Avira expounded, sometimes in the name of R. Assi and sometimes in the name of R. Ammi, "Whoever is arrogant in the end will be diminished,

"as it is said, 'They are exalted, there will be a diminution' (Job 24:24).

"And lest you maintain that they continue in the world [alive], Scripture states, 'And they are gone' (Job. 24:24).

"But if [the arrogant person] repents, he will be gathered up [in death] at the time allotted to him [and not before],

"as was the case with our father, Abraham,

"as it is said, 'But when they are lowly, they are gathered in like all' (Job 24:24)—like Abraham, Isaac, and Jacob, concerning whom 'all' is written [at Gen. 24:1, 27:33, 33:11].

"And if not: 'They are cut off as the tops of the ears of corn' (Job 24:24)."

"With him also who is of a contrite and humble spirit" (Isa. 57:15).

R. Huna and R. Hisda:

One said, "I [God] am with the contrite."

The other said, "I [God] am the contrite."

Logic favors the view of him who has said, "I [God] am with the contrite," for lo, the Holy One, blessed be he, neglected all mountains and heights and brought his Presence to rest on Mount Sinai,

and he did not raise Mount Sinai upward [to himself].

R. Joseph said, "A person should always learn from the attitude of his Creator, for lo, the Holy One, blessed be he, neglected all mountains and heights and brought his Presence to rest on Mount Sinai,

"and he neglected all valuable trees and brought his Presence to rest in the bush."

And R. Eleazar said, "Whoever is arrogant—his dust will not be stirred up [in the resurrection of the dead].

"For it is said, 'Awake and sing, you that dwell in the dust' (Isa. 26:19).

"It is stated not 'you who lie in the dust' but 'you who dwell in the dust,' meaning, one who has become a neighbor to the dust [by constant humility] even in his lifetime."

And R. Eleazar said, "For whoever is arrogant the Presence of God laments,

"as it is said, 'But the haughty he knows from afar' (Ps. 138:6)."

R. Avira expounded, and some say it was R. Eleazar, "Come and take note of the fact that not like the trait of the Holy One, blessed be he, is the trait of flesh and blood.

"The trait of flesh and blood is that those who are high take note of those who are high, but the one who is high does not take note of the one who is low.

"But the trait of the Holy One, blessed be he, is not that way. He is high, but he takes note of the low,

"as it is said, 'For though the Lord is high, yet he takes note of the low' (Ps. 138:6)."

Said R. Hisda, and some say it was Mar Uqba, "Concerning whoever is arrogant, said the Holy One, blessed be he, he and I cannot live in the same world,

"as it is said, 'Whoever slanders his neighbor in secret—him will I destroy; him who has a haughty look and a proud heart I will not endure' (Ps. 101:5).

"Do not read, 'him [I cannot endure]' but 'with him [I cannot endure].'"

There are those who apply the foregoing teaching to those who slander, as it is said, "Whoever slanders his neighbor in secret—him will I destroy" (Ps. 101:5).

Said R. Alexandri, "Whoever is arrogant—even the slightest breeze shakes him,

"as it is said, 'But the wicked are like the troubled sea' (Isa. 57:20).

"Now if the sea, which is so vast [lit.: which has so many quarter-logs (of water)]—the slightest breeze shakes it, a man, who is not so vast—all the more so [that the slightest breeze would shake him]."

Said Hezekiah, "The prayer of a person is heard only if he makes his heart as soft as flesh,

"as it is said, 'And it shall come to pass, that from one new moon to the next, all flesh shall come to worship' (Isa. 66:23)."

Said R. Zira, "In regard to flesh, it is written, 'And it is healed' (Lev. 13:18). In regard to man, it is not written, 'And he is healed.'"

Said R. Joshua b. Levi, "Come and take note of how great are the humble in the sight of the Holy One, blessed be he.

"For when the sanctuary stood, a person would bring a burnt-offering, gaining thereby the reward for bringing a burnt-offering, or a meal-offering, and gaining the reward for a meal offering.

"But a person who is genuinely humble does Scripture treat as if he had made offerings of all the sacrifices,

"as it is said, 'The sacrifices [plural] of God are a broken spirit' (Ps. 51:19).

"And not only so, but his prayer is not rejected, as it is said, 'A broken and contrite heart, O God, you will not despise' (Ps. 51:19)."

BAVLI TO MISHNAH-TRACTATE SOTAH 1:1/5A-B

Astrology and Its Antidote: A Difference of Opinion

Despite the admonishment against conceit stated in the section just preceding, we find here the sages debating their relative importance on this earth. In this passage, largely about the role played by stars in fate, the primary point—do the constellations mean anything?—raises a deeper issue of humility and generosity.

It was written in R. Joshua b. Levi's notebook, "One who is born on Sunday will be a man without 'one thing' in him."

What is the meaning of a man without "one thing" in him?

Should I say, without one good quality? But didn't R. Ashi say, "I was born on Sunday"? So it must be, "A man without one thing to his disgrace."

But didn't R. Ashi say, "I and Dimi bar Qaquzeta were born on Sunday, I am a king and he is *a capo di capi*"?

Rather, it means, either wholly good or wholly bad. How come? Because light and darkness were created on that day.

"One who is born on Monday will be contentious. How come? Because the waters were divided that day. One who was born on a Tuesday will be wealthy and promiscuous. How come? Because herbs were created that day [which multiply rapidly and mix with other herbs (Freedman)]. One who was born on Wednesday will be wise and have a great memory. How come? Because that is the day on which the Heavenly luminaries were hung up. One who was born on Thursday will do deeds of generosity. How come? Because fish and birds were created that day [Freedman: which are fed by God's generosity]. One who was born on Friday will be someone who makes the rounds [in his search for learning]."

[Reverting to the notes:] "One who is born on the Sabbath will die on the Sabbath, because the preeminent Sabbath day was desecrated on his account."

Said Raba bar R. Shila, "And he will be called a great saint."

R. Hanina said to [his disciples], "Go and tell Bar Levi [R. Joshua], 'It is not the star that rules over the day in general on which one was born that governs, but the star that controlled that very hour that governs. He who was born under the sun will be an outstanding person; he will eat and drink of his own property, and his secrets will be uncovered; if he is a thief, he will not succeed. He who is born under Venus will be wealthy and promiscuous. How come? Because fire was created under that star. He who was born under Mercury will have a wonderful memory and be smart. How come? Because Mercury is the scribe of the sun. He who is born under the moon will be a man to suffer evil, building and destroying, destroying and building, eating and drinking what is not his, and his secrets will remain hidden. If he is a thief, he will be successful. He who is born under Saturn will be a man who never accomplishes what he sets out to do."

Others say, "All plans against him will be frustrated."

"He who is born under Jupiter [called 'righteous'] will be a person who habitually does righteousness."

R. Nahman bar Isaac said, "Doing righteousness in good deeds."

"He who is born under Mars will shed blood."

R. Ashi said, "That means he'll be a surgeon, thief, slaughterer, or circumciser."

Rabbah said, "I was born under Mars."

Said Abbayye, "Yeah, and you inflict punishment and kill [with words]."

It has been stated:

R. Hanina says, "One's star is what makes one smart, one's star is what gives wealth, and Israel is subject to the stars."

R. Yohanan said, "Israel is not subject to the stars."

And R. Yohanan is consistent with views expressed elsewhere, for said R. Yohanan, "How on the basis of Scripture do we know that Israel is not subject to the stars? As it is said, 'Thus says the Lord, Do not learn the way of the gentiles, nor be dismayed at the signs of the Heavens, for the nations are dismayed at them' (Jer. 10:2). They are dismayed, but the Israelites are not dismayed."

And so Rab takes the view that Israel is not subject to the stars, for said R. Judah said Rab, "How on the basis of Scripture do we know that Israel is not subject to the stars? As it is said, 'And he brought him forth outside' (Gen. 15:5). Said Abraham before the Holy One, blessed be He, 'Lord of the world, "Someone born in my household is my heir" (Gen. 15:3).' He said to him, 'Not at all. "But he who will come forth out of your own loins" (Gen. 1:4).' He said before him, 'Lord of the world, I have closely examined my star, and I have seen that I am destined to have no children.' He said to him, 'Abandon this astrology of yours—Israel is not subject to astrology. Now what's your calculation? Is it that Jupiter stands in the west [and that is your constellation]? I'll turn it back and set it up in the East.' And so it is written, 'Who has raised up Jupiter from the east? He has summoned it for his sake' (Isa. 41:2)."

It is also the position of Samuel that Israel is not subject to the stars.

For Samuel and Ablat were in session, and some people going along to a lake. Said Ablat to Samuel, "That man is going but won't come back, a snake will bite him and he'll die."

Said to him Samuel, "Yeah, well, if he's an Israelite, he will go and come back."

While they were in session, he went and came back. Ablat got up and took of the man's knapsack and found in it a snake cut up and lying in two pieces.

Said Samuel to the man, "What did you do [today in particular]?"

He said to him, "Every day we tossed our bread into one pot and ate, but today one of us had no bread, and he was shamed. I said to him, 'I will go and collect the bread.' When I came to him, I made as if to go and collect the bread, so he shouldn't be ashamed."

He said to him, "You have carried out a religious duty."

Samuel went forth and expounded, "'But charity delivers from death' (Prov. 10:2)—not from a grotesque death, but from death itself."

It is also the position of Aqiba that Israel is not subject to the stars.

For R. Aqiba had a daughter. Chaldaeans [astrologers] told him, "On the day that she goes into the bridal canopy, a snake will bite her and she'll die."

This worried him a lot. On that day she took a brooch and stuck it into the wall, and by chance it sank into the eye of a snake. The next day when she took it out, the snake came trailing along after it.

Her father said to her, "What did you do [today in particular]?"

She said to him, "In the evening a poor man came to the door, and everyone was busy with the banquet so no one could take care of him, so I took some of what was given to me and gave it to him."

He said to her, "You have carried out a religious duty."

R. Aqiba went forth and expounded, "'But charity delivers from death' (Prov. 10:2)—not from a grotesque death, but from death itself."

BAVLI TO MISHNAH-TRACTATE SHABBAT 24:3/156A-B

Attitude: Better Sincere Sin Than Hypocritical Virtue

Yohanan Hassandelar says, "Any gathering which is for the sake of Heaven is going to endure. And any which is not for the sake of Heaven is not going to endure."

TRACTATE ABOT 4:11

"Now it happened that when Moses held up his hand, Israel prevailed, and when he let his hand fall, Amalek prevailed" (Exod. 17:11).

Now do Moses's hands make war or stop it?

But the purpose is to say this to you:

So long as the Israelites would set their eyes upward and submit their hearts to their Father in Heaven, they would grow stronger. And if not, they fell.

In likewise, you may say the following:

"Make yourself a fiery serpent and set it on a standard, and it shall come to pass that everyone who is bitten, when he sees it, shall live" (Num. 21:8).

Now does that serpent [on the standard] kill or give life? [Obviously not.]

But: So long as the Israelites would set their eyes upward and submit to their Father in Heaven, they would be healed. And if not, they would pine away.

MISHNAH-TRACTATE ROSH HASHANAH 3:8

Said R. Nahman bar Isaac, "A transgression committed for its own sake, in a sincere spirit, is greater in value than a religious duty carried out not for its own sake, but in a spirit of insincerity.

"For it is said, 'May Yael, wife of Hever the Kenite, be blessed above women, above women in the tent may she be blessed' (Judg. 5:24).

"Now who are these women in the tent? They are noneother than Sarah, Rebecca, Rachel, and Leah." [The murder she committed gained more merit than the matriarchs' great deeds.]

But is this really true that a transgression committed for its own sake, in a sincere spirit, is greater in value than a religious duty carried out not for its own sake, but in a spirit of insincerity. And did not R. Judah say Rab said, "A person should always be occupied in study of the Torah and in practice of the commandments, even if this is not for its own sake [but in a spirit of insincerity], for out of doing these things not for their own sake, a proper spirit of doing them for their own sake will emerge"?

Say: it is equivalent to doing them not for their own sake.

Said R. Judah said Rab, "A person should always be occupied in study of the Torah and in practice of the commandments, even if this is not for its own sake [but in a spirit of insincerity], for out of doing these things not for their own sake, a proper spirit of doing them for their own sake will emerge."

For as a reward for the forty-two offerings that were presented by the wicked Balak to force Balaam to curse Israel, he was deemed worthy that Ruth should descend from him.

For said R. Yosé b. R. Hanina, "Ruth was the grand daughter of Eglon, the grandson of Balak, king of Moab."

BAVLI TO MISHNAH-TRACTATE HORAYOT 3:3/10B-11A

Blessings

R. Simeon says, "There are three crowns: and these are they: the crown of the Torah, the crown of priesthood, and the crown of sovereignty. But the crown of a good name is best of them all."

The crown of the priesthood: how so? Even if one should give all the silver and gold in the world, people still cannot bestow on him the crown of the priesthood, for it is said, "And he and his descendants after him shall have the covenant of an everlasting priesthood" (Num. 25:13).

The crown of sovereignty: Even if one should give all the silver and gold in the world, people still cannot bestow on him the crown of sovereignty, as it is said, "And my servant David shall be their prince forever" (Ezek. 37:25).

But the crown of the Torah is not that way. As to the labor of the Torah, whoever wants to undertake it may come and undertake it, as it is said, "Let all who thirst come for water" (Isa. 51:1).

THE FATHERS ACCORDING TO RABBI NATHAN XLI:I.1

Booksmarts

We have here a different version of a universally held truth: It is better to do things than to know things. But while the sages take a conventional view towards knowledge—it is nothing without action—it is left to the reader to interpret what are "good deeds." In the context of the sages' many other discussions about the activity of learning, it is hard to imagine how anyone could achieve true knowledge without committing good deeds as well. After all, if obtaining knowledge is a divine exercise, achievable only through the honored relationship between a sage and his disciple, knowledge is itself a product of good deeds. Nevertheless, the following passage offers a wonderful metaphor for knowledge, one that has been recirculated effectively for centuries: the tree of life.

Simeon his son says: "All my life I grew up among the sages, and I found nothing better for a person [the body] than silence. And not the learning is the thing, but the doing. And whoever talks too much causes sin."

TRACTATE ABOT 1:17

R. Hanina b. Dosa says, "For anyone whose fear of sin takes precedence over his wisdom, his wisdom will endure. And for anyone whose wisdom takes precedence over his fear of sin, wisdom will not endure, as it is said, 'The beginning of wisdom is the fear of the Lord' (Ps. 111:10)."

He would say, "Anyone whose deeds are more than his wisdom—his wisdom will endure. And anyone whose wisdom is more than his deeds—his wisdom will not endure, as it is said, 'We will do and then we will listen' (Exod. 24:7)."

TRACTATE ABOT 3:9

People said before Rabban Yohanan ben Zakkai, "A sage who fears sin—to what is [he comparable]?"

He said to them, "Lo, such a one is a craftsman with his tools in hand."

"A sage who does not fear sin?"

He said to them, "Lo, this is a craftsman without his tools."

"One who fears sin but is no sage?"

"This is not a craftsman, but he has tools in hand."

R. Eleazar b. Azariah says, "If there is no learning of Torah, there is no proper conduct, if there is no proper conduct, there is no learning in Torah. If there is no wisdom, there is no reverence. If there is no reverence, there is no wisdom."

He would say, "A person who has good works and has studied much Torah—to what is he likened? To a tree that stands by water, with few branches but deep roots. Even though the four winds of the world come, they cannot move it from its place,

"as it is said, 'He shall be as a tree planted by the waters, and that spreads out its roots by the river, and shall not fear when heat comes, and his leaf shall be green, and shall not be careful in the year of drought, neither shall cease from yielding fruit' (Jer. 17:8).

"A person in whom are no good deeds but who has studied much Torah—to what is he compared? To a tree that stands in the wilderness, with abundant branches but shallow roots. When the winds blow, they will uproot it and blow it down,

"as it is said, 'He shall be like a tamarisk in the desert and shall not see when good comes, but shall inhabit the parched places in the wilderness' (Jer. 17:6)."

THE FATHERS ACCORDING TO RABBI NATHAN XXII:I-III

Elisha b. Abuyah says, "One who has good deeds to his credit and has studied the Torah a great deal—to what is he to be likened?

"To someone who builds first with stones and then with bricks. Even though a great flood of water comes and washes against the foundations, the water does not blot them out of their place.

"One who has no good deeds to his credit but has studied the Torah—to what is he to be likened?

"To someone who builds first with bricks and then with stones. Even if only a little water comes and washes against the foundations, it forthwith overturns them."

He used to say, "One who has good deeds to his credit and has studied the Torah a great deal—to what is he to be likened?

"To lime spread over stones. Even if vast rain storms come down on them, they do not stir the lime from its place.

"One who has no good deeds to his credit but has studied the Torah a great deal—to what is he to be likened?

"To lime spread over bricks. Even if a sporadic rain falls on the lime, it is forthwith melted and disappears."

He used to say, "One who has good deeds to his credit and has studied the Torah a great deal—to what is he to be likened?

"To a cup with a base.

"One who has no good deeds to his credit but has studied the Torah a great deal—to what is he to be likened?

"To a cup with no base. When the cup is filled, it turns on its side and whatever is in it pours out."

He used to say, "One who has good deeds to his credit and has studied the Torah a great deal—to what is he to be likened?

"To a horse that has a bridle.

"One who has no good deeds to his credit but has studied the Torah a great deal—to what is he to be likened?

"To a horse without a bridle. When someone rides on the horse, it throws him off with a toss of the head [Goldin: headlong]."

He used to say, "He who studies the Torah in his youth—the words of the Torah are absorbed in his blood and come out of his mouth fully spelled out.

"He who studies the Torah in his old age—the words of the Torah do not get absorbed in his blood and do not come out of his mouth fully spelled out.

"And so is the apophthegm: 'If in your youth you did not want them, how will you get them in your old age?'"

THE FATHERS ACCORDING TO RABBI NATHAN CXXIV:I-V

Busy-ness and Real Achievement

Rabbi Tarfon says: "The day is short, the work formidable, the workers lazy, the wages high, the employer impatient."

He would say: "It's not your job to finish the work, but you are not free to walk away from it. If you have learned much Torah, you will be given a good reward. And your employer can be depended upon to pay your wages for what you do. And know what sort of reward is going to be given to the righteous in the coming time."

TRACTATE ABOT 2:15-16

Charity and Righteousness

The Hebrew word for righteousness is used also to refer to charity or philanthropy. That is the basis of all that follows.

It has been taught on Tannaite authority:

R. Judah says, "Great is charity, for it draws redemption nearer: 'Thus says the Lord, keep judgment and do righteousness [charity], for my salvation is near to come and my righteousness to be revealed' (Isa. 56:1)."

He would say, "Ten strong things have been created in the world. Rock is strong, iron shatters it. Iron is strong, fire melts it. Fire is strong, water quenches it. Water is strong, clouds carry it. Clouds are strong, wind scatters them. Wind is strong, the body can withstand it. The body is strong. Fear crushes it. Fear is strong, wine overcomes it. Wine is strong, sleep removes it. Death is strongest of all, but charity saves from death: 'Righteousness delivers from death' (Prov. 10:2)."

Expounded R. Dosetai b. R. Yannai, "Come and note that the trait of the Holy One, blessed be he, is not like the trait of a mortal. If someone brings a splendid gift to the king, it may or may not be accepted from him, and should it be accepted from him, he may or may not see the king. But the Holy One, blessed be he, is not that way. Someone gives a penny to a poor person, and he has the merit of receiving the face of the Presence of God: 'And I shall behold your face in righteousness, I shall be satisfied when I awake with your likeness' (Ps. 17:15)."

Said R. Yohanan, "What is the meaning of the clause, 'He who has pity on the poor lends to the Lord' (Prov. 19:17)?

"Were the matter not explicitly written down in a verse of Scripture, it would not be possible to state it! It is, as it were, to say, 'The borrower is a slave to the lender' (Prov. 22:7)."

Said R. Hiyya bar Abba [said] R. Yohanan, "It is written, 'Riches do not profit in the day of wrath, but righteousness delivers from death' (Prov. 11:4), and further, 'Treasures of wickedness profit nothing, but righteousness delivers from death' (Prov. 10:2). Why make reference to righteousness two times? One delivers from an unnatural death, the other from punishment of Gehenna.

"Which one delivers from Gehenna? It is the one in which 'wrath' is used, as it is written, 'A day of wrath is that day' (Zeph. 1:15).

"Which delivers someone from an unnatural death?

"When someone gives without knowing to whom he is giving, when someone gets without knowing from whom he gets."

"When someone gives without knowing to whom he is giving": this excludes the practice of Mar Uqba.

"When someone gets without knowing from whom he gets": this excludes what R. Abba would do.

So what should one do?

Put the money in the charity box.

BAVLI TO MISHNAH-TRACTATE BABA BATRA 1:5/BAVLI 10A-B

Collegiality: Going Along to Get Along

The temptation to stray, an issue of sin, nevertheless has its roots in social instincts. The sages deal here succinctly with the pressure to go along, and ultimately praise the impulse to go it alone, in study.

R. Nehuniah b. Haqqanneh used to recite a short prayer when he entered the study hall and when he exited.

They said to him, "What is the nature of this prayer?"

He said to them, "When I enter, I pray that I will cause no offense. And when I exit, I give thanks for my portion."

MISHNAH-TRACTATE BERAKHOT 4:2

When he enters [the study hall] what does he say? "May it be thy will, Lord my God, God of my fathers that I shall not be angry with my associates, and that my associates shall not be angry with me; that we not declare the clean to be unclean, that we not declare the unclean to be clean; that we not declare the permissible to be forbidden, that we not declare the forbidden to be permissible; lest I find myself put to shame in this world and in the world to come [for rendering a wrong decision]."

And when he exits [the study hall] what does he say? "I give thanks to thee, Lord my God, God of my fathers, that you cast my lot with those who sit in the study hall and the synagogues, and you did not cast my lot with those who sit in the theaters and circuses. For I toil and they toil. I arise early and they arise early. I toil so that I shall inherit [a share of] paradise [in the world to come] and they toil [and shall end up] in a pit of destruction. As it says, 'For thou dost not give me up to Sheol, or let thy godly one see the pit' (Ps. 16:10)."

R. Pedat in the name of R. Jacob bar Idi, "R. Eleazar used to recite three prayers after his recitation of the Prayer [of Eighteen]. What did he say? 'May it be thy will, Lord my God, and God of my fathers, that no person come to hate us, nor that we come to hate any person, and that no person come to envy us, not that we come to envy any person. And let [the study of] your Torah be our occupation all the days of our lives. And let our words be supplications before you.'"

R. Hiyya bar Abba adds [to this prayer recited after the recitation of the Prayer of Eighteen], "And unite our hearts to fear your name. And keep us far from that which you despise. And bring us near to that which you love. And deal justly with us for the sake of your name."

YERUSHALMI BERAKHOT 4:2

Counsel: Wise Advice of Sages to Their Children and Disciples

Our rabbis have taught on Tannaite authority:

Seven things did R. Aqiba command his son R. Joshua, "My son, don't take up residence at the high point of a town or study there, and don't take up residence in a town that is headed by disciples of sages, and don't enter your own home suddenly, all the more so your neighbor's home, and don't hesitate to wear shoes. Get up early to eat, in summer because of the heat, in winter because of the cold. Treat your Sabbath as a weekday but don't fall into need of support from other people. Make every effort with someone on whom the hour smiles."

Five things did R. Aqiba command R. Simeon b. Yohai when he was imprisoned. He said to him, "My lord, teach me Torah."

He said to him, "I'm not going to teach you."

He said to him, "If you don't teach me, I will tell my father Yohai, and he will hand you over to the government."

He said to him, "My son, more than the calf wants to suck, the cow wants to suckle."

He said to him, "But if [the mother] is in danger, the calf also is in danger [so I can take the risk of learning if you can take the risk of teaching]."

He said to him, "Well, if you really want to be strangled, then get yourself hung from a big tree, and when you teach your son, teach him from a scroll that has been carefully proofread."

And what might that be?

Said Raba, and some say, R. Mesharshayya, "A new one; when a mistake gets in, it sticks."

"Don't cook in a pot that your neighbor has used."

And what might that be?

A divorcée while her ex- is still alive.

For a master has said, "A divorced man who married a divorced woman—there are four opinions in that bed."

If you wish, I shall say, even a widow, since not all "fingers" are the same.

"Enjoying the produce without interest is a religious duty and a good investment.

"A religious duty that leaves the body pure is marrying a woman when he already has children."

Said Rab to R. Kahana, "Deal in carcasses but not in words; flay carcasses in the market and earn a living, but don't say, 'I'm a priest and I'm an eminent authority, and it's beneath my dignity.' Even if you merely go up to the roof, take food with you. Even if a hundred pumpkins cost only a *zuz* [a small denomination of currency] in town, start hoarding them."

Our rabbis have taught on Tannaite authority:

There are three that are not to be provoked, and these are they: an inconsequential gentile, a little snake, and a humble disciple.

How come? Because their kingdom is standing behind their ears [they will grow up and take revenge].

Said Rab to Aibu his son, "I have worked hard with you in learning traditions, but nothing has come of it. Come, and I'll teach you things of this world: sell your wares with sand yet on your feet [as soon as you come to market with what you've bought], you may sell anything and regret it except for wine, which you should sell without regret; untie your purse, then open your sacks [pocket the money, then deliver the goods]; better a qab from the ground than a kor from the roof [stay near home]. When the dates are in your bag, go running to the brewery" [to make them into beer, but don't eat them; beer will bring more return].

Said R. Yohanan, "Over three does the Holy One, blessed be he, issue a proclamation every day: a single man who lives in a big city without sin, a poor man who returns lost and found to the owner, and a wealthy man who tithes his produce in secret."
R. Safra was a single man living in a big city.
A Tannaite authority recited that statement [of Yohanan] before Raba and R. Safra. R. Safra's face lit up. Said to him Rab, "That doesn't refer to someone like the master, but to such as R. Hanina and R. Oshayya, cobblers in the Land of Israel, who lived on Whore Street and made shoes for the whores and went to them. The whores looked at them, but they wouldn't raise their eyes to look at them, and the whore's oath was 'by the life of the holy rabbis of the Land of Israel.'"

There are three whom the Holy One, blessed be he, loves: he who doesn't lose his temper, he who doesn't get drunk, and he who doesn't insist on his viewpoint.

There are three whom the Holy One, blessed be he, hates: he who is insincere, he who knows testimony for his fellow but doesn't testify for him, and he who sees something improper in his neighbor and gives sole testimony against him [ruining his name but not inflicting legal punishment on him].

That is illustrated by the case of Tobias. He sinned, and Zigud came all by himself to testify against him before R. Pappa, who flogged Zigud. He said to him, "Tobias sinned and Zigud is flogged?"

"Yes: 'one witness shall not rise up against a man' (Deut. 19:15), but you have testified against him all on your own; so all you do is ruin his reputation."

Our rabbis have taught on Tannaite authority:
There are three whose lives are no lives: the lugubrious, the temperamental, and the picky.
And said R. Joseph, "All three traits are in me."

BAVLI TO MISHNAH-TRACTATE PESAHIM 10:1/BAVLI 112B-113B

Creation of Man [Adam] All Alone

Why are we different if we emerged from the same ancestor? The answers of the sages provide an insightful view of diversity and unity.

Therefore man was created alone, to teach you that whoever destroys a single Israelite soul is deemed by Scripture as if he had destroyed a whole world.

And whoever saves a single Israelite soul is deemed by Scripture as if he had saved a whole world.

And it was also for the sake of peace among people, so that someone should not say to his fellow, "My father is greater than your father."

And it was also on account of the minim, so that the *minim* [heretics] should not say, "There are many domains in Heaven."

And to portray the grandeur of the Holy One, blessed be he. For a person mints many coins with a single seal, and they are all alike one another, But the King of kings of kings, the Holy One, blessed be he, minted all human beings with that seal of his with which he made the first person, yet not one of them is like anyone else. Therefore everyone is obligated to maintain, "On my account the world was created."

MISHNAH-TRACTATE SANHEDRIN 4:5J-N

Therefore [man was created alone]:

Our rabbis have taught on Tannaite authority:

On what account was man created alone?

And why was he created one and alone in the world? Because of the righteous and the wicked

so that the righteous should not say, "We are the sons of the righteous one," and so that the evil ones should not say, "We are the sons of the evil one."

Another matter: Why was he created one and alone? So that families should not quarrel with one another. For if now, that man was created one and alone, they quarrel with one another, had there been two created at the outset, how much the more so!

Another matter: Why was he created one and alone? Because of the thieves and robbers. And if now, that he was created one and alone, people steal and rob, had there been two, how much the more so!

TOSEFTA SANHEDRIN 8:4A-E

To portray the grandeur . . .

Our rabbis have taught on Tannaite authority:

Why was he created one and alone?

To show the grandeur of the King of the kings of kings, blessed be he.

For if a man mints many coins with one mold, all are alike.

But the Holy One, blessed be he, mints every man with the mold of the first man [T: for with a single seal, he created the entire world], and not one of them is like another [T: from a single seal all those many diverse seals have come forth],

as it is said, "It is changed as clay under the seal, and all these things stand forth as in a garment." (Job 38:14)

And on what accounts are faces not like one another?

On account of imposters,

so no one should see a lovely house or woman and say "It is mine" [or: jump into his neighbor's field or jump in bed with his neighbor's wife],

as it is said, "And from the wicked their light is withheld and the strong arm is broken" (Job 38:15).

It has been taught on Tannaite authority: R. Meir says, "The omnipresent has varied a man in three ways: appearance, intelligence, and voice

intelligence, because of robbers and thieves, and appearance and voice, because of the possibilities of licentiousness."

Our rabbis have taught on Tannaite authority:

Man was created on Friday [last in order of creation].

And why was man created last?

So that he should not grow proud.

For they can say to him, "The mosquito came before you in the [order of the] works of creation."

Another matter: So that he might immediately take up the doing of a religious duty.

Another matter: So that he might enter the banquet at once [with everything ready for him].

They have made a parable: To what is the matter comparable?

To a king who built a palace and dedicated it and prepared a meal and [only] afterward invited the guests.

And so Scripture says, "The wisest of women has built her house" (Prov. 9:1).

This refers to the King of the kings of kings, blessed be He, who built his world in seven [days] by wisdom.

"She has hewn out her seven pillars" (Prov. 9:1)—these are the seven days of creation.

"She has killed her beasts and mixed her wine" (Prov. 9:2)—these are the oceans, rivers, wastes, and all the other things which the world needs.

And afterwards: She has sent forth her maidens, she cries on the high places of the city, Who is simple—let him turn in hither, and he who is void of understanding (Prov. 3:4)—these refer to Adam and Eve.

BAVLI TO MISHNAH-TRACTATE SANHEDRIN 4:5J/BAVLI SANHEDRIN 38A

Criticism

He would say, "If you have friends, some of whom give you criticism and some of whom give you praise, love the ones who give you criticism and hate the ones who give you praise.

"For the ones who give you criticism will bring you to the life of the world to come, while the ones who give you praise will remove you from the world."

THE FATHERS ACCORDING TO RABBI NATHAN XXIX

Death of a Loved One

The sages had a gift for euology—not simply because they understood how to bestow honor, but because they understood death.

When R. Hiyya bar Adda, the nephew of Bar Qappara, died R. Simeon Laqish accepted [condolences] on his account because he [Resh Laqish] had been his teacher. We may say that [this action is justified because] a person's student is as beloved to him as his son.

And he [Resh Laqish] expounded concerning him [Hiyya] this verse: "My beloved has gone down to his garden, to the bed of spices, to pasture his flock in the gardens, and to gather lilies" (Song of Sol. 6:2). It is not necessary [for the verse to mention, 'To the bed of spices']. [It is redundant if you interpret the verse literally, for most gardens have spice beds.]

Rather [interpret the verse as follows:] My beloved—this is God; has gone down to his garden—this is the world; to the beds of spices— this is Israel; to pasture his flock in the gardens—these are the nations of the world; and to gather lilies—these are the righteous whom he takes from their midst.

They offer a parable [relevant to this subject]. To what may we compare this matter [of the tragic death of his student]? A king had a son who was very beloved to him. What did the king do? He planted an orchard for him.

As long as the son acted according to his father's will, he would search throughout the world to seek the beautiful saplings of the world, and to plant them in his orchard. And when his son angered him he went and cut down all his saplings.

Accordingly, so long as Israel acts according to God's will, he searches throughout the world to seek the righteous persons of the nations of the world and bring them and join them to Israel, as he did with Jethro and Rahab. And when they [the Israelites] anger him he removes the righteous from their midst.

Once R. Hiyya bar Abba and his associates, and some say it was R. Yosé b. Halafta and his associates, and some say it was R. Aqiba and his associates, were sitting discussing Torah under a certain fig tree. And each day the owner of the fig tree would awaken early and gather [the ripe figs].

They said, "Perhaps he suspects [that we are taking his figs]. Let us change our place."

The next day the owner of the fig tree came and said to them, "My masters, you have deprived me of the one commandment which you were accustomed to fulfill with me [i.e. under my tree]."

They said to him, "We feared perhaps you suspected us [of taking your figs.]"

The next morning he [thought he would] let them see [why he picked the figs early]. He waited until the sun shined upon them and his figs got worm-eaten.

At that time they said, "The owner of the fig tree knows when it is the right time to pick a fig, and [at that time] he picks it."

So too God knows when it is the right time to take the righteous from the world, and [at that time] he takes them.

When R. Bun bar R. Hiyya died [at a young age] R. Zeira came up and eulogized him [by expounding this verse]: "Sweet is the sleep of a laborer [whether he eats little or much; but the surfeit of the rich will not let him sleep]" (Qoh.* 5:12). It does not say whether he sleeps [little or much] but rather whether he eats little or much. [Even though R. Bun died young and did not study for too many years, he will still have a sweet repose in the world to come.]

---

* Qohelet = the Book of Ecclesiastes

To what [story] may [the life of] R. Bun bar R. Hiyya be compared? [To this story.] A king hired many workers. One worker excelled very much in his work. What did the king do? He took him and walked with him back and forth [through the rows of crops and did not let him finish his day's work]. Towards evening, when all the workers came to be paid, he gave him a full day's wages along with [the rest of] them.

The workers complained and said, "We toiled all day, and this one toiled only two hours, and he gave him a full day's wages!"

The king said to them, "This one worked [and accomplished] more in two hours than you did in a whole day."

So R. Bun toiled in the study of the Torah for twenty-eight years, [and he learned] more than an aged student could learn in a hundred years."

When R. Levi bar Sisi died Samuel's father came up and eulogized him [by expounding]: "The end of the matter; all has been heard. Fear God . . . " (Qoh. 12:13).

To what [may the life of] R. Levi bar Sisi be compared? [To the story of] a king who had a vineyard, and in it were one hundred vines, which produced one hundred barrels of wine each year. [As his estate dwindled] he was left with fifty, then forty, then thirty, then twenty, then ten, then one [vine]. And still it [alone] produced one hundred barrels of wine. And he loved this vine as much as the whole vineyard.

In this way was R. Levi bar Sisi was beloved to God as much as all other persons together. This is as it is written, "For this is the whole of man [ibid.]." (Var.: Meaning [he loved] this one as much as all mankind [for he was a great God-fearing person].)

YERUSHALMI BERAKHOT 2:8

Deceit

There are seven kinds of thieves.

The first among all of them is the one who deceives people.

He who presses his fellow to come as his guest but does not intend to receive him properly.

He who overwhelms him with gifts and knows concerning him that he will not accept them.

He who opens for someone jars of wine which already had been sold to a storekeeper.

He who falsifies measures.

He who pads the scales.

He who mixes up seeds of St. John's bread in seeds of fenugrec, and vinegar in oil, even though they have said, oil does not mix with anything; therefore they use it for anointing kings.

And not only so, but they hold him culpable as if he [supposed he] were able to deceive the Most High and fool [him].

He who deceives people is called a thief, and it is said, "So Absalom stole the hearts of the men of Israel" (2 Sam. 15:6).

Who is the greater? The thief or the one who is the victim? One must say it is the one who is the victim, who was well aware that he was the victim of thievery but who kept silent.

So too we find when the Israelites were standing at Mount Sinai, they sought to deceive the Most High, as it is said, "All that the Lord has spoken we will do and we will hear" (Exod. 24:7).

It is as if he were the victim of stealing by them.

Scripture says, "Oh that they had such a mind as this always, to fear me and to keep all my commandments, that it might go well with them and with their children forever" (Deut. 5:29).

Now if you should want to claim that all things are not revealed before him, it already has been stated, "But they flattered him with their mouths; they lied to him with their tongues. Their heart was not steadfast toward him; they were not true to his covenant" (Ps. 78:36–37).

Nonetheless: "Yet he, being compassionate, forgave their iniquity, and did not destroy them" (Ps. 78:38).

And it says, "Like the glaze covering an earthen vessel are smooth lips with an evil heart.

"He who hates, dissembles with his lips, and harbors deceit in his heart; when he speaks graciously, believe him not, for there are seven abominations in his heart" (Prov. 26:23–25).

TOSEFTA BABA QAMMA 7:7

Discretion

"Even in your thought do not curse the king, nor in your bed-chamber curse the rich; [for a bird of the air will carry your voice, or some winged creature tell the matter]" (Qoh. 10:20).

Said R. Abin, "[God says,] 'You should not curse and blaspheme before me with that very capacity for thought that I gave you beyond [what I gave] to domesticated beasts, wild animals, and fowl.

"'For you I created two eyes and for them two eyes, for you two ears and for them two ears. I made you like them. [Yet] to him [namely, to man] they must keep silent.

"'He is like the beasts that keep silent' (Ps. 49:21). [God speaks], 'I have silenced them on account of the honor owing to you.'

"'How many favors have I done for you, and yet you do not understand.' 'Man in his honor does not understand' (Ps. 49:20)."

Another interpretation: "Even in your thought do not curse the king" (Qoh. 10:20). Do not curse the king who came before you.

"Nor in your bed-chamber curse the rich." Do not curse the rich man who came before you.

"For a bird of the air will carry your voice" (Qoh. 10:20).

Said R. Jeremiah bar Eleazar, "This refers to a raven and the art of bird divination."

"Or some winged creature will tell the matter" (Qoh. 10:20).

R. Levi said, "The wall has ears, the road along the ground has ears."

Another interpretation: "Even in your thought do not curse the king" (Qoh. 10:20). Do not curse the king [who rules] in your own generation.

"Nor in your bed-chamber curse the rich." Do not curse the rich man [who thrives] in your own generation.

"For a bird of the air will carry your voice" (Qoh. 10:20).

Said R. Judah bar Simon, "Said the Holy One, blessed be he, to David, 'David, is this the [appropriate] way you should have spoken before me: "All my enemies shall be ashamed and sorely troubled" (Ps. 6:10)? Who is your enemy? Is it not Saul? Is this not written: "On the day on which the Lord saved him from the hand of all his enemies and from the hand of Saul"' (Ps. 18:1)?

"At that moment David said before the Holy One, blessed be he, 'Lord of the ages. Do not count it against me as a deliberate sin but as an error.'

"For it is written, 'An error of David'" (Ps. 7:1).

Another interpretation: "Even in your thought do not curse the king" (Qoh. 10:20):

The King of the world you should not curse.

"Nor in your bed-chamber curse the rich" (Qoh. 10:20): The Rich One of the world you should not curse.

"For a bird of the air will carry your voice" (Qoh. 10:20).

Said R. Levi, "There is a voice that goes forth for good and there is a voice that goes forth for evil.

"There is a voice that goes forth for good: 'And the Lord heard the voice of your speaking, when you spoke to me, and the Lord said to me, "They have spoken well in all that they have said""" (Deut. 5:253).

[Levi resumes his discourse:] "There is a voice that goes forth for evil: 'And the Lord heard all the voice of your words and he grew angry'" (Deut. 1:34).

R. Hama in the name of R. Tahalipa, his father-in-law, said, "The Holy One, blessed be he, said, 'To you it appears to be anger, but to me it does not appear to be anger.'

"'Wherefore I swore in my anger' (Ps. 95:11). 'In my anger I swore, but I retract.'

"'If they shall come to my rest' (Ps. 95:11). 'To this rest they will not come, but they shall come to another rest [in the age to come].'"

R. Levi in the name of Bar Qappara said, "The matter may be compared to the case of a king who grew angry with his son and made a decree that he might not join him in his palace.

"What did the king then do [when he regretted his wrathful oath]? He went and tore down the palace and rebuilt it and brought his son [to live] with him into the [new palace].

"Thus he turned out to carry out his [original] oath and at the same time to bring his son in.

"So said the Holy One, blessed be he, 'Wherefore I swore in my anger that they should not enter into my rest' (Ps. 95:11).

"'To this rest they will not enter, but they will enter another rest.'"

"[For a bird of the air will carry your voice] or some winged creature tell the matter" (Qoh. 10:20):

Said R. Abin, "When a man sleeps, the body tells it to the soul, the soul to the spirit, the spirit to the angel, the angel to the cherub, the cherub to the winged creature, and the winged creature will tell the matter before Him who spoke and brought the world into being."

LEVITICUS RABBAH XXXII:II.1ff

Dogs: Our Best Friends

When a man's ways please the Lord, even his enemies are at peace with him (Prov. 16:7):

R. Meir says, "This [his enemies] refers to a dog."

R. Joshua b. Levi says, "This [his enemies] refers to a snake."

R. Meir says, "This refers to a dog. There was a herdsman who milked a cow. A snake came and drank from the milk. A dog saw it. The [herdsman and his family] sat down to eat. The dog began to bark at them, but they paid no attention to it. So the dog went and lapped up some of the milk and died. They buried him and set up a gravestone, and even now it is called 'the dog's gravestone.'"

R. Joshua b. Levi said, "It refers to a snake. There was a man who ground up garlic. A wild snake came along and ate of it. The house-snake saw this. They sat down to eat. The house-snake began to spit dirt at them, but they did not pay attention. In the end the snake threw itself into the garlic-mush [and died]."

R. Abbahu went to Caesarea. He happened by a certain person's house. The householder placed the dog by the visitor. He [Abbahu] said to him, "Do I owe you all this humiliation [that you inflict on me? Have I earned it?]"

He said to him, "My lord, I pay you only the greatest respect. On one occasion kidnappers came to town, and one of them came and wanted to drag off my wife. The dog went and bit off the man's balls."

PESIQTA DERAB KAHANA XI:I.1

Doubt: Giving People the Benefit of the Doubt

Our rabbis have taught on Tannaite authority:

To him who gives one's fellow the benefit of the doubt, they give the benefit of the doubt. And there was the case of someone who came down from Upper Galilee and was employed by someone in the South for three years. On the eve of the Day of Atonement he said to him, "Pay me my wages so that I can go and feed my wife and children."

He said to him, "I don't have any ready cash."

He said to him, "Then pay me in produce."

He said to him, "I don't have any."

"Give me land."

"I don't have any."

"Give me cattle."

"I don't have any."

"Give me pillows and blankets."

"I don't have any."

So he tossed his things over his shoulder and went home depressed. After the festival the householder took the man's salary in hand and with it three loaded asses, one bearing food, another drink, the third, various goodies, and he went to the man's house. After they had eaten and drunk, he gave him his salary. He said to him, "When you said to me, 'Give me my wages,' and I said to you, 'I don't have any ready cash,' of what did you suspect me?"

"I thought that you might have come upon a real bargain to buy with the cash."

"And when you said to me, 'Give me cattle,' and I said to you, 'I don't have cattle,' of what did you suspect me?"

"I thought that it might have been hired out to third parties."

"When you said to me, 'Give me land,' and I said to you, 'I don't have any land,' of what did you suspect me?"

"I thought that it might have been sharecropped by a third party."

"And when I said to you, 'I don't have produce,' of what did you suspect me?"

"I thought that they might not be tithed."

"And when I said to you, 'I don't have pillows and blankets,' of what did you suspect me?"

"I thought that you might have sanctified all your property to Heaven."

He said to him, "By the Temple service! That's just how things were. I vowed all my property [to others] on account of my son, Hyrcanus, who does not engage in Torah study, and when I went to my fellows in the South, they released me from my vow, and you, just as you gave me the benefit of the doubt, may the Omnipresent give you the benefit of the doubt."

Our rabbis have taught on Tannaite authority:

There was the case of a certain pious man who ransomed an Israelite woman [from kidnappers]. At the inn he had her lie at his feet. In the morning he went down, immersed, and repeated [Torah traditions] to his disciples.

He said to them, "When I had her lie down at my feet, of what did you suspect me?"

They said, "Perhaps among us is a disciple who is not thoroughly known by the master."

"When I went down and immersed, of what did you suspect me?"

"We thought that because of the rigors of the journey the master may have had a seminal emission."

He said to them, "By the Temple service! That's just how things were. Just as you gave me the benefit of the doubt, may the Omnipresent give you the benefit of the doubt."

Our rabbis have taught on Tannaite authority:

Once disciples of sages needed something from a Roman courtesan, with whom all the great men of Rome were intimate. They said, "Who will go?"

Said to them R. Joshua, "I will go."

R. Joshua and his disciples went. When they got to the door of her house, he took off his phylacteries at a distance of four cubits and went in and locked the door before them. When he came out, he went down and immersed and then he repeated Torah traditions for his disciples. And he said to them, "When I took off my phylacteries, of what did you suspect me?"

"We thought that the master was thinking that one should not bring holy words into an unclean place."

"When I locked the door, of what did you suspect me?"

"We thought that perhaps some matter of government may be dealt with between him and her."

"When I went down and immersed, of what did you suspect me?"

"We thought, maybe a bit of spit from her mouth landed on the garments of the master."

He said to them, "By the Temple service! That's just how things were. Just as you gave me the benefit of the doubt, may the Omnipresent give you the benefit of the doubt."

BAVLI TO MISHNAH-TRACTATE SHABBAT 18:2

Dreams and Their Interpretation

The following discussion, while extensive, is linked not only by the theme of dream-interpretation, but also by the issue of how one reaches those interpretations. The act of predicting future events for dreamers can be flawed, the sages warn us, giving a number of reasons why. Then, as a rejoinder to the theme at hand, they show how dream-interpretation is done right, and ultimately, whether it makes any difference.

When Samuel would have a bad dream, he would say, "Dreams speak falsely" (Zech. 10:2).

When he had a good dream, he would say, "Do dreams speak falsely? For it is written, 'I speak with him in a dream' (Num. 12:6)."

Raba contrasted these two verses: "'I speak with him in a dream' (Num. 12:6), but it also is written, 'Dreams speak falsely' (Zech. 10:2).

"But [Raba said] there is no contradiction. In the one case we speak of a message in a dream brought by an angel; in the other one brought by a shade."

Said R. Bizna bar Zabeda, said R. Aqiba, said R. Paneda, said R. Nahum, said R. Birim in the name of a sage, and who is it? it is R. Benaah, "There were twenty-four dream-interpreters in Jerusalem.

"Once I had a dream and I went to each one of them, and what one of them said by way of interpretation did not correspond to what the next one told me, but all of them came true for me.

"That serves to illustrate what is said: 'All dreams accord with what people have to say about them.'"

Said R. Samuel bar Nahmani said R. Jonathan, "What a man is shown [in a dream] is only his own fantasy [what is suggested by his own thoughts].

"For it is said, 'As for you, O King, your thoughts come into your mind upon your bed' (Dan. 2:29).

"If you prefer, I offer proof from the following verse: 'That you may know the thoughts of your heart' (Dan. 2:30)."

Said Raba, "You may know that that is so, for people are not shown in dreams [such impossibilities as] either a golden palm tree or an elephant going through the eye of a needle."

Bar Hedya was a dream-interpreter. If someone gave him a fee, he would interpret his dream in a good way, and if someone did not pay him a fee, he interpreted it in a bad way.

Abbayye and Raba had dreams. Abbayye paid him a fee of a *zuz*, and Raba did not give him anything.

They said to him, "In our dream we recited the verse, 'Your ox shall be slain before your eyes' (Deut. 28:31)."

To Raba he said, "You will go bankrupt and will not even want to eat because of depression."

To Abbayye he said, "You will make a killing, and you will not want to eat because of excitement."

They said to him, "We recited [in our dreams] the verse, 'You shall beget sons and daughters but they will not be yours' (Deut. 28:41)."

To Raba he said that it is an unfavorable sign.

To Abbayye he said, "Your sons and daughters will be many. Your daughters will get married to others and it will seem to you as if they go into captivity."

"We recited, 'Your sons and your daughters will be given to another people' (Deut. 28:32)."

To Abbayye he said, "Your sons and daughters will be many. You will want to marry them to your relations, and your wife will want to marry them off to hers, and she will force you to give them to her relations, so that it will seem as if it is to another people."

To Raba he said, "Your wife will die, and your sons and daughters will fall into the hands of another woman [when you remarry]."

For Raba said R. Jeremiah bar Abba said Rab said, "What is the meaning of the verse of Scripture, 'Your sons and your daughters will be given to another people' (Deut. 23:32)?

"This speaks of a stepmother."

"We recited in our dreams: 'Go your way, eat your bread with joy' (Qoh. 9:7)."

To Abbayye he said, "You will make a killing and eat and drink and recite that verse out of great joy."

To Raba he said, "You will go bankrupt. You will have to kill a beast but not eat the meat and drink, and you will recite the verse of Scripture to [Simon:] allay your anxiety."

"We recited this verse: 'You shall carry much seed out into the field [and gather little in, for the locusts will consume it]' (Deut. 28:38)."

To Abbayye he cited the first half of the verse, to Raba, the second half.

"We recited, 'You shall have olive trees throughout your borders [but you shall not anoint yourself]' (Deut. 28:40)."

To Abbayye he cited the first half of the verse, to Raba the second half.

"We recited, 'And all the peoples of the earth shall see that the name of the Lord is called upon you' (Deut. 28:10)."

To Abbayye he said, "Your reputation will go forth as head of a court, and respect for you will fall upon everybody."

To Raba he said, "The royal treasury will be broken into, and you will be arrested as a thief, and everyone will make an argument *a fortiori* based upon you [Simon: If Raba is suspect, how much more so are we]."

The next day the royal treasury was broken into, and they came and arrested Raba.

They said to [Bar Hedya], "We saw lettuce on the mouth of the jar."

To Abbayye he said, "Your profits will double like lettuce."

To Raba he said, "Your business will be as bitter as lettuce."

They said to him, "We saw meat on the mouth of the jar."

To Abbayye he said, "Your wine will be sweet, and everyone will come to buy meat and wine from you."

To Raba he said, "Your wine will turn, and everyone will come to buy meat to eat with it [as a cheap condiment]."

They said, "We saw a cask hanging on a palm."

To Abbayye he said, "Your business will thrive like a palm."

To Raba he said, "Your merchandise will be as sweet as dates [to the customers, who will find it very cheap]."

They said to him, "We saw a pomegranate growing on the mouth of a jar."

To Abbayye he said, "Your goods will fetch high prices like pomegranates."

To Raba he said, "Your merchandise will turn stale, like a [dry] pomegranate."

They said to him, "We saw a cask fall into a pit."

To Abbayye he said, "Your merchandise will fetch a good market, as in the saying, 'The madder has fallen into a well and cannot be found. [Simon: Your goods will be in demand like something which has fallen into a pit.]"

To Raba he said, "Your merchandise will spoil and be thrown into a pit."

They said to him, "We saw a young ass standing by our pillow and braying."

To Abbayye he said, "You will become king and an Amora [as your spokesman] will stand at your side [to repeat in a loud voice what you say]."

To Raba he said, "The words, 'The first born of an ass' [a passage written in the phylacteries] have been erased from your phylactery."

[Raba then] said to him, "I examined them, and those words are there." He said to him, "The letter W from the word '[first-born of] an ass' certainly has been erased from your phylactery."

In the end Raba came by himself to [Bar Hedya]. He said to him, "I saw that the outer door fell down."

He said to him, "Your wife will die."

He said to him, "I saw that my front and back teeth fell out."

He said to him, "Your sons and daughters will die."

He said to him, "I saw two pigeons flying away."

He said to him, "You will divorce two wives."

He said to him, "I saw two turnip tops."

He said to him, "You will be hit twice with a club."

That day Raba went and stayed at the session of the school house all day long. He came upon two blind men fighting with one another. Raba went to separate them, and they hit Raba twice. They were going to hit him again, but he said, "Two are enough. That is all that I saw in my dream."

In the end Raba came and paid [Bar Hedya] a fee. He said to him, "I saw a wall fall down."

He said to him, "Goods without limit you will get."

He said to him, "I saw Abbayye's house fall down and get covered with dirt."

He said to him, "Abbayye will die and his entire court will come to you."

He said to him, "I saw my house fall down and everybody came and took a brick."

He said to him, "Your traditions will be scattered [and known] everywhere."

He said to him, "I saw that my skull was split open and my brains fell out."

He said to him, "The stuffing will come out of your pillow."
He said to him, "In my dream I recited the Hallel-Psalms for [the exodus from] Egypt."

He said to him, "A miracle will happen to you."

[Bar Hedya] was going along with [Raba] on a boat. [Bar Hedya] said [to himself], "What business do I have traveling with someone for whom a miracle will be done? [It will be necessary to save us all, but only he will be saved]."

As he got off the boat, a scroll fell from his hand. Raba found it and saw that written in it were the words, "All dreams accord with the interpretation [that someone gives to them]."
He said, "Wicked one! It was your fault that the dreams came true as they did, and you made all this trouble for us. I forgive you for everything except for what happened to the daughter of R. Hisda [my wife, who died on your account]. May it be God's will that that man [you] be handed over to the government, and that the government have no pity for you."

He said, "What shall I do? It is a tradition that a curse of a sage, even if it is for nothing, comes true. That is all the more so the case with Raba's curse, for he cursed me quite justly."

He said, "I'll go and escape into exile. For a master has said, 'Exile atones for sin.'"

He went and into exile, to Roman territory. He went and sat at the door of the [Simon:] keeper of the king's wardrobe. The wardrobe keeper had a dream. He said to him, "I had a dream that a needle pricked my finger."

He said to him, "Pay me a *zuz*."

The other would not hand it over to him, so he would not say anything to him.

He said to him, "I saw in a dream that a worm fell between my two fingers."

He said to him, "Pay me a *zuz*."

The other would not hand it over to him, so he would not say anything to him.

He said to him, "I saw in a dream that a worm fell in my hand."

He said to him, "Worms have fallen all over the silks [of the wardrobe]."

The word spread throughout the palace, and they took the wardrobe keeper to kill him. He said to them, "Why are you taking me? You should take the one who knew what was going on and said nothing."

They took Bar Hedya and said to him, "On account of your *zuz* the king's silks have been ruined. They tied together two cedar trees with a rope. They tied one of his legs to one cedar and the other to the other one. Then they cut the cedars loose, and he split into two. Each tree popped up, and he lost his head and split into two.

BAVLI TO MISHNAH-TRACTATE BERAKHOT 9:1/55B-56B

A Samaritan set himself up as a dream-interpreter, ridiculing people.

Said R. Ishmael b. R. Yosé, "I shall go and see how this Samaritan is ridiculing people."

He went.

Someone came to him and said, "I saw in my dream an olive tree feeding oil."

He said to him, "The olive means light and oil means light; you will see a lot of light."

Said R. Ishmael b. R. Yosé, "May your spirit explode! That man has known [has committed incest with] his mother."

Someone else came to him, saying to him, "I saw in my dream one eye swallowing the other."

He said to him, "Your one eye is light and so the other, you will see much light."

Said R. Ishmael b. R. Yosé, "May your spirit explode! That man has two children, and one of them has committed incest with the other."

Someone else came to him, saying to him, "I saw in my dream that I swallowed a star."

He said to him, "You are light and a star is light, so light is added to light."

Said R. Ishmael b. R. Yosé, "May your spirit explode! That man has killed a Jew."

How did he know it? From the following: "Look now toward Heaven and count the stars" (Gen. 15:5).

Another came to him and said, "I saw in my dream that I had three eyes."

He said to him, "You will see much light."

Said R. Ishmael b. R. Yosé, "May your spirit explode! That man is a baker; two eyes are his own, the third, the oven's."

Another came to him and said, "I saw in my dream that I had four ears, and everybody was listening to me."

He said to him, "You will be very famous."

Said R. Ishmael b. R. Yosé, "May your spirit explode! That man is a thorn-gatherer, and when he carries them everybody runs away from him."

Another came to him and said, "I saw in my dream that I was carrying a notebook with twenty-four pages, written on one side and erased on the other."

He said to him, "You are rising to greatness, and your business affairs will be so many that you will have to write and erase."

Said R. Ishmael b. R. Yosé, "May your spirit explode! That man has a garment of twenty-four patches, and he sews in one place and the garment is torn in another."

Another came to him and said, "I saw in my dream that I was carrying a pole, with a bundle of lettuce tied to it."

He said to him, "You are rising to greatness."

Said R. Ishmael b. R. Yosé, "May your spirit explode! That man has a store of wine that is going to sour, and everybody will come and take some of it in bottles and use it for pickling lettuce."

Another came to him and said, "I saw in my dream that everybody was pointing at me.

He said to him, "You are rising to greatness and everybody is going to point at you as a gesture of praise."

Said R. Ishmael b. R. Yosé, "Pay me the fee, and I'll interpret the dream for you."

He said to him, "It has already been interpreted."

The same man came back and said, "I saw in my dream that everybody was puffing at me with their cheeks and praising me with gestures of their fingers."

He said to him, "You will become great, and everybody will praise you with his cheeks."

Said R. Ishmael b. R. Yosé, "May your spirit explode! That man has a store of wheat, and when he dreamed people were pointing at him in praise, what it meant was that rain had dripped on it, and when he dreamed that people were puffing at him with their cheeks, it meant that the wheat had swelled up, and when he dreamed that people praised him with their fingers, it meant that the wheat had already sprouted, so he would get no profit from it."

A Samaritan said, "I want to go to see a certain sage of the Jews who makes fun of everybody."

He said to him, "I saw in my dream four cedars, four sycamores, a hide stuffed with straw, and an ox riding on them."

Said to him R. Ishmael b. R. Yosé, "The four cedars stand for four bedposts, the four sycamores stand for four legs of the bed, the hide stuffed with straw, the cords, the ox riding on them, the leather mattress on which you sleep. You are going to climb up into bed but not get out of it."

And so it happened.

Another came and said to him, "In planting season I dreamed of an olive tree."

He said to him, "You will see a lot of light."

Another came and said to him, "In beating season I dreamed of olives."

He said to him, "Prepare your loins for blows."

He said to him, "My lord, the other got a good interpretation and I got a bad one!?

He said to him, "May your spirit explode! He saw it at planting time, you at beating time."

There was the case of a disciple who was in session before R. Yohanan, who explained matters to no avail.

He said to him, "What's wrong that you don't understand?"

He said to him, "I saw in my dream three bad things, and I don't know what they mean."

He said to him, "What are they?"

He said to him, "In my dream I was told I would die in the month of Adar, would not see the month of Nisan, and would sow but not reap."

He said to him, "These are good omens. 'Dying in Adar' means you will die in the glory of the Torah. 'Not seeing Nisan' means you will not experience trials [the words for "Nisan" and "trials" use the same consonants].' 'Sowing but not reaping' means you will not bury children who are born to you."

Another one said to him, "I dreamed that I did not have pants on."
He said to him, "That is not a bad sign but a good one. When the Festival [of Tabernacles] comes, you will have nothing."
How did he know? Because the word for "leg" and the word for "festival" are the same.

Someone came to R. Yosé b. Halafta and said, "I was shown in my dream, 'Go to Cappadocia and find your father's property.'"
He said to him, "Did your father ever go to Cappadocia?"
He said to him, "No."
He said to him, "Go, count the twentieth beam in your house."
He said to him, "There aren't twenty in all."
He said to him, "Go, count from top to bottom and from bottom to top, and at the twentieth you will find your father's treasure."
He did so and found the money and got rich.
How did R. Yosé know? Because in Greek *kappa* means twenty and *dokoi* means beams.

There was the case of a woman who came to R. Eleazar and said, "I saw in my dream that the beam of the house was split."
He said to her, "You will have a son."
And that's what happened.

Another time she came and did not find him there, but did find his disciples. She said to them, "Where is your master?"
They said to her, "What do you want of him?"
She said to them, "Maybe you are as smart as your teacher about interpreting a dream I saw."
They said to her, "Tell us what you want and we'll make sense of it for you."
She said to them, "I saw in my dream that the beam of the house was split."
They said to her, "You will bury your husband."
She left, weeping.
R. Eleazar heard and asked, "Why is she crying?"
They said to him, "She came to bring you a question but did not find you."
He said to them, "What did she want?"
"The interpretation of a dream."

"And what did you tell her?"

They told him, and he said to them, "You have killed him, for is it not written, 'And it came to pass, as he interpreted it to us, so it was' (Gen. 41:13)?

"And has not R. Yohanan said, 'A dream follows its interpretation, except in the case of wine. Some dream of drinking wine and it is a good sign, others dream of it and it is a bad sign.'"

R. Abbahu said, "Dreams mean nothing for either good or ill."

LAMENTATIONS RABBATI XXXV:VII.4

Drunkenness

"Do not look upon wine when it is red [when it sparkles in the cup and goes down smoothly. At the last it bites like a serpent and stings like an adder" (Prov. 23:31–2). "You will be like one who lies down in the midst of the sea, like one who lies on the top of a mast. 'They struck me,' you will say, 'but I was not hurt; they beat me, but I did not feel it. When shall I awake? I will seek another drink'" (Prov. 23:34–35). "Who has woe? who has sorrow? who has strife? who has complaining? who has wounds without cause? who has redness of eyes? Those who tarry long over wine, those who go to try mixed wine" (Prov. 23:29–30). "In the end it bites like a snake and stings [PRS, also: separates] like an adder" (Prov. 23:32).]

"Do not look upon wine when it is red": it certainly makes one red.

"When it sparkles in the cup": the passage is written not *kos*, "cup," but *kis*, "at the bag."

[The drinker] looks at the cup, the storekeeper at the purse.

"and goes down smoothly": in the end he will make his house bare.

He will say, "What this brass pot can do, a clay pot can do." So he sells the brass pot and drinks wine with the proceeds. "What this copper ladle can do a clay ladle can do," so he sells it and drinks wine with the proceeds.

R. Isaac b. Radipa in the name of R. Ammi said, "In the end he will sell everything in his house so as to drink wine with the proceeds."

Said R. Aha, "There is the case of a man who sold all his household goods to buy wine with the proceeds, the very beams of his house to buy wine with the proceeds.

"His children complained, saying, 'Will this old man of ours leave the world without leaving us a thing after he dies? What can we do with him? Let's go and make him drink and get him drunk and put him on a slab and take him out and say he's dead and lay him on his bier in the graveyard.' They did just that, taking him and getting him drunk and bringing him out and leaving him in the cemetery.

"Wine merchants passed by the gate of the graveyard. They heard that the *corvée* tax [of personal service to the crown] was being levied in that town. They said, 'Come and let's unload the wine skins in this grave and get out of here.' That's just what they did. They unloaded their burdens in the cemetery and went off to find out about the uproar in the town. Now that man was lying there, [and the merchants] saw him and took for granted that he was dead.

"When the man woke up from his sleep, he saw a skin of wine hanging above his head. He untied it and put the spout in his mouth and drank. When he was feeling good, he began to sing. After three days, his children said to one another, 'Shouldn't we go and see how father's doing—whether he's alive or dead!'

"They came and found him with a wine skin spout in his mouth, and he was sitting and drinking. They said to him, 'Even here your Creator has not abandoned you among the dead, but he has left you among the living. Since this is what Heaven has meted out to you, we don't know what we can do for you.' They agreed among themselves to provide for him and arrange some sort of permanent provision for him. They set things up so that each one would provide him with a drink per day."

It is written, "You will be like one who lies down in the midst of the sea, like one who lies on the top of a mast. ['They struck me,' you will say, 'but I was not hurt; they beat me, but I did not feel it. When shall I awake? I will seek another drink']" (Prov. 23:34–35):

"You will be like one who lies down in the midst of the sea": like a boat tossed on the high seas, going down and up, down and up.

Just as a ship is shaken in the ocean, so in the end a habitual drunkard is shaken out of his wits.

"like one who lies on the top of a mast": like a helmsman who sits on top of the masthead and falls asleep, as the mast sways to and fro underneath him.

Another interpretation: "like one who lies on the top of a mast": like a cock that sits on the top of a pole and falls asleep, as the pole sways to and fro underneath it.

["'They struck me,' you will say, 'but I was not hurt; they beat me, but I did not feel it. When shall I awake? I will seek another drink'"]: "they beat me, but I did not feel it": they hit him, but he did not feel it.

"they beat me, but I did not feel it":

They overcharge him, but he does not know it.

If he drank five *xestes* of beer, they say to him, "You drank ten."

If he drank ten, they say to him, "You drank twenty."

Should you wish to say, when he wakes up from his sleep, he will forget [wine], Scripture states, "When shall I awake? I will seek another drink."

["Who has woe? who has sorrow? who has strife? who has complaining? who has wounds without cause? who has redness of eyes? those who tarry long over wine, those who go to try mixed wine" (Prov. 23:29–30)]:

"Who has woe? who has sorrow":

R. Huna said, "He who does not work hard at studying Torah."

"who has strife? who has complaining": one who is sued, one who has quarrels.

"who has wounds without cause": one who has causeless injuries.

"who has redness of eyes": one who has irritated eyes.

There was a case of a man who would ordinarily drink twelve *xestes* of wine every day.

One day he drunk only eleven. He wanted to go to sleep, but sleep did not come. He got up in the darkness and went to the innkeeper, saying to him, "Sell me an *xestes* of wine."

He said to him, "No, I am not able to open for you, because it's already dark."

He said to him, "If you don't give it to me, my sleep will not come to me."

He said to him, "Just now the town watchmen went by here, and I am afraid on account of the watchmen, so I can't give you what you want."

The man looked up and saw a hole in the door. He said to him, "Push a straw through that hole, then you pour on the inside, and I'll drink out here."

The man pressed him. What did he do? He stuck a straw through the hole in the door, and as the innkeeper poured out wine inside, the man drank it outside. When he had finished, he fell asleep in a corner before the door.

The watchman came upon him by the door and found him asleep. Thinking that he was a thief, they beat him, but he did not feel it, and they wounded him, but he did not know it. They reddened his eye, and he did not see a thing.

People recited concerning him the following verse: "who has wounds without cause?"—who has causeless injuries?

"who has redness of eyes?": Who has irritated eyes?

Whom do such things afflict? "those who tarry long over wine, those who go to try mixed wine."

"those who tarry long over wine": They are the ones who get into the bar first and leave last.

"those who go to try mixed wine": These are people who go looking for wine.

When they hear that someone has a fine vintage, they go running after him and say, "So-and-so's wine is great, so-and-so's wine is red. Give us some and let's drink. So-and-so's wine is sparkling, give us some and let's drink it."

LEVITICUS RABBAH XII:I.1=ESTHER RABBAH I XXXII:I.1

Dying a Good Death

Said R. Hiyya the Elder, "[When a righteous man takes his leave of the world,] three bands of angels take care of him.

"One says, 'Let him come in peace' (Isa. 57:2).

"One says, 'Let him rest on his bier' (Isa. 57:2).

"One walks before him in silence, as it is said, '. . . . walking before him' (Isa. 57:2)."

Said R. Judah bar Simon in the name of R. Josiah, "The Holy One, blessed be he, as it were, says to him, 'Let him come in peace [whole and in one piece] from the wicked.'

"You derive the fact that the Holy One, blessed be he, says to the wicked, 'You [wicked] will have no peace,' from the verse, There is no peace, says my God to the wicked (Isa. 57:21).

"Now if with his own mouth the Holy One, blessed be he, says to the wicked, 'You will have no peace,' all the more so that to the righteous he will say, 'Let him come in peace.'"

On that account it is said, "Holy men exult in glory, they sing for joy on their beds (Ps. 149:5).

"In what glory will they exult? It is in the glory that the Holy One, blessed be he, does with the righteous when they take their leave of the world."

PESIQTA RABBATI II.III.2

R. Seorim, brother of Raba, was sitting before Raba at his death-bed, and saw him falling into a coma. Raba said to him, "Tell [the angel of death] not to torment me as I die."

He said to him, "But aren't you his good buddy?"

He said to him, "Since my star has been handed over into his control, he doesn't pay any attention to me any more."

He said to him, "Show yourself to me in a dream." [Raba] did so.

He asked him, "Did you suffer when you were dying?"

He said to him, "No more than the prick of the leech."

Raba was sitting before R. Nahman at his deathbed, and saw him falling into a coma. He said to him, "Tell [the angel of death] not to torment me as I die."

He said to him, "But aren't you an eminent authority?"

He said to him, "So who is eminent, who is regarded, who is treated as distinguished [by the angel of death]?"

He said to him, "Show yourself to me in a dream." He did so.

He asked him, "Did you suffer when you were dying?"

He said to him, "No more than taking a piece of hair out of the milk, and, I have to tell you, if the Holy One, blessed be he, said to me, 'Now go back to that world as you were before,' I wouldn't do it, for the fear of death is too much to take."

R. Eleazar was engaged in eating food in the status of priestly rations [which have to be protected from corpse-uncleanness] at the moment at which the angel of death made his appearance. He said to him, "Am I not eating food in the status of priestly rations? And is this not classified as Holy Things?!"

So the hour passed.

The angel of death made his appearance to R. Sheshet in the marketplace. He said to him, "Are you going to take me in the marketplace like a dumb cow? Come to me at my home!"

The angel of death made his appearance to R. Ashi in the marketplace. He said to him, "Give me thirty days' more so I can review my learning, since you say up there, 'Happy is he who comes up here bringing his learning all ready at hand.'"

So he came along thirty days later. He said to him, "So what's the rush?"

He said to him, "R. Huna bar Nathan is on your heels, and 'no regime may impinge upon its fellow, even by so much as a hair's breadth.'"

The angel of death could not overcome R. Hisda, because his mouth never ceased to recite his learning. He went out and sat on a cedar tree by the house of study. The branch of the cedar cracked, R. Hisda stopped, and the other overcame him.

The angel of death could not get near R. Hiyya. One day he appeared to him in the form of a poor beggar. He came and knocked on the door, saying, "Bring out some food for me." Others brought it out to him.

He said to R. Hiyya, "Aren't you, my lord, going to treat with mercy this man who is standing outside?"

He opened the door to him, and he showed him a fiery rod and made him give up his soul.

BAVLI TO MOED QATAN 3:8.III

When Joshua b. Levi lay dying, they said to the angel of death, "Go, do what he wants."

He went and showed himself to him. He said to him, "Show me my place [in Paradise]."

He said to him, "Well and good."

"Give me your knife, on the way you might otherwise frighten me."

He gave it to him.

When they got there, he raised him up [above the wall surrounding Paradise] and showed him his place. Joshua b. Levi leapt to the other side of the wall. The angel of death grabbed him by the corner of his cloak, but Joshua b. Levi exclaimed, "By an oath! I'm not going back!"

Said the Holy One, blessed be He, "If this man ever received remission for an oath of his, he has to go back, but if not, he may not go back."

[The angel of death said,] "Well, at least, give me back my knife." Joshua b. Levi wouldn't give it back.

An echo came forth and said to him, "Give it back to him, it's needed for ordinary mortals."

Elijah proclaimed before him, "Make place for the son of Levi, make place for the son of Levi!"

As [R. Joshua b. Levi] made his way, he came across R. Simeon b. Yohai, seated [Slotki:] at thirteen tables of gold. He said to [R. Joshua b. Levi], "Are you the son of Levi?"

He said to him, "Indeed so."

"Did a rainbow appear in your lifetime?"

"Yes."

"Then you're not the son of Levi."

But that's not so. In fact there was no such thing as a rainbow in his lifetime, but [R. Joshua b. Levi] thought to himself, "I don't want to take any credit for myself."

R. Hanina bar Pappa was [R. Joshua b. Levi's] friend. When he was dying, they said to the angel of death, "Go, do what he wants."

He went and showed himself to him. He said to him, "Let me have thirty days more, so I can review my learning, for it is said, 'Happy is he who comes here in full command of what he knows.'"

He allowed him the extra time, and thirty days later he appeared to him again. He said to him, "Show me my place [in Paradise]."

He said to him, "Well and good."

"Give me your knife, on the way you might otherwise frighten me."

He said to him, "Do you want to do to me what your friend did?"

He said to him, "Well, then, bring a scroll of the Torah, and look and see whether there's anything written in there that I didn't carry out?"

"Well, then, did you attach yourself to those who suffered from the dreadful skin ailment and study Torah?"

Even so [for he had done no such thing], when he died, a pillar of fire stood between him and the world, and we have learned as a tradition that a pillar of fire will form a partition only for one who was unique in his generation, or perhaps for two. R. Alexandri approached him and said, "Do something for the honor of the sages [and let us bury you]."

He ignored him.

"Do it for the honor of your father."

He ignored him.

"Do it for the honor owing to yourself!"

The pillar of fire departed.

BAVLI TO MISHNAH-TRACTATE KETUBOT 7:10

Ecology and Residence

Wisdom guides us not only in conduct, but even in choice of home. Some situations lack the elementary necessities of a decent life. For our sages knowing where to live matters, as does knowing how.

Said R. Huna, "Any city that has no vegetables —a disciple of a sage has no right to live there."

Said R. Judah said Rab, "Any town that has lots of ups and downs— men and beasts who live there die in half the normal lifetime."

They die? Do you really imagine it? Rather, they age in the prime of life.

Said R. Huna b. R. Joshua, "The crags between Be Bari and Be Nersh made me old."

BAVLI TO MISHNAH-TRACTATE ERUBIN 5:1/55B-56A

Envy

People naturally are competitive, but for many, competition spills over into contention. For if the other accomplishes something more, the one feels diminished. Envy fuels hatred, contempt, fear, and loathing; it is the single most common emotion. Whether among siblings or in clubs or in businesses, offices, and professions, no single emotion brings more malice or ill-will than sheer loathing of someone who has more, or does more, than the norm. Envy is the price of excellence, and the one who is envied, whether proud or humble, cannot do much about it.

Rabbi Joshua says: Envy, desire of bad things, and hatred for people push a person out of the world.

Envy: how so?

This teaches that in the way in which someone sees to his own household, so should we see to the household of another person.

And just as a person does not want a bad name to circulate against his wife and children, so he should not want to circulate a bad name against the honor owing to his fellow's wife and children.

Another matter concerning envy: how so?

A person should not begrudge another person the learning that that person has achieved.

There is the case of someone who envied the learning of his fellow. His life was shortened, he died and went his way.

THE FATHERS ACCORDING TO RABBI NATHAN XVI

Ephemerality of Glory: The Case of Adam

This an extended argument, which focuses on Adam's violation of the Garden of Eden, but applies to the very contemporary issue of wasted blessings. The sages lay out a sequence of events to illustrate Adam's fortune, not simply to be created by God, but to be created just before the Sabbath, when all creatures would delight in God's work. Yet Adam fails God, and is immediately sent from Eden. Glory is fleeting, indeed, and there is no patience in God's Heaven for those who squander a divine inheritance. The message is illustrated with examples closer to sages' contemporaries, but no less significant today.

What was the order of the creation of the first Man? [The entire sequence of events of the creation and fall of Man [Adam] and Woman took place on a single day, illustrating a series of verses of Psalms that are liturgically utilized on the several days of the week.]

In the first hour [of the sixth day, on which Man was made] the dirt for making him was gathered, in the second, his form was shaped, in the third, he was turned into a mass of dough, in the fourth, his limbs were made, in the fifth, his various apertures were opened up, in the sixth, breath was put into him, in the seventh, he stood on his feet, in the eighth, Eve was made as his match, in the ninth, he was put into the Garden of Eden, in the tenth, he was given the commandment, in the eleventh, he turned rotten, in the twelfth, he was driven out and went his way.

This carries out the verse: 'But Man does not lodge overnight in honor' (Ps. 49:13).

On the first day of the week [with reference to the acts of creation done on that day], what Psalm is to be recited? 'The earth is the Lord's and the fullness thereof, the world and they who dwell in it' (Ps. 24:1). For [God] is the one who owns it and transfers ownership of it, and he is the one who will judge the world.

On the second day? 'Great is the Lord and greatly to be praised in the city of our God' (Ps. 48:2). He divided everything he had made [between sea and dry land] and was made king over his world.

On the third day? 'God is standing in the congregation of the mighty, in the midst of the mighty he will judge' (Ps. 82:1). He created the sea and the dry land and folded up the land to its place, leaving a place for his congregation.

On the fourth day? 'God of vengeance, O Lord, God of vengeance, appear' (Ps. 94:1). He created the sun, moon, stars, and planets, which give light to the world, but he is going to exact vengeance from those who serve them.]

On the fifth? 'Sing aloud to God our strength, shout to the God of Jacob' (Ps. 81:2). He created the fowl, fish, mammals of the sea, who sing aloud in the world [praises of God].

On the sixth? 'The Lord reigns, clothed in majesty, the Lord is clothed, girded in strength, yes, the world is established and cannot be moved' (Ps. 93:1). On that day he completed all his work and arose and took his seat on the heights of the world.

On the seventh? 'A Psalm, a song for the Sabbath day' (Ps. 92:1). It is a day that is wholly a Sabbath, on which there is no eating, drinking, or conducting of business, but the righteous are seated in retinue with their crowns on their heads and derive sustenance from the splendor of God's presence, as it is said, 'And they beheld God and ate and drank' (Exod. 24:11), like the ministering angels.

And why [was man created last]?

So that [immediately upon creation on the sixth day] he might forthwith take up his Sabbath meal.

R. Simeon b. Eleazar says, "I shall draw a parable for you. To what may the first Man be compared? He was like a man who married a proselyte, who sat and gave her instructions, saying to her, 'My daughter, do not eat a piece of bread when your hands are cultically unclean, and do not eat produce that has not been tithed, and do not profane the Sabbath, and do not go around making vows, and do not walk about with any other man. Now if you should violate any of these orders, lo, you will be subject to the death penalty.'

"What did the man himself do? He went and in her presence ate a piece of bread when his hands were cultically unclean, ate produce that had not been tithed, violated the Sabbath, went around taking vows, and with his own hands placed before her [an example of what he had himself prohibited].

"What did that proselyte say to herself? 'All of these orders that my husband gave me to begin with were lies.' So she went and violated all of them."

R. Simeon b. Yohai says, "I shall draw a parable for you. To what may the first Man be compared? He was like a man who had a wife at home. What did that man do? He went and brought a jug and put in it a certain number of dates and nuts. He caught a scorpion and put it at the mouth of the jug and sealed it tightly. He left it in the corner of his house.

"He said to her, 'My daughter, whatever I have in the house is entrusted to you, except for this jar, which under no circumstances should you touch.' What did the woman do? When her husband went off to market, she went and opened the jug and put her hand in it, and the scorpion bit her, and she went and fell into bed. When her husband came home from the market, he said to her, 'What's going on?'

"She said to him, 'I put my hand into the jug, and a scorpion bit me, and now I'm dying.'

"He said to her, 'Didn't I tell you to begin with, "Whatever I have in the house is entrusted to you, except for this jar, which under no circumstances should you touch."' He got mad at her and divorced her.

"So it was with the first man.

"When the Holy One, blessed be he, said to him, 'Of all the trees of the garden you certainly may eat, but from the tree of knowledge of good and evil you may not eat, for on the day on which you eat of it, you will surely die' (Gen. 2:17),

"On that day he was driven out, thereby illustrating the verse, 'Man does not lodge overnight in honor' (Ps. 49:24)."

On the very same day Man was formed, on the very same day man was made, on the very same day his form was shaped, on the very same day he was turned into a mass of dough, on the very same day his limbs were made and his various apertures were opened up, on the very same day breath was put into him, on the very same day he stood on his feet, on the very same day Eve was matched for him, on the very same day he was put into the Garden of Eden, on the very same day he was given the commandment, on the very same day he went bad, on the very same day he was driven out and went his way, thereby illustrating the verse, "Man does not lodge overnight in honor" (Ps. 49:24).

THE FATHERS ACCORDING TO RABBI NATHAN I:XII-XIV

Father's Blessing of His Daughter

Irony can be illustrative; in this case, a father's apparent apathy can be understood later as deep caring. Rabban Gamaliel issues two blessings for his daughter—one, never to return home, and two, never to stop worrying for her own family. The blessings are commingled: they both mean the same thing. A good parent knows when a child has to become a parent, too.

Rabban Gamaliel married off his daughter, She said to him, "Father, pray for me."

He said to her, "May you never come back here."

She produced a son. She said to him, "Father, pray for me."

He said to her, "May the cry of 'woe' never leave your lips."

She said to him, "Father, on two occasions for rejoicing which have come to me, you curse me!"

He said to her, "Both of them were blessings. Because there will be peace in your home, may you never come back here, and because your son will live, may you never stop saying, 'Woe.' [That is,] 'Woe, my son has not yet eaten!' 'Woe, he has not yet drunk!' 'Woe, he has not yet gone to the school!'"

GENESIS RABBAH XXVI:IV.4

Flattery

These passages define flattery in reverse; not by what it is, but by who did it, for what purposes, and what can the word be compared to. Thus leaving us somewhere in the dark—with no definition, we should take care to impart our understanding of the word—the sages move to textual issues. An underlying argument remains however: flattery has its purpose only in strategic matters, when it would surely alleviate a dangerous situation. Otherwise, the sages imply, it is merely a tool for the wicked.

R. Judah, the Westerner, and some say, R. Simeon b. Pazzi, expounded, "It is permitted to flatter the wicked in this world, as it is said, 'The vile person shall no longer be called generous, nor the churl said to be bountiful' (Isa. 32:5). That reference [to what is no longer to be done] indicates that in this world, it is permitted [to do just that]."

R. Simeon b. Laqish said, "[Proof of that fact derives] from here: 'As one sees the face of God, and you were pleased with me' (Gen. 33:10) [this being what Jacob said by way of flattery to Esau]."

That statement differs from what R. Levi said, for R. Levi said, "To what may one compare the case of Jacob and Esau? To a man who invited his friend but realized that he wanted to kill him. He said to him, 'Taste this dish which I am tasting. It is like the dish I tasted when I was at the king's house.'

"The other party said, 'The king knows him?!' He thereupon became afraid [of the host] and did not kill him."

R. Eleazar said, "Whoever practices flattery brings anger upon the world, as it is said, "But they who are flatterers at heart lay up anger' (Job 36:13).

"Not only so, but the prayer of such a person is not heard, as it is said, 'They cry not for help when he chastens them' (Job 36:16)."

R. Eleazar said, "Whoever practices flattery—even foetuses in their mother's womb curse such a person,

"As it is said, 'He says to the wicked, "You are righteous"—peoples shall curse him, nations shall abhor him' (Prov. 24:24). Now the word for 'abhor' means only 'curse,' as it is said, 'Whom God has not cursed' (Num. 23:8). The word for nation refers only to foetus, as it is said, 'And the one nation [in context, foetus in the womb] shall be stronger than the other' (Gen. 25:23)."

R. Eleazar said, "Whoever practices flattery goes to Gehenna, as it is said, 'Woe to those who call evil good and good evil' (Isa. 5:20).

"What follows that verse? 'Therefore as the tongue of fire devours stubble and as the dry grass sinks down in the flame . . . .' (Isa. 5:20)."

And R. Eleazar said, "Whoever flatters his fellow in the end will fall into his power; if he does not fall into his power, he will fall into the power of his sons; and if he does not fall into the power of his sons, he will fall into the power of his grandson,

"So it is said, 'And Jeremiah said to Hananiah, "Amen. The Lord do so, the Lord perform your words"' (Jer. 28:6).

"And it is written immediately afterward, 'And when he was in the gate of Benjamin, a captain of the guard was there, whose name was Irijah, son of Shelemiah, son of Hananiah [grandson of the one Jeremiah had flattered], and he laid hold on Jeremiah the prophet, saying, "You go over to the Chaldeans." Then Jeremiah said, "It is false, I am not going over to the Chaldeans"' (Jer. 37:13). And it is written, 'So he laid hold of Jeremiah and brought him to the princes' (Jer. 37:14)."

And R. Eleazar said, "Any congregation in which there is flattery is to be avoided as a menstruating woman, as it is said, 'For the community of flatterers is separated' (Job. 15:34), and overseas they call a menstruating woman 'separated' [using the same word].

"What is the meaning of the word for barren? She is separated from her husband."

And R. Eleazar said, "Any community in which there is flattery in the end will go into exile.

"For here it is written, 'For the community of flatterers is barren' (Job 15:34), and elsewhere it is written, 'Then you shall say in your heart, "Who has gotten me these, since I have been bereaved of my children, and I am barren, an exile, and wandering to and fro"' (Isa. 49:21)."

Said R. Jeremiah bar Abba, "There are four categories who will not receive the face of the Presence of God:

"The category of scoffers, flatterers, liars, and slanderers.

"The category of scoffers, as it is written, 'He has stretched out his hand against scorners' (Hos. 7:5).

"The category of flatterers, as it is written, 'For a flatterer shall not come before him' (Job. 13:16).

"The category of liars, as it is written, 'He who speaks lies shall not be established in my sight' (Ps. 101:7).

"The category of slanderers, as it is written, 'For you are not a God who has pleasure in wickedness; evil will not dwell with you' (Ps. 5:5). 'You are righteous, O Lord, and evil will not dwell in your house.' [Psalm 5 addresses slander.]"

BAVLI TO MISHNAH-TRACTATE SOTAH 7:6/41B–42A

Foolishness

Typically, the sages find definition in comparison: not simply stating what something is, but what it is not. And while there is ample reason to define foolishness in terms of itself, the sages have chosen to compare it to wisdom. But the wisdom here appears to the modern eye more savvy than reflection. Nevertheless, these three arguments illustrate in a charming manner how foolishness and wisdom are well within the reach of anyone, at any time.

"His locks are wavy": (Song of Sol. 5:11):

[With reference to the word for wavy, the letters of which yield the word heaps,] R. Yohanan of Sepphoris interpreted the verse to speak of heaps of dirt:

"What does a fool say? 'Who can ever hope to remove this pile of dirt?'

"What does a smart person say? 'Lo, today, I'll take away two basket loads, and tomorrow I'll take away two, and in the end I'll take away the entire pile.'

"So a stupid person says, 'Who in the world can study the whole Torah? The tractate of Damages [referring to Baba Qamma, Baba Mesia, and Baba Batra] has thirty chapters and the tractate of Utensils has thirty chapters [of Mishnah teachings].'

"What does a smart person say? 'Lo, I'll learn two laws today, and two laws tomorrow, until I have finished reciting the entire Torah.'"

R. Yannai said, "'Wisdom is unattainable to the fool' (Prov. 24:7).

"The matter may be compared to the case of a loaf of bread suspended in the air in a house.

"What does a fool say? 'Who can bring it down?'

"What does a smart person say? 'Didn't somebody else go and hang it up? So I'll go and bring two sticks and tie them together and I'll pull it down.'

"So what does a fool say? 'Who can ever learn the Torah which is in the heart of a sage?'

"What does a wise man say? 'Didn't he learn it from somebody else? So I'll study two laws by day and two laws by night until I have learned the entire Torah just like him.'"

Said R. Levi, "The matter may be compared to a basket with a hole. The owner hired workers to fill it up.

"What does a fool say? 'What good can I do? The basket takes in here what it lets out there.'

"What does a smart person say? 'Do I not collect a wage for each barrel?'

"So what does a fool say? 'What good do I do if I learn Torah and then forget it?'

"But what does a wise man say? 'Does the Holy One, blessed be He, not pay a reward for the effort?'"

Forbearance

*Spite, or the desire to wish poorly on one's enemies, visits both God and
his lowliest servants in the following three sections. But the distinctions
between gradations of spite serve a purpose and teach a lesson. In the
first discussion, which has a striking philosophical utility, God does not
spite his creation for the sins of some of his creations. And in the final
discussion, a true sage does not spite his ex-wife for her own sins. Clearly,
we are reading about two kinds of relationships. But, as we have seen
before, the divine sets up the model, which can be replayed by the mortal.*

They asked sages in Rome, "If [God] is not in favor of idolatry, why
does he not wipe it away?"

They said to them, "If people worshipped something of which the
world had no need, he certainly would wipe it away.

"But lo, people worship the sun, moon, stars, and planets.

"Now do you think he is going to wipe out his world because of idiots?"

They said to them, "If so, let him destroy something of which the
world has no need, and leave something which the world needs!"

They said to them, "Then we should strengthen the hands of those who
worship these [which would not be destroyed], for then they would say, 'Now
you know full well that they are gods, for lo, they were not wiped out!' "

MISHNAH-TRACTATE ABODAH ZARAH 4:7A

". . . be prudent in judgment":

How so? This teaches that a person should be forbearing in his
opinions and should not be too captious in sticking to his opinions, for
whoever is captious in sticking to his opinions forgets his opinions.

For so we find in the case of Moses, our master, that when he was
captious in sticking to his views, he forgot his learning. [Goldin: This
teaches that a man should be patient in his speech and not short tempered in his speech, for whoever is short tempered in his speech forgets
what he has to say.]

Where do we find with respect to Moses, our master, that when he
was captious in sticking to his views, he forgot his learning?

As it is said, And Eleazar the priest said to the men of the army, who
had gone out to battle, "This is the law of the Torah which the Lord
commanded Moses" (Num. 31:22). "It was Moses whom he commanded, and not me whom he commanded, Moses, my father's brother,
whom he commanded, and not me, whom he commanded."

And where do we find with respect to Moses, our master, that he was captious in sticking to his views?

Lo, it says in respect to the officers of the army, 'And Moses was angry with the officers of the host, and Moses said to them, Have you saved all the women alive?' (Num. 31:14) [Remember, it was they who, in Balaam's departure, set about seducing the Israelites into disloyalty to the Lord that day at Peor, so that the plague struck the community of the Lord].

THE FATHERS ACCORDING TO RABBI NATHAN I:v.2

R. Yosé the Galilean had a bad wife, who was the daughter of his sister [so it was an act of merit that he married her] but who used to embarrass him. His disciples said to him, "Master, divorce her, for she does not treat you with respect."

He said to them, "Her dowry is too big for me, so I cannot divorce her."

One time he and R. Eleazar b. Azariah were in session. When they had finished their studies, he said to him, "Master, will you allow me to go with you to your house?"

He said to him, "Yes."

When they got there, she looked down and left the house [angrily]. [Yosé] looked into the pot that was standing on the range and asked her, "Is there anything in the pot?"

She said to him, "In the pot there is hash." But when he went and peeked, he found chicken.

R Eleazar b. Azariah understood what he was hearing. They sat down together and ate. He said to him, "My lord, did she not say that in the pot was hash, while we found chicken in it?"

He said to him, "It was a miracle."

When they had finished eating, he said to him, "My lord, divorce that woman, for she does not treat you with respect."

He said to him, "Sir, her dowry is too much for me to pay, so I cannot divorce her."

He said to him, "We [your disciples] will divide up her dowry so that you can divorce her." They did so and divided among themselves the cost of her dowry, and he divorced her and married another woman, far better than she had been.

The sins of that first wife caused it to happen that she went and married the town watchman. After some time trouble came upon the man, and [since he was blind] she would lead him all over town [to go begging]. But when they would come in the neighborhood in which R. Yosé the Galilean lived, she led him away from it.

Since that man had been the town watchman and knew the entire town, he said to her, "Why do you not bring us to the neighborhood in which R. Yosé the Galilean lives? I heard that he carries out his religious duties [and so will support us, since we are poor]."

She said to her, "I am his divorced wife, and I haven't got the strength to face him."

One time they came begging to the neighborhood of R. Yosé the Galilean, and the husband began to beat her, and her cries brought embarrassment all over town. R. Yosé the Galilean looked out and saw that the couple was being ridiculed in the marketplaces of the town. He took them and gave them housing in a room that he owned and provided them with food so long as they lived.

This was on the count of the verse: "And that you do not hide yourself from your own flesh" (Isa. 58:7).

Genesis Rabbah XVII:iii.2

Foretaste of Ultimate Things

Wisdom tells us how to see much in little, how to discern in what is here a glimpse at what is coming. Simple experiences give us the flavor of complex and profound ones.

R. Hinena bar Isaac said, "There are three kinds of partial realization [of a complete experience].

"The partial realization of the experience of death is in sleep.

"The partial realization of the experience of prophecy is in a dream."

"The partial realization of the world to come is in the Sabbath."

R. Abin added two more: "The partial realization of light from above is in the orb of the sun, and the partial realization of wisdom from on high is the Torah."

Genesis Rabbah XLIV:xvii.3

Forgiveness

To forbear, as we have seen, means to withstand from mocking or punishing a vanquished rival. Here, the sages explain how to resolve sin— less an act of contrition than one of meaningful sorrow. The sages acknowledge that, in certain cases, sense dictates that the sinner is lost, but they also argue that God absolves, above all, when contrition is honest. And, as is the custom, the sages offer a story, and then a metaphor, to make this point whole.

Said R. Phineas: "' Good and upright [is the Lord; therefore he instructs sinners in the way]' (Ps. 25:8).

"Why is he good? Because he is upright.

"And why is he upright? Because he is good.

"' Therefore he instructs sinners in the way—that is, he teaches them the way to repentance."

They asked wisdom, "As to a sinner, what is his punishment?" She said to them, "Evil pursues the evil" (Prov. 13:21).

They asked prophecy, "As to a sinner, what is his punishment?" She said to them, "The soul that sins shall die" (Ezek. 18:20).

They asked the Holy One, blessed be he, "As to a sinner, what is his punishment?"

He said to them, "Let the sinner repent, and his sin will be forgiven for him."

This is in line with the following verse of Scripture: "Therefore he instructs sinners in the way" (Ps. 25:8).

"He shows the sinners the way to repentance."

YERUSHALMI MAKKOT 2:6

There is the case of R. Simeon b. Eleazar, who was coming from the house of his master in Migdal Eder, riding on an ass and making his way along the seashore. He saw an unusually ugly man. He said to him, "Empty head! what a beast you are! Is it possible that everyone in your town is as ugly as you are?"

He said to him, "And what can I do about it? Go to the craftsman who made me and tell him, 'How ugly is that utensil that you have made!'"

When R. Simeon b. Eleazar realized that he had sinned, he got off his ass and prostrated himself before the man, saying to him, "I beg you to forgive me."

He said to him, "I shall not forgive you until you go to the craftsman who made me and tell him, 'How ugly is that utensil that you have made!'"

He ran after the man for three miles. The people of the town came out to meet him. They said toward him, "Peace be to you, my lord."

He said to them, "Whom do you call, 'my lord'?"

They said to him, "To the one who is going along after you."

He said to them, "If this is a 'my lord,' may there not be many more like him in Israel."

They said to him, "God forbid! and what has he done to you?"

He said to them, "Thus and so did he do to me."

They said to him, "Nonetheless, forgive him."

He said to them, "Lo, I forgive him, on the condition that he not make a habit of acting in that way."

On that same day R. Simeon entered the great study-house that was his and gave an exposition: "'One should always be as soft as a reed and not as tough as a cedar.'

"In the case of a reed, all the winds in the world can go on blowing against it but it sways with them, so that when the winds grow silent, it reverts and stands in its place. And what is the destiny of a reed? In the end a pen is cut from it with which to write a scroll of the Torah.

"But in the case of a cedar it will not stand in place, but when the south wind blows against it, it uproots the cedar and turns it over. And what is the destiny of a cedar? Foresters come and cut it down and use it to roof houses, and the rest they toss into the fire.

"On the basis of this fact they have said, 'One should always be as soft as a reed and not as tough as a cedar.'"

THE FATHERS ACCORDING TO RABBI NATHAN XLI:III.1

Free Will and Predestination

How to hold together the competing principles that God is all-powerful and that we can make choices? That is the problem that wisdom addresses in recognition of paradoxes. If God sees the future, then what difference do our choices make? That is the issue worked out in the sayings of Aqiba and other sages on the matter of predestination.

R. Aqiba would say, "Everything is foreseen, and free choice is given. In goodness the world is judged. And all is in accord with the abundance of deed[s]."

He would say, "(1) All is handed over as a pledge, (2) and a net is cast over all the living. (3) The store is open, (4) the storekeeper gives credit, (5) the account-book is open, and (6) the hand is writing.

"(1) Whoever wants to borrow may come and borrow. (2) The

charity-collectors go around every day and collect from man whether he knows it or not. (3) And they have grounds for what they do. (4) And the judgment is a true judgment. (5) And everything is ready for the meal."

TRACTATE ABOT 3:15-16

R. Eleazar Haqqappar says, "Jealousy, lust, and ambition drive a person out of this world."

He would say, "Those who are born are [destined] to die, and those who die are [destined] for resurrection. And the living are [destined] to be judged—so as to know, to make known, and to confirm that (1) he is God, (2) he is the one who forms, (3) he is the one who creates, (4) he is the one who understands, (5) he is the one who judges, (6) he is the one who gives evidence, (7) he is the one who brings suit, (8) and he is the one who is going to make the ultimate judgment.

"Blessed be he, for before him are no (1) guile, (2) forgetfulness, (3) respect for persons, or (4) bribe-taking, for everything is his. And know that everything is subject to reckoning. And do not let your evil impulse persuade you that Sheol is a place of refuge for you. For (1) despite your wishes were you formed, (2) despite your wishes were you born, (3) despite your wishes do you live, (4) despite your wishes do you die, and (5) despite your wishes are you going to give a full accounting before the King of kings of kings, the Holy One blessed be he."

TRACTATE ABOT 4:22

Generosity

Giving, in the sages' wisdom, is not absolute. There is good and bad, and while generosity as a rule is encouraged, it must be tempered by good sense and respect. To give recklessly causes more harm than good, since it can mislead or encourage sloth.

Anyone in whom are these three traits is one of the disciples of Abraham, our father; but [if he bears] three other traits, he is one of the disciples of Balaam, the wicked; (1) a generous spirit, (2) a modest mien, and (3) a humble soul—he is one of the disciples of Abraham, our father. He who exhibits (1) a grudging spirit, (2) an arrogant mien, and (3) a proud soul—he is one of the disciples of Balaam, the wicked. What is the difference between the disciples of Abraham our father and the disciples of Balaam the wicked? The disciples of Abraham our father enjoy the benefit [of their learning] in this world and yet inherit the world to come, as it is said, 'That I may cause those who love me to inherit substance, and so that I may fill their treasures' (Prov. 8:21). The disciples of Balaam the wicked inherit Gehenna and go down to the Pit of Destruction, as it is said, 'But you, O God, shall bring them down into the pit of destruction; bloodthirsty and deceitful men shall not live out half their days' (Ps. 55:24).

TRACTATE ABOT 5:19

It was taught on Tannaite authority:

R. Meir used to say, "A person should not implore his friend to dine with him if he knows that he will not dine with him. And one should not proffer him favors if he knows that he will not accept. And one should not open for him casks of wine [whose remains] were already sold to a merchant without apprising him of the arrangement". And one should not suggest [to his friend] that he anoint himself with oil if the flask is empty. [In each case he misleads the friend into thinking that he is willing to do something special for him]. But if [he does any of these things] as a sign of respect for him, it is permitted."

Is that so? Lo, Ulla came to the house of R. Judah. He opened for him casks of wine [whose remains] were already sold to a merchant. He must have apprised him of the arrangement. And if you prefer you can maintain that [this incident concerning R. Judah and] Ulla is an exception. He was so beloved to R. Judah that he surely would have opened them for him even without [the arrangement with the merchant].

Our rabbis taught on Tannaite authority: A person should not go to a house of mourning [or a house of rejoicing] with a wine flagon that resonates [from its emptiness] and he should not fill it with water [and go to a house of mourning] because he misleads him [i.e., the mourner or celebrant to think that he is doing something special for him]. But if there is a fellowship of the city [there], he is permitted [to do this out of respect].

Our rabbis taught on Tannaite authority: A person should not sell to his fellow a sandal [made from the hide] of an animal that died as if it came from a live animal that had been slaughtered for two reasons. One, because he misleads him. And the other, because of the danger [that the hide is tainted in some way].

A person should not send to his fellow a cask of wine with oil floating at the opening. And once a person sent his fellow a cask of wine with oil floating at its opening. And he went and invited guests [thinking it was a barrel of oil]. And they came. When he found out that it was wine he hanged himself.

And guests are not permitted to give from what is brought before them to the son or the daughter of the householder unless they asked for permission from the householder. And once a person invited three guests during a year of famine and he had only three eggs to serve them. The son of the household came in. One of the guests took his portion and gave it to him [i.e., the son]. And so did the second [guest] and so did the third. The father of the child came and found him with one egg gorged in his mouth and one in each hand. [Enraged] he threw him to the ground and he died. When his mother saw what happened she went up to the roof and jumped off and died. Then even he went up to the roof and jumped off and died.

BAVLI TO MISHNAH-TRACTATE HULLIN 7:2A

God and the Persecuted

The single most moving insight that wisdom offers on God's nature is contained in the demonstration that God favors the pursued over the pursuer, the one that is driven away over the one who does the expulsion. The entire record of Scripture is adduced to demonstrate that fact, deeply meaningful to the people, Israel, through its history.

"God seeks what has been driven away" (Qoh. 3:15):

R. Huna in the name of R. Joseph said, "The Holy One, blessed be he, is destined to avenge the blood of the pursued through punishing the pursuer.

"[You find that] when a righteous man pursues a righteous man, God seeks what has been driven away.

"When a wicked man pursues a wicked man, God seeks what has been driven away.

"All the more so when a wicked man pursues a righteous man, God seeks what has been driven away.

"[The same principle applies] even when you come around to a case in which a righteous man pursues a wicked man, God seeks what has been driven away.'"

R. Yosé b. R. Yudan in the name of R. Yosé b. R. Nehorai says, "It is always the case that the Holy One, blessed be he, demands an accounting for the blood of those who have been pursued from the hand of the pursuer.

"You may know that this is the case, for lo, Abel was pursued by Cain, God seeks what has been driven away [and God sought an accounting for the pursued]: 'And the Lord looked [favorably] upon Abel and his meal offering' (Gen. 4:4).

"Noah was pursued by his generation, God seeks what has been driven away: 'Noah found favor in the eyes of God' (Gen. 6:8). 'You and all your household shall come into the ark' (Gen. 7:1). And it says, 'For this is like the days of Noah to me, as I swore [that the waters of Noah should no more go over the earth]' (Isa. 54:9).]

"Abraham was pursued by Nimrod,God seeks what has been driven away: 'You are the Lord, the God who chose Abram and brought him out of Ur' (Neh. 9:7).

"Isaac was pursued by the Ishmael, God seeks what has been driven away. And they said, 'We have certainly seen that the Lord is with you' (Gen. 26:28) 'For through Isaac will seed be called for you' (Gen. 21:12)].

"Jacob was pursued by Esau, God seeks what has been driven away. 'For the Lord has chosen Jacob, Israel for his prized possession' (Ps. 135:4).

"Joseph was pursued by his brothers, God seeks what has been driven away. 'The Lord was with Joseph, and he was a successful man' (Gen. 39:2).

"Moses was pursued by Pharaoh, but 'Moses, the man God had chosen, threw himself into the breach to turn back his wrath lest it destroy them' (Ps. 106:23).

"David was pursued by Saul, God seeks what has been driven away. 'And he chose David, his servant' (Ps. 78:70).

"Israel is pursued by the nations, God seeks what has been driven away. 'And you has the Lord chosen to be a people to Him' (Deut. 14:2).

R. Judah bar Simon in the name of R. Yosé bar Nehorai, "And the rule applies also to the matter of offerings. A bull is pursued by a lion, a sheep is pursued by a wolf, a goat is pursued by a leopard.

"Therefore the Holy One, blessed be he, has said, 'Do not make offerings before me from those animals that pursue, but from those that are pursued: When a bull, a sheep, or a goat is born (Lev. 22:27).

PESIQTA DERAB KAHANA IX.II.3

God's Love and God's Jealousy

Akin to forbearance, God's love, completed by God's jealousy, forms the highest compliment humanity has ever received. For, the wisdom of Judaism maintains, out of all of creation, God most loves humanity. That is why God craves our love and is jealous when we give it elsewhere than to God.

"For I the Lord your God am a jealous God":
Rabbi says, "God in charge of jealousy: 'I rule jealousy, but jealousy does not rule me.'
"'I rule sleep, but sleep does not rule me.'
"So Scripture says, 'Behold, he who keeps Israel neither slumbers nor sleeps' (Ps. 121:4)."

Another comment concerning "for I the Lord your God am a jealous God":
"It is with jealousy that I exact punishment from idolatry.
"But as to other matters, 'showing steadfast love.'"

A philosopher asked Rabban Gamaliel, "It is written in your Torah, 'for I the Lord your God am a jealous God.'
"Now does an idol have any power to arouse jealousy against itself? A great athlete is jealous of another athlete, a sage is jealous of another sage, a rich man is jealous of another rich man. Then does an idol have any power to arouse jealousy against itself?"
He said to him, "If someone calls his dog by his father's name, so that, when he takes a vow, it is by the life of this dog, against whom will the father feel jealousy? The son or the dog?"
He said to him, "There is some value in some of them."
He said to him, "What evidence do you have?"
He said to him, "Lo, there was a wildfire in a certain town, but the temple of idolatry of that town was saved. Did idolatry not stand up for itself?"
He said to him, "Let me give you a parable. To what is the matter to be compared? To the case of a mortal king who goes out to make war. With whom does he make war? With the living or the dead?"
He said to him, "With the living."
He said to him, "If there is no value in any one of them, why does he not simply wipe it all out?"

He said to him, "Now is it only one thing that you people worship? Lo, you worship the sun and the moon, the stars and the planets, the mountains and hills, springs and glens, and even man. Is he then going to destroy his entire world on account of idiots? 'Shall I utterly consume all things from off the face of the earth, says the Lord' (Zeph. 1:2)."

[With reference to "and stumbling blocks with the wicked" (Zeph. 1:3):], he said to him, "Since the wicked stumble therein, why does he not remove it from the world?"

He said to him, "On account of fowls? If so, they also worship man: 'Shall I cut off man from off the face of the earth' (Zeph. 1:3)."

MEKHILTA LII:II.5

God's Many Faces

Anthropomorphism, imagining something to have the qualities of man, is not unique to the sages, or any culture. But here, as the sages recount for themselves the many ways God is envisioned as a warrior, they struggle to develop another image of God consistent with the text: one who is so powerful that he need not use armaments to do his battles.

"The Lord is a man of war; the Lord is his name":

R. Judah says, "Lo, this verse of Scripture is rich in numerous passages [that serve to amplify the picture].

"It indicates that he appeared to them with every sort of armament.

"He appeared to them like a mighty hero, girded with sword: 'Gird your sword upon your thigh, O mighty one' (Ps. 45:4).

"He appeared to them like a horseman: 'And he rode on a cherub and flew' (Ps. 18:11).

"He appeared to them coated in mail and garbed in a helmet: 'And he put on righteousness as a coat of mail and a helmet of salvation on his head' (Isa. 59:17).

"He appeared to them carrying a spear: 'At the shining of your glittering spear' (Hab. 3:11); 'Draw out also the spear and battle-axe' (Ps. 35:3).

"He appeared to them bearing bow and arrow: 'Your bow is made bare' (Hab. 23:9); 'And he sent out arrows and scattered them' (2 Sam. 22:15).

"He appeared to them with shield and buckler: ''His truth is a shield and a buckler' (Ps. 91:4); 'Take hold of shield and buckler' (Ps. 35:2).

"Shall I then infer that he needs any of these measures?

"Scripture says, 'The Lord is a man of war, the Lord is his name,'

"meaning, it is with his name that he does battle, and he does not need any of these means of making war.

"If that is the case, then how come Scripture articulates each one of these measures by itself?

"If the Israelites are in need, the Omnipresent makes war for them.

"And woe for the nations of the world for what their ears are going to hear, for lo, the One who spoke and brought the world into being is going to make war on them."

Since when he appeared at the sea, it was in the form of a mighty soldier making war, as it is said, "The Lord is a man of war,"

and when he appeared to them at Sinai, it was as an elder, full of mercy, as it is said, "And they saw the God of Israel" (Exod. 24:10,

and when they were redeemed, what does Scripture say? "And the like of the very Heaven for clearness" (Exod. 24:10); "I beheld until thrones were placed and one that was ancient of days sat" (Dan. 7:9); "A fiery stream issued" (Dan. 7:10) —

[so God took on many forms.] It was, therefore, not to provide the nations of the world with an occasion to claim that there are two dominions in Heaven

that Scripture says, "The Lord is a man of war, the Lord is his name."

[This then bears the message:] The one in Egypt is the one at the sea, the one in the past is the one in the age to come, the one in this age is the one in the world to come: "See now that I, even I, am he" (Deut. 32:39); "Who has wrought and done it? He who called the generations from the beginning. I the Lord who am the first and with the last I am the same" (Isa. 41:4).

There is a mighty soldier in a town, bearing all manner of weapons but without strength or courage, without know-how and experience in battle.

But the One who spoke and brought the world into being is not that way. He has strength, courage, know-how and experience in battle:

"For the battle is the Lord's and he will give you into our hand" (1 Sam. 17:47); "A Psalm of David: blessed be the Lord my rock, who trains my hands for war and my fingers for battle" (Ps. 144:4).

There is a mighty soldier in a town, whose strength at forty is not the same as [but more than] his strength at sixty, or whose strength at sixty is not the same as his strength at eighty, but as he goes along, his strength diminishes.

But the One who spoke and brought the world into being is not that way. "I the Lord do not change" (Mal. 3:6).

There is a mighty soldier in a town, who, when clothed in passion and might, even his mother or his dear one strikes, raging on.

But the One who spoke and brought the world into being is not that way.

"The Lord is a man of war, the Lord is his name":

"The Lord is a man of war" in making war against the Egyptians,

[but] "the Lord is his name," in that [nonetheless] he shows mercy to his creatures: "The Lord, the Lord is a merciful god and gracious" (Exod. 34:6).

There is a mighty soldier in a town, who, once he shoots an arrow, cannot retrieve it, since it is gone from his hand.

But the One who spoke and brought the world into being is not that way.

When the Israelites do not carry out the will of the Omnipresent, it is as though a decree goes forth from his presence: "If I whet my glittering sword" (Deut. 32:41), while when the Israelites carry out repentance, he can immediately call it back: "And my hand takes hold on judgment" (Deut. 32:41).

Should I then suppose that he brings it back empty? Scripture is explicit: "I will render vengeance upon my enemies" (Deut. 32:41).

On whom then does he turn it? On the names of the world: "And I will pay back those who hate me" (Deut. 32:41).

A mortal king goes forth to war, and [if at that time] the towns near by come and ask what they need from him and they say to them, "The king is preoccupied in preparing for war. When he returns victorious, you can come and ask for what you need from him."

But the One who spoke and brought the world into being is not that way:

"The Lord is a man of war" when fighting against the Egyptians,

[but] "the Lord is [still] his name," for he hears the cry of everyone in the world: "O you who hear prayer, to you all flesh comes" (Ps. 65:3).

A mortal king goes forth to war, and he may not be able to provision his troops and provide all their daily rations.

But the One who spoke and brought the world into being is not that way.

"The Lord is a man of war" when fighting against the Egyptians,

[but] "the Lord is [still] his name," for he sustains and provides for everything he created: "To whom who divided the Red Sea in two . . . who gives food to all flesh" (Ps. 136:13, 25).

"The Lord is a man of war":
It is not possible to say so, for is it not stated: "Do I not fill Heaven and earth, says the Lord" (Jer. 23:24); "And one called the other and said" (Isa. 6:3); "And behold the glory of the God of Israel came" (Ezek. 43:2).
How then can Scripture say, "The Lord is a man of war"?
"On account of the love that I bear for you, and on account of the sanctification that you bear, I shall sanctify my name through you."
Thus Scripture says, "Though I am God and not man, still I, the Holy One, am in the midst of you" (Hos. 11:9),
"I shall sanctify my name through you."

"The Lord is his name":
With his name he makes war, and he hardly needs any of those measures.
So David says, "You come to me with sword and with spear and with javelin, but I come against you in the name of the Lord of hosts" (1 Sam. 17:45); "Some trust in chariots, some in horses, but we call on the name of the Lord our God" (Ps. 20:8); "And Asa cried to the Lord his God" (2 Chron. 14:10).

MEKHILTA 29/SHIRATA I

God's Presence

Where does wisdom find God's presence, advising us to look for God there too? It is, predictably, where words of Torah—God's teaching—are spoken. God is present in those words.

Hananiah b. Teradion says, "[If] two sit together and between them do not pass teachings of the Torah, lo, this is a seat of the scornful, as it is said, 'Nor sits in the seat of the scornful' (Ps. 1:1). But two who are sitting, and words of the Torah do pass between them—the Presence is with them, as it is said, 'Then they that feared the Lord spoke with one another, and the Lord hearkened and heard, and a book of remembrance was written before him, for them that feared the Lord and gave thought to his name' (Mal. 3:16). I know that this applies to two. How do I know that even if a single person sits and works on the Torah, the Holy One, blessed be he, set aside a reward for him? As it is said, 'Let him sit alone and keep silent, because he has laid it upon him' (Lam. 3:28)."

R. Simeon says, "Three who ate at a single table and did not talk about teachings of the Torah while at that table are as though they ate from dead sacrifices (Ps. 106:28), as it is said, 'For all tables are full of vomit and filthiness [if they are] without God' (Ps. 106:28). But three who ate at a single table and did talk about teachings of the Torah while at that table are as if they ate at the table of the Omnipresent, blessed is he, as it is said, 'And he said to me, This is the table that is before the Lord' (Ezek. 41:22)."

R. Halafta of Kefar Hananiah says, "Among ten who sit and work hard on the Torah the Presence comes to rest, as it is said, 'God stands in the congregation of God' (Ps. 82:1). And how do we now that the same is so even of five? For it is said, 'And he has founded his group upon the earth' (Amos 9:6). And how do we know that this is so even of three? Since it is said, 'And he judges among the judges' (Ps. 82:1). And how do we know that this is so even of two? Because it is said, 'Then they that feared the Lord spoke with one another, and the Lord hearkened and heard' (Mal. 3:16). And how do we know that this is so even of one? Since it is said, 'In every place where I record my name I will come to you and I will bless you' (Exod. 20:24)."

R. Eleazar of Bartota says, "Give him what is his, for you and yours are his. For so does it say about David, 'For all things come of you, and of your own have we given you' (1 Chron. 29:14)."

TRACTATE ABOT 3:2

God's Steadfast Love

Explaining suffering in a world ruled by God vexes the sages, but to make the explanation easier, they use a simple analogy: what would you do to save your fellow? In this regard, the sages seem somewhat optimistic, but their logic remains consistent. The question is not "Where was God?" but, "Where was faith in God?"

[Regarding this [relationship between God and his people,] R. Yudan in the name of R. Isaac gave four discourses [in the form of parables]:

[1] A person had a human patron. [One day] they came and told him [the patron], "A member of your household has been arrested." He said to them, "Let me take his place."

They said to him, "Lo, he is already going out to trial."

He said to them, "Let me take his place."

They said to him, "Lo, he is going to be hanged."

Now where is he and where is his patron [when ultimately he needs him]?

But the Holy One, blessed be He, [will save his subjects, just as he] saved Moses from [execution by] the sword of Pharaoh.

This is in accord with what is written, 'He delivered me from the sword of Pharaoh' (Exod. 18:4).

Said R. Yannai, "It is written, 'Moses fled from Pharaoh' (Exod. 2:15). Is it possible for a person to flee from the government? [No.] But when Pharaoh arrested Moses, he ordered that they decapitate him. But [when they tried to do so,] the sword bounced off Moses' neck and broke.

"This accords with what is written, 'Your neck is like an ivory tower' (Song of Sol. 7:4). This refers to Moses' neck."

Rabbi said, R. Abyatar [said], "Moreover, the sword bounced off Moses' neck, and it fell on Quaestionarius' [the executioner's] neck, and killed him. This accords with that which is written, 'He delivered me from the sword of Pharaoh' (Exod. 18:4). He delivered me, and the executioner was killed."

R. Berekhiah recited concerning [the story of this incident] the verse, "The ransom of the righteous is the wicked" (Prov. 21:18).

R. Abun recited, "The righteous is delivered from trouble; and the wicked gets into it instead" (Prov. 11:8).

Taught Bar Qappara, "An angel came down, and took Moses' appearance. And they arrested the angel, and Moses escaped."

Said R. Joshua b. Levi, "When Moses fled from Pharaoh, all his people became either dumb, deaf, or blind. He said to the mute ones, 'Where is Moses?' And they could not speak. He asked the deaf ones, and they could not hear. He asked the blind ones, and they could not see.

"This accords with what the Holy One, blessed be He, said to Moses [when Moses was afraid to go before Pharaoh], 'Who has made a man's mouth? Who makes him dumb, or deaf, or seeing, or blind? Is it not I, the Lord?' (Exod. 4:11).

"[God told Moses,] 'I saved you there [when you fled from Pharaoh]. Shall I not stand up for you now [when you go before Pharaoh to bring down the plagues on Egypt]?'

"In this regard [the verse says], 'For what great nation is there that has a god so near to it as the Lord our God is to us, whenever we call upon him' (Deut. 4:7)."

R. Yudan in the name of R. Isaac gave another discourse [in the form of a parable]:

[2] A person had a human patron. [One day] they came and told the patron, "A member of your household has been arrested."

He said, "Let me take his place."

They said to him, "Lo, he is already going out to trial."

He said to them, "Let me take his place."

They said to him, "Lo, he is going to be thrown into the water [to be executed]."

Now where is he and where is his patron?

But the Holy One, blessed be he, [saves his subjects, just as he] saved Jonah from the belly of the fish. Lo it says, "And the Lord spoke to the fish, and it vomited out Jonah upon dry land" (Jon. 2:10).

R. Yudan in the name of R. Isaac gave another discourse [in the form of a parable]:

[3] A person had a human patron. [One day] they came and told the patron, "A member of your household has been arrested."

He said to them, "Let me take his place."

They said to him, "He is going out to trial."

He said to them, "Let me take his place."

They said to him, "Lo, he is going to be thrown into the fire [to be executed]."

Now where is he and where is his patron?

But the Holy One, blessed be he, is not like that. He [saves his subjects, just as he] saved Haninah, Mishael, and Azariah [Shadrach, Meshach, Abednego] from the fiery furnace.

In this regard [it says], "Nebuchadnezzar said, 'Blessed be the God of Shadrach, Meshach, and Abednego, [who has sent his angel and delivered his servants, who trusted in him]'" (Dan. 3:28).

R. Yudan in the name of R. Isaac gave another discourse [in the form of a parable]:

[4] A person had a human patron. [One day they came and told the patron, "A member of your household has been arrested."

He said to them, "Let me take his place."

They said to him, "He is going out to trial."

He said to them, "Let me take his place."]

They said to him, "He is to be thrown to the beasts [to be executed]."

[Now where is he and where is his patron?]

But the Holy One, blessed by He, [saves his subjects, just as he] saved Daniel from the lions' den.

In this regard [it says], "My God sent his angels and shut the lions' mouths, and they have not hurt me" (Dan. 6:22).

R. Yudan [gave another discourse in the form of a parable] in his own name:

[5] A man has a human patron. When this man faces trouble, he does not suddenly burst in [on his patron to ask for help]. Rather he comes and stands at his patron's gate and calls to his patron's servant or some member of his household. And he [the servant] in turn informs the patron, "So and so is standing at the gate of your courtyard. Do you wish me to let him enter, or shall I let him stand outside?"

But the Holy One, blessed by He, is not like that. [God says,] "If a person faces trouble, he should not cry out to the angels Michael or Gabriel. But he should cry out to me and I will immediately answer him."

In this regard [it says], "All who call upon the name of the Lord shall be delivered" (Joel 2:32).

Said R. Pinhas, "This incident occurred to Rab.

"He was coming up from the hot spring of Tiberias. He met some Romans. They asked him, 'Who are you?'

"He said to them, 'I am a member of [the governor] Severus' [entourage].' They let him pass.

"That night they came to [the governor] and said to him, 'How much longer will you put up with these Jews?'

"He said to them, 'What do you mean?'

"They said to him, 'We encountered a person. He said he was a Jew. We asked him who he was. And he said he was from Severus' [entourage].'

"He [the governor] said to them, 'What did you do for him?'

"They said to him, 'Is it not enough that we let him alone?'

"He said to them, 'You acted very well.'

[The lesson of this story is:] One who relies on the protection of mere flesh and blood may be saved. How much more will one who relies on the protection of the Holy One, blessed be he, [be saved from harm]. In this regard [it says,] "All who call upon the name of the lord shall be delivered" [ibid.].

Said R. Alexander, "This incident occurred concerning an archon named Alexandrus."

"He was presiding over the trial of a thief. He [the judge] asked [the defendant], 'What is your name?'

"[He responded,] 'Alexandrus.'

"He said to him, 'Alexandrus [you are free to go]. Be off to Alexandria.'"

[The lesson is] if a man is saved because he invokes the name of a mere human judge, all the more will a person be saved if he invokes the name of the Holy One, blessed be He.

In this regard [it says,] "All who call upon the name of the Lord shall be delivered" [ibid.].

YERUSHALMI BERAKHOT 9:1

The Golden Rule

The wisdom of Judaism, treasured by holy Israel as much as by Jesus, frames the Golden Rule of Lev. 19:18—"You shall love your neighbor as yourself"—in its own distinctive way. This formulation is in the negative, as that of Jesus is in the affirmative, but the sense is the same. Here is how Scripture teaches Judaism and Christianity alike to treat "man as the measure of all things"—but with a particularly Israelite twist.

There was a case of a gentile who came before Shammai. He said to him, "Convert me on the stipulation that you teach me the entire Torah while I am standing on one foot." He drove him off with the building cubit that he had in his hand.

He came before Hillel: "Convert me."

He said to him, "'What is hateful to you, to your fellow don't do.' That's the entirety of the Torah; everything else is elaboration. So go, study."

BABLI TO MISHNAH-TRACTATE SHABBAT 2:5/31A

Rabbi Yosé says: "Let your companion's property be as precious to you as your own. And get yourself ready to learn Torah, for it does not come as an inheritance to you. And may everything you do be for the sake of Heaven.

"Let your companion's property be as precious to you as your own: how so?

"This teaches that just as someone looks out for his own property, so he should look out for the property of his fellow, "and just as a person does not want a bad name to circulate concerning his property, so he should not want a bad name to circulate concerning the property of his fellow."

Another comment on "Let your companion's property be as precious to you as your own": how so?

When a disciple of a sage comes to you, saying, "Teach me," if you have something to teach him, repeat the tradition, and if not, send him away right off, and do not take his money.

For it is said, "Do not say to your neighbor, Go and come again, and tomorrow I will give; when you have it with you all along" (Prov. 3:28).

THE FATHERS ACCORDING TO RABBI NATHAN XVII:II.1

Rabbi Eliezer says: "Let the respect owing to your companion be as precious to you as the respect owing to yourself. And don't be easy to anger. And repent one day before you die.

"Let the respect owing to your companion be as precious to you as the respect owing to yourself: how so?

"This teaches that just as someone sees to the honor owing to himself, so he should see to the honor owing to his fellow.

"And just as a person does not want a bad name to circulate against his honor, so he should not want to circulate a bad name against the honor owing to his fellow.

"Another explanation of the statement, Let the respect owing to your companion be as precious to you as the respect owing to yourself: how so?

"When a person has a myriad and all his money is taken away from him, he should nonetheless not lower himself for something worth a mere penny [but should retain his dignity]. [Let him not discredit himself over so much as a perutah's worth.]"

THE FATHERS ACCORDING TO RABBI NATHAN XV:I.1-XV:II.1

Gossip

Second only to envy as the source for the destruction of the social order, gossip takes malice and gives it body and power. When someone gossips about another, the victim of the gossip cannot mount a defense, and when, as is often the case, the gossip is false or—still worse—half-

true, the victim is helpless to recover the truth. Communities and familiars, organizations and institutions—these are hotbeds of gossip, which is the aggression of the weak, the method of destruction of others that is the preferred weapon of cowards.

"Death and life are in the power of the tongue" (Prov. 18:21).

Aqilas translated, "A spoon-knife, [that is, a utensil that has a knife at one end, a spoon at the other, thus] death on one side, life on the other."

Bar Sira said, "[If a person] had before him a coal, if he blows on it, it burns higher. [If] he spits on it, it goes out [Ben Sira 28:12]. [Both come from the same mouth, that is, breath or spit.]"

R. Hiyya bar Abba said, "[If] there was a basket of dates before a person, [if] he ate [of the dates] before [by stating the required formula] he tithed [the basket], there is 'death in the power of the tongue,' while [if] he tithed [the basket, also by merely stating a required formula], and then ate [of the dates], there is 'life in the power of the tongue.'"

Said R. Yannai, "[If] before a person was a loaf of bread from which tithes and offerings had not been designated, if he ate [of the bread] before [by stating the required formula] he tithed [the bread], there is 'death in the power of the tongue,' while [if] he tithed [the bread, as above] and then ate it, there is 'life in the power of the tongue.'"

Rabban Gamaliel said to Tabi, his slave, "Go, buy us a good piece of meat from the market."

He went and brought him tongue.

After a while he said to him, "Go and buy us a poor piece of meat from the market."

He went and brought him tongue.

He said to him, "When I said to you, 'Go, buy us a good piece of meat from the market,' you went and brought us tongue, and when I said to you, 'Go, buy us a poor piece of meat from the market,' you went and brought us tongue!"

He said to him, "My lord, from [tongue comes] good things, and from [tongue comes] bad things.

"When it is good, there is nothing better, and when it is bad, there is nothing worse."

Rab made a banquet for his disciples. He brought before them soft tongues and hard tongues. They began to select the soft ones and to leave the hard ones. He said to them, "My disciples, note what you are doing when you select the soft ones and leave the hard ones.

"So should your tongues be, soft for one another."

LEVITICUS RABBAH XXXIII:I.1-3

Said R. Yohanan in the name of R. Yosé b. Zimra, "What is the meaning of the following verse of Scripture: 'What shall be given to you and what more shall be done for you, you lying tongue' (Ps. 120:3).

"Said the Holy One, blessed be he, to the tongue, 'All the parts of the human body stand upright, but you recline. All the parts of the human body are outside, but you are inside. Not only so, but I have set up as protection for you two walls, one of bone [the teeth] and one of flesh [the cheeks]. 'What shall be given to you and what more shall be done for you, you lying tongue!'"

Said R. Yohanan in the name of R. Yosé b. Zimra, "Whoever repeats slander is as if he denied the very principle [of God's rule], as it is said, 'Who has said, Our tongue will we make mighty, our lips are with us, who is lord over us' (Ps. 12:5)."

And R. Yosé b. Zimra said, "Whoever repeats slander—plagues come upon him, as it is said, 'Whoever slanders his neighbor in secret him will I destroy,' and elsewhere it is written, 'For destruction' [in perpetuity] (Lev. 25:30), which is translated as 'permanently.' And we have learned: The only difference between a mesora who is shut up and one who is permanent[ly afflicted] is the matter of the messing up of the hair and the tearing of the clothing.'" [Jung, p. 87, n. 6: The Hebrew for the words "I will destroy" and "in perpetuity" are both derived from one and the same root. Hence the suggestion that, since the word is used in connection with leprosy "absolutely" (the Aramaic version of "in perpetuity") and the word "destroy" refers to the same thing, the punishment of destruction will take the form of [the skin ailment described at Lev. 13].

Said R. Hisda said Mar Uqba, "Whoever speaks slander is worthy of being stoned.

"Here it is written, 'Him will I destroy' (*asmit*), and there it is written, 'They have destroyed (*smtw*) my life in the dungeon and cast stones on me' (Lam. 3:53)."

And R. Hisda said Mar Uqba said, "Concerning whoever speaks slander, the Holy One, blessed be he, has said, 'He and I cannot live in the same world.'

"For it is said, 'Whoever slanders his neighbor in secret, him will I destroy, whoever is haughty of eye and proud of heart, him I cannot suffer' (Ps. 101:5). Do not read, 'Him (*'wtw*) I will not suffer' but 'With (*'tw*) him I will not suffer' [to be together in the same world]."

There are those who repeat this interpretation in regard to the arrogant.

Said R. Hisda said Mar Uqba, "Concerning whoever speaks slander, the Holy One, blessed be he, says to the [angelic] prince in charge of Gehenna, 'Let us get together to judge him, I from above and you from below.'

"For it is said, 'Sharp arrows of the mighty, with coals of broom' (Ps. 120:4).

"'Arrow' means only the tongue, as it is said, 'Their tongue is a sharpened arrow, it speaks deceit' (Jer. 9:7).

"'Mighty' refers only to the Holy One, blessed be he, as it is said, 'The Lord will go forth as a mighty one' (Isa. 52:13).

"'Coals of broom' refer to Gehenna."

Said R. Hama bar Hanina, "What remedy is there for those who speak slander?

"If it is a disciple of a sage, let him keep busy in Torah, as it is said, 'The healing for a tongue is the tree of life' (Prov. 15:4), and 'tongue' means an evil tongue [slander], as it is said, 'Their tongue is a sharpened arrow' (Jer. 9:7). 'Tree of life' refers only to the Torah, as it is said, 'It is a tree of life to those who hold on to it' (Prov. 3:18).

"If it is an ordinary person, let him become humble, for it is said, 'But perverseness therein is a wound to the spirit' (Prov. 15:4)."

R. Aha b. R. Hanina says, "If one already has slandered, he has no remedy.

"For David through the Holy Spirit has already [pronounced him] cut off, as it is said, 'May the Lord cut off all flattering lips, the tongue that speaks proud things' (Ps. 12:4)."

Rather, what remedy may one seek so that he may not become guilty of slander?

If is is a disciple of a sage, let him keep busy in Torah.
If it is an ordinary person, let him become humble, for it is said, "But perverseness therein is a wound to the spirit" (Prov. 15:4).

A Tannaite authority of the house of R. Ishmael [taught], "Whoever speaks slander inflates his sins [so that they are as great] as the three cardinal sins of idolatry, fornication, and bloodshed.

"Here in Scripture it is written, 'The tongue that speaks great things' (Ps. 12:4), and in regard to idolatry, 'Oh, this people has sinned a great sin' (Exod. 32:31).

"In respect to incest, it is written, 'How shall I commit this great sin' (Gen. 39:9), and in respect to bloodshed, 'My punishment is greater than I can bear' (Gen. 4:13)."

"And might I say [that the cited verse concerning slander] indicates that slander is only as weighty as two (of the three sins listed.) The framer deduces this from the fact that Scripture calls each of the other sins "great," but with respect to slander, Scripture only uses the word great once in the plural form.]

Which of the sins would possibly be excluded? [No answer is given.]

In the West they say, "Slander about a third party kills three: the one who says it, the one who receives it, and the one about whom it is said."

R. Hama bar Hanina said, "What is the meaning of the verse of Scripture, 'Death and life are in the hands of the tongue' (Prov. 18:21)?

"Now does the tongue have a hand? Rather it is to indicate to you that just as the hand can commit murder, so the tongue can commit murder.

"If you wish then to reason that just as the hand can commit murder only in the case of one who is nearby, also the tongue can commit murder only in the case of one who is nearby, [to prevent one's reaching that false conclusion,] Scripture states, 'Their tongue is a sharpened arrow' (Jer. 9:7). [It can commit murder even from a distance like an arrow.]

"If you wish then to reason that just as the arrow can reach only what is forty or fifty cubits away, so the tongue can reach only for forty or fifty cubits, [to prevent one's reaching that false conclusion,] Scripture states, 'They have set their mouth against the Heaven and their tongue walks through the earth' (Ps. 73:9)."

[Pursuing the analysis of the cited verse], since it is written, "They have set their mouth against the Heaven," why did the author find it necessary to say as well, "Their tongue is a sharpened arrow"?

In this latter part of the verse, we are informed that [the tongue] kills like an arrow.

And since it is written, "Their tongue is a sharpened arrow," why was it necessary to state, "Death and life are in the hands of the tongue" (Prov. 18:21)?

It is in accord with what Raba said.

For Raba said, "Whoever wants life will find it in his tongue, whoever wants death will find it in his tongue."

How shall we define slander?

Raba said, "It would, for example, be like one's saying, 'There is a fire in so-and-so's house.'"

Said to him Abayye, "What in the world has this man done? All he is doing is telling people a matter of public knowledge.

"Rather, slander would be committed in what sort of case? For example, if one said, 'Where should there be a fire, if not in so-and-so's house! For there [you] always [find] meat and fish [in the ovens, which are always lit]!'"

Said Rabbah, "Whatever is said before the person [to whom it pertains] does not fall into the category of slander."

Said he said to him, "It is all the more so a matter of impudence [than] slander."

He said to him, "I concur with R. Yosé."

For R. Yosé said, "I never in my life said something and then turned around [to see who might have heard it]."

Said Rabbah bar R. Huna, "Anything that is said before three persons does not fall into the category of slander.

"What is the reason [for this view]? Your friend has a friend, and your friend's friend has a friend."

When R. Dimi came, he said, "What is the meaning of the verse of Scripture, 'He who blesses his friend with a loud voice, rising early in the morning, it shall be regarded as a curse to him' (Prov. 27:14)?

"It would be exemplified in the case of one who came as a guest, and the householders took a great deal of trouble for him. The next day he goes out and sits in the marketplace and says, 'May the All-Merciful bless so and so, for all the trouble he took in my behalf.' Then people will hear me and go and importune [the host to take care of them as well]."

R. Dimi, brother of R. Safra, repeated as a Tannaite teaching. "One should never speak in praise of his fellow, for out of saying good things about him, bad things will come out."

There are those who say, R. Dimi, brother of R. Safra, fell ill. R. Safra came up to visit him. [Dimi] said to them, "May something bad happen to me, if I have not carried out everything that our rabbis have said, [so there is no religious reason for my illness]."

He said to him, "But did you carry out the teaching, 'One should never speak in praise of his fellow, for out of saying good things about him, bad things will come out'?"

He said to him, "I never heard that statement. But if I had heard it, I would have carried it out."

BAVLI TO MISHNAH-TRACTATE ARAKHIN 3:5/15B-16A

Gratitude

To be grateful is an act of humility and generosity, a way of acknowledging how much others, like God, give us. The richest, happiest people we know are those with the gift to be grateful.

[When] Ben Zoma saw a crowd on steps of the Temple Mount, he said, "Blessed is he who is wise in knowing secrets. Blessed is he who created [all] these [people] to serve me."

He would say, "How hard did Adam toil before he could taste a morsel [of food]: he seeded, plowed, reaped, sheaved, threshed, winnowed, separated, ground, sifted, kneaded, and baked, and only then could he eat. But I arise in the morning and find all these [foods ready] before me.

"How hard did Adam toil before he could put on a garment: he sheared, bleached, separated, dyed, spun, and wove, and only then could he put it on. But I arise in the morning and find all these [garments ready] before me.

"How many skilled craftsmen are industrious and rise early [to their work] at my door. And I arise in the morning and find all these [ready] before me."

And so [Ben Zoma] would say, "What does a good guest say? '[May my host be remembered [by God] for good!] How much trouble did he take for me! How many kinds of wine did he bring before us! How many kinds of cuts [of meat] did he bring before us! How many kinds of cakes did he bring before me! And all the trouble that he took he took for me!'

"But what does a bad guest say? 'How little trouble did this household take. [And what have I eaten of his?] I ate only a loaf of his bread. I drank only a cup of his wine. He went to all this trouble only to provide for his wife and children.'"

TOSEFTA BERAKHOT 6:2F-J

Guardians of the Public Interest

For a different version of the same theme, see Politicians. Do not misinterpret the following as a simple statement of mistrust for government. Rather, it is an assertion of the importance of learning and knowledge.

Yudan the Patriarch sent R. Hiyya, R. Assi, and R. Ammi to travel among the towns of the Land of Israel to provide for them scribes and teachers. They came to one place and found neither a scribe nor a teacher. They said to the people, "Bring us the guardians of the town." The people brought them the citizens of senatorial class in the town.

They said to them: "Do you think these are the guardians of the town? They are nothing other than the destroyers of the town."

They said to them, "And who are the guardians of the town?"

They said to them, "The scribes and teachers."

That is in line with what is written: "Unless the Lord builds the house [those who build it labor in vain. Unless the Lord watches over the city, the watchman stays awake in vain]" (Ps. 127:1).

YERUSHALMI HAGIGAH 1:7

Honesty

If wisdom has a single lesson of ethics to impart, it is that honesty never costs, but deceit, lying, deception, thievery never cease to exact their charges. Telling the truth, exact honesty in transactions with others, returning what does not belong to us, refraining from keeping what belongs to others—these elementary forms of honesty bring rich rewards to the social order and build the conscience and character of those that do them.

Simeon b. Shetah was employed in flax [to support himself]. His disciples said to him, "Rabbi, remove [this work] from yourself. and we shall buy for you an ass, and you will not have to work so much."

They went and brought him an ass from a Saracen. Hanging on it was a pearl.

They came to him and told him, "From now on you do not have to work any more."

He said to them, "Why?"

They told him, "We bought you an ass from a Saracen, and hanging on it was a pearl."

He said to them, "Did its master know about it?"

They said to them, "No."

He said to them, "Go, and return it."

Did not R. Huna Bibi bar Goslon in the name of Rab state, "They replied before Rabbi, 'Even in accord with the one who has said, 'Stealing from an idolator is prohibited,' all parties concur that it is permitted [to retain] what he has lost. [Accordingly why did Simeon b. Shetah return the pearl?]"

[He replied,] "Now do you think that Simeon b. Shetah was a barbarian? More than Simeon b. Shetah wanted all the money in the world, he wanted to hear the gentile say, 'Blessed be the God of the Jews.'"

And whence did he [learn that such a thing was possible

From the following story which R. Haninah tells:

Some old rabbis bought a pile of wheat from some soldiers, and found in it a pouch filled with money, and they returned it to them. The soldiers said, "Blessed be the God of the Jews."

Abba Oshaiah was a laundryman [in a bathhouse]. The queen came to wash there and lost her jewels and gold pieces. He found them and returned them to her.

She said, 'They are yours [for you have acquired possession of them]. As to me, what are these worth to me? I have many which are even better than these."

He said to her, 'The Torah has decreed that we should return [what we find]."

She said, "Blessed be the God of the Jews."

R. Samuel bar Suseretai went to Rome. The queen had lost her jewelry. He found it. A proclamation went forth through the city: "Whoever returns her jewelry in thirty days will receive thus and so. [If he returns it] after thirty days, his head will be cut off."

He did not return the jewelry within thirty days. After thirty days, he returned it to her.

She said to him, "Weren't you in town?"

He said to her, "Yes [I was here]."

She said to him, "And didn't you hear the proclamation?"

He said to her, "Yes [I heard it]."

She said to him, "And what did it say?"

He said to her that it said, "Whoever returns her jewelry in thirty days will receive thus-and-so. [If he returns it] after thirty days his head will be cut off."

She said to him, "And why didn't you return it within thirty days?"

"So that people should not say, 'It was because I was afraid of you that I did so.' But it was because I fear the All-Merciful."

She said to him. "Blessed be the God of the Jews."

YERUSHALMI BABA MESIA 1:5

Honesty in Government

In this remarkable story, sages portray the just and the unjust government. They show how the greatest king of all time, Alexander, learned wisdom in a remote, obscure place, and from the women of that place.

Alexander of Macedonia went to the king of Kasia, beyond the mountains of darkness. He came to a certain town, called Cartagena, and it was populated entirely by women.

They came out before him and said to him, "If you make war on us and conquer us, word will spread about you that you destroyed a town of women. But if we do battle with you and conquer you, word will spread about you that you made war on women and they beat you. And you'll never again be able to hold up your head among kings."

At that moment he turned away and left. After he went away, he wrote on the door of the gate of the city, saying, "I, Alexander the Macedonian, a king, was a fool until I came to the town called Cartagena, and I learned wisdom from women."

He came to another town, called Africa. They came out and greeted him with apples made out of gold, golden pomegranates, and golden bread.

He said, "Is this gold what you eat in your country?"

They said to him, "And is it not this way in your country, that you have come here?"

He said to them, "It is not your wealth that I have come to see, but it is your justice that I have come to see."

While they were standing there, two men came before the king for justice.

This one kept himself far from thievery, and so did that. One of them said, "I bought a rubbish heap from this man. I dug it open and found a jewel in it. I said to him, 'Take your jewel. I bought a rubbish heap. A jewel I didn't buy.'"

The other said, "When I sold the rubbish heap to that man, I sold him the rubbish heap and everything that is in it."

The king called one of them and said to him, "Do you have a male child?"

He said to him, "Yes."

The king called the other and said to him, "Do you have a daughter?"

He said to him, "Yes."

Then the king said to them, "Let this one marry that one, and let the two of them enjoy the jewel."

Alexander of Macedonia began to express surprise.

He said to him, "Why are you surprised? Did I not give a good judgment."

He said to him, "Yes, you did."

He said to him, "If this case had come to court in your country, how would you have judged it?"

He said to him, "We should have cut off the head of this party and cut off the head of that party, and the jewel would have passed into the possession of the crown."

He said to him, "Does rain fall on you?"

He said to him, "Yes."

"And does the sun rise for you?"

He said to him, "Yes."

He said to him, "Are there small cattle in your country?"

He said to him, "Yes."

"Woe to you! It is on account of the merit of the small cattle that you are saved."

That is in line with the following verse of Scripture: "Man and beast you save, O Lord" (Ps. 36:7).

"Man on account of the merit of the beast do you save, O Lord."

Pesiqta deRab Kahana IX.i.8

Honoring Parents

Almost everyone remembers the commandment to honor one's parents, but these discussions give full amplification to the meaning of "honor." It is not always what one expects, and offers some insights into the parent–child relationship.

"Honor your father and your mother [that your days may be long in the land which the Lord your God gives you]":

Might I infer that this is with words?

Scripture says, "Honor the Lord with your substance" (Prov. 3:9). That means, with food, drink, and fresh garments.

Another interpretation of the verse, "Honor your father and your mother [that your days may be long in the land which the Lord your God gives you]":

"Why is this stated?

"Since it is said, 'For whatever man curses his mother or his father . . .' (Lev. 20:9), I know only that subject to the law is only a man.

"How do I know that a woman, one of undefined gender-traits, one who exhibits gender traits for both genders [are subject to the law]?

"Scripture says, 'Honor your father and your mother'—under all circumstances.

"Just as in the case of honor, there is no distinction between a man and a woman, so as to fearing parents, there should be no distinction between man and woman," the words of R. Ishmael.

R. Judah b. Batera says, "Scripture says, 'You shall fear every man his mother and his father, and you shall keep my Sabbaths' (Lev. 19:3):

"Just as in the case of the Sabbath, the law does not distinguish between a man, a woman, one of undefined gender-traits, and one who exhibits gender traits for both genders, so in the case of fear of parents, there should be no distinction between man and woman, one of undefined gender-traits, and one who exhibits gender traits for both genders."

Rabbi says, "Precious before the One who spoke and brought the world into being is the honor owing to father and mother,

"for he has declared equal the honor owing to them and the honor owing to him, the fear owing to them and the fear owing to him, cursing them and cursing him.

"It is written: 'Honor your father and your mother,' and as a counterpart: 'Honor the Lord with your substance' (Prov. 3:9).

"Scripture thus has declared equal the honor owing to them and the honor owing to him.

"'You shall fear every man his mother and his father' (Lev. 19:3), and, as a counterpart: 'You shall fear the Lord your God' (Deut. 6:13).

"Scripture thus has declared equal the fear owing to them and the fear owing to him.

"'And he who curses his father or his mother shall surely be put to death' (Exod. 21:17), and correspondingly: 'Whoever curses his God' (Lev. 24:15).

"Scripture thus has declared equal the cursing them and cursing him."

[Rabbi continues,] "Come and note that the reward [for obeying the two commandments is the same].

"'Honor the Lord with your substance . . . so shall your barns be filled with plenty' (Prov. 3:9–10, and 'Honor your father and your mother that your days may be long in the land which the Lord your God gives you.'

"'You shall fear the Lord your God' (Deut. 6:13), as a reward: 'But to you that fear my name shall the sun of righteousness arise with healing in its wings' (Mal. 3:20).

"'You shall fear every man his mother and his father and you shall keep my Sabbaths' (Lev. 19:3).

"And as a reward? 'If you turn away your foot because of the Sabbath, then you shall delight yourself in the Lord' (Isa. 58:13–14)."

Rabbi says, "It is perfectly self-evident before the One who spoke and brought the world into being that a person honors the mother more than the father, because she brings him along with words. Therefore Scripture gave precedence to the father over the mother as to honor.

"And it is perfectly self-evident before the One who spoke and brought the world into being that a person fears his father more than the mother, because the father teaches him Torah. Therefore Scripture gave precedence to the mother over the father as to fear.

"In a case in which something is lacking, [Scripture] thereby made it whole.

"But might one suppose that whoever takes precedence in Scripture takes precedence in deed?

"Scripture says, 'You shall fear every man his mother and his father' (Lev. 19:3),

"indicating that both of them are equal to one another."

"Honor your father and your mother that your days may be long in the land which the Lord your God gives you":

If you have honored them, "that your days may be long in the land which the Lord your God gives you."

And if not, "that your days may be cut short."

For thus words of the Torah are so interpreted that from an affirmative statement one derives the negative, and from the negative, the affirmative.

"in the land which the Lord your God gives you":

In this connection sages have said, "In the case of every religious duty in which Scripture specifies the reward along side, the earthly court is not admonished to enforce the rule."

MEKHILTA ATTRIBUTED TO RABBI ISHMAEL LIV:I.1

"Every one [Hebrew: man] [of you shall revere his mother and his father, and you shall keep my Sabbaths]":

I know only that a man [is subject to the instruction].

How do I know that a woman is also involved?

Scripture says, ". . . shall revere" [using the plural].

Lo, both genders are covered.

If so, why does Scripture refer to "man"?

It is because a man controls what he needs, while a woman does not control what she needs, since others have dominion over her.

It is said, "Every one of you shall revere his mother and his father," and it is further said, "The Lord your God you shall fear" (Deut. 6:13).

Scripture thereby establishes an analogy between the reverence of father and mother and the reverence of the Omnipresent.

It is said, "Honor your father and your mother" (Exod. 20:12), and it is further said, "Honor the Lord with your substance" (Prov. 3:9).

Scripture thereby establishes an analogy between the honor of father and mother and the honor of the Omnipresent.

It is said, "He who curses his father or his mother will certainly die" (Prov. 20:20), and it is said, "Any person who curses his God will bear his sin" (Lev. 24:15).

Scripture thereby establishes an analogy between cursing father and mother and cursing the Omnipresent.

But it is not possible to refer to smiting Heaven [in the way in which one is warned not to hit one's parents].

And that is entirely reasonable, for all three of them are partners [in a human being].

Simeon says, "Sheep take precedence over goats in all circumstances.

"Is it possible that that is because they are more choice?

"Scripture says, 'If he brings a sheep as his offering for sin' (Lev. 4:32), teaching that both of them are of equivalent merit.

"Pigeons take precedence over turtledoves under all circumstances.

"Might one suppose that that is because they are more choice?

"Scripture says, 'Or a pigeon or a turtledove for a sin-offering' (Lev. 12:6), teaching that both of them are of equivalent merit.

"The father takes precedence over the mother under all circumstances.

"Is it possible that the honor owing to the father takes preference over the honor owing to the mother?

"Scripture says, 'Every one of you shall revere his mother and his father,' teaching that both of them are of equivalent merit."

But sages have said, "The father takes precedence over the mother under all circumstances, because both the son and the mother are liable to pay respect to his father."

What is the form of reverence that is owing?

The son should not sit in his place, speak in his place, contradict him.

What is the form of honor that is owing?

The son should feed him, give him drink, dress him, cover him, bring him in and take him out.

Since it says, "Every one of you shall revere his mother and his father," might one suppose that if his father and mother told the son to violate one of any of the commandments that are stated in the Torah, he should obey them?

Scripture says, "And you shall keep my Sabbaths; I am the Lord your God" (Lev. 19:3):

"All of you are liable to pay due respect to me."

SIFRA CXCV:II.1-6

Our rabbis have taught on Tannaite authority:

Three form a partnership in the creation of a human being, the Holy One, blessed be he, one's father, and one's mother. When someone honors father and mother, said the Holy One, blessed be he, "I credit it to them as though I had lived among them and they honored me."

It has been taught on Tannaite authority:

Rabbi says, "It is perfectly self-evident to the One who spoke and brought the world into being that the son honors his mother more than his father, because she influences him with kind words. Therefore the Holy One, blessed be he, gave precedence to honoring the father over honoring the mother. But it also is perfectly self-evident before the One who spoke and brought the world into being that the son fears the father more than the mother, because he teaches him Torah. Therefore the Holy One, blessed be he, gave priority to fear of the mother over fear of the father."

A Tannaite authority repeated before R. Nahman: "When someone gives anguish to his father or his mother, said the Holy One, blessed be he, 'I did well in not living among them, for if I lived among them, they would have given me anguish, too.'"

They asked R. Ulla, "To what extent is one obligated to honor father and mother?"

He said to them, "Go and observe how a certain gentile has treated his father in Ashkelon, and Dama b. Netinah is his name. On one occasion sages wanted to do business with him in the amount of six hundred thousand, but the keys were lying under his father's pillow, and he would not disturb him."

Said R. Judah said Samuel, "They asked R. Eliezer, to what extent is one obligated to honor one's father and one's mother? He said to them, 'Go and observe how a certain gentile has treated his father in Ashkelon, and Dama b. Netinah is his name. On one occasion they wanted to buy from him precious stones for the ephod, in the amount of six hundred thousand (R. Kahana repeated as the Tannaite version, eight hundred thousand) but the keys were lying under his father's pillow, and he would not disturb him. Another year the Holy One, blessed be he, gave him his reward, for a red cow was born to him in his corral, and sages of Israel came to him. He said to them, "I know full well of you that if I should demand of you all the money in the world, you will give it to me. But now I ask of you only that sum of money that I lost in honor of my father."'"

And said R. Hanina, "Now if someone who is not subject to commandments acts in such a way, then if someone who is subject to the commandment acts in such a way, all the more so! For said R. Hanina, 'Greater is he who is commanded and acts on that account than he who is not commanded and acts on that account.'"

Said R. Joseph, "To begin with, I thought that if someone said to me, the decided law accords with R. Judah, that a blind person is exempt from the obligation of the commandments, I should have made a big party for all the rabbis, since I'm not obligated to do them, but I do them anyhow. But now that I've heard the statement of R. Hanina, 'Greater is he who is commanded and acts on that account than he who is not commanded and acts on that account,' to the contrary, if someone will tell me that the decided law is not in accord with R. Judah, I'll make a big party for all the rabbis."

When R. Dimi came, he said, "Once [Dama] was dressed in a gold embroidered silk coat, sitting among the Roman nobles, and his mother came along and tore it from him and hit him on the head and spat in his face, but he did not in any way answer back to her."

A Tannaite statement of Abimi b. R. Abbahu: There is he who feeds his father pheasant to eat but this drives the son from the world, and there is he who binds his father up to the grinding wheel, and this brings the son into the world to come. [Someone fed the father pheasants, but when the father asked how he could afford them, said, "It's none of your business, chew and eat." By contrast, someone was grinding on a mill and the father was summoned for the *corvée*, so the son said to the father, "You grind for me and I'll go in your place."]

Said R. Abbahu, "For instance, my son Abimi carried out in an exemplary manner the religious duty of honor of parents."
Abimi had five ordained sons when his father was yet alive, but when R. Abbahu came and called at the gate, he ran and opened for him, saying, "Coming, coming," until he got there.
Once he said to him, "Bring me a glass of water." Before he got there, the father dozed off. So he bent over him until he woke up. This brought it about that Abimi succeeded in explaining "a song of Asaph" (Ps. 79:1).

R. Assi had an aged mother. She said to him, "I want some jewelry." So he made it for her.
"I want a man."
"I'll go looking for someone for you."
"I want a man as handsome as you."
At that he left her and went to the Land of Israel. He heard that she was coming after him. He came to R. Yohanan and asked him, "What is the law on my leaving the Land and going abroad?"
He said to him, "It is forbidden."

"What is the law as to going to greet my mother?"

He said to him, "I don't know."

He waited a bit and then went and came back. He said to him, "Assi, you obviously want to go. May the Omnipresent bring you back here in peace."

Assi came before R. Eleazar. He said to him, "God forbid! Maybe he was mad?"

"What did he say to you?"

"May the Omnipresent bring you back here in peace."

He said to him, "Well, if he had been angry, he wouldn't have given you a blessing."

In the meanwhile he heard that it was her coffin that was coming. He said, "If I had known that, I wouldn't have gone out."

BAVLI TO MISHNAH-TRACTATE QIDDUSHIN 1:7/30B-31B

Hospitality

R. Eliezer, R. Joshua, R. Sadoq were reclining at the banquet of the son of Rabban Gamaliel. Rabban Gamaliel mixed the cup of wine for R. Eliezer, but the latter did not want to take it from him.

R. Joshua took it. Said to him R. Eliezer, "What's this Joshua! Is it right that we should recline, while Gamaliel, the noble, should stand over us and serve us?"

R. Joshua said to him, "Let him do his service. Abraham was the greatest man of the age but served the ministering angels, even though he thought that they were idol-worshipping Arabs?."

"For it is said, 'And he lifted up his eyes and looked, and behold, three men stood over against him' (Gen. 18:2).

"Now that yields an argument *a fortiori*:

"If Abraham, who was the greatest man of the age, served ministering angels thinking that they were idol-worshipping Arabs, Gamaliel, the noble, should surely serve me!"

Said to them R. Sadoq, "You have neglected the honor owing to the Omnipresent and occupied yourselves with the honor owing to mortals.

"If he who spoke and brought the world into being, restores the winds and brings clouds and brings down rain, raises the crops and sets a table for each and every person, should not Gamaliel, the honored man, serve us?"

SIFRÉ DEUTERONOMY. XXXVIII:I.4

Humble Gifts

King Agrippas wanted to offer a thousand bird offerings on a single day. He sent a message to the priest, "Let no one beside me make an offering on this day."

A poor man came, with two birds in his hand, and said to [the priest], "Offer these for me."

[The priest] said to him, "The king ordered me not to permit anyone but him to make an offering today."

[The poor man] said to him, "My Lord, priest, I catch four birds every day, two which I offer, and two which I use for a living. If you do not offer these two up, you cut my living in half."

The priest took them and offered them up.

In a dream King Agrippas foresaw [this message], "A poor man's offering came before yours."

He sent a message to the priest, "Didn't I tell you not to let anyone but me make an offering that day?"

He sent words to him, "My lord, king, a poor man came, with two birds in his hand and said to me, 'Offer these for me. I said to him, 'The king ordered me no to permit anyone but him to make an offering today.' He said to me, 'I catch four birds every day, two which I offer, and two which I use for a living. If you do not offer these two up, you cut my living in half.' Now should I not have offered them up?!"

He said to him, "You did things right."

People were leading an ox to be offered, but it would not be led. A poor man came with a bundle of endive in his hand, and held it out to the beast, which ate it. [The ox] sneezed and expelled a needle, and it then allowed itself to be led on to be offered. [If the needle had not been expelled, it would have caused an internal perforation, resulting in a blemish invalidating the animal for sacrificial purposes.]

The owner of the ox saw a message in his dream: "The offering of a poor man came before yours."

A woman brought a handful of fine flour [for a cereal offering, in line with Lev. 2:1]. But the priest ridiculed her and said, "See what these women are bringing as their offerings! In such a paltry thing what is there to eat? And what is there to offer up?"

The priest saw a message in his dream: "Do not ridicule her on such an account, for it is as if she was offering up her own soul."

Now is it not a matter of an argument *a fortiori*? If concerning someone who doesn't offer up a living soul [of a beast], Scripture uses the word, "Soul" [When any soul (RSV: one) brings a cereal offering"], if someone brings a [contrite] soul, how much the more is it as if this one has offered her own soul."

LEVITICUS RABBAH III:V.2

Humiliating Others

R. Yosé ben Hanina said, "He who exalts himself at the cost of his fellow's humiliation has no share in the World to Come. How much more he who exalts himself against the Life of the Worlds! What is written after it? 'How abundant is your goodness, which you have laid up for those who fear you' (Ps. 31:20). Let him have no [share] in your abundant goodness."

YERUSHALMI HAGIGAH 2:1

Humility

Lo, all the other rivers say to the Euphrates, "How come you don't sound off as you flow, the way in which the rest of us make our flow heard from a distance?"

The river said to them, "My deeds give evidence concerning me [so I don't have to announce how great I am]. If someone sews seed by me, the seed comes up in three days. If he puts a sapling nearby, it comes up in thirty days.

"Even Scripture praises me, [calling me great]: '. . . as far as the Great River, the river Euphrates'" (Deut. 1:7).

SIFRÉ DEUTERONOMY VI:III.3

Our rabbis have taught on Tannaite authority:
A person always should be humble, like Hillel the Elder, and not captious, like Shammai the Elder.

There was the case of two people, who went and made a bet with one another for four hundred *zuz*.

They stipulated, "Whoever can go and infuriate Hillel will get the four hundred *zuz*."

One of them went [to try]. That day was a Friday, toward nightfall, and Hillel was washing his hair. The man came and knocked on the door, saying, "Where is Hillel, where is Hillel?"

Hillel wrapped himself up in his cloak and came to meet him. He said to him, "My son, what do you require?"

He said to him, "I have a question to ask."

He said to him, "Ask, my son, ask."

He said to him, "How come the Babylonians have round heads?"

He said to him, "My son, you have asked quite a question: It's because they don't have skilled midwives."

He went and waited a while and came back and knocked on the door. He said, "Who's here? Who's here?"

Hillel wrapped himself up in his cloak and come out.

He said to him, "My son, what do you need?"

He said to him, "Why are the eyes of the people of Palmyra [Tadmor] bleary?"

He said to him, "My son, you've asked quite a question. It's because they live in the sands of the desert and the winds blow and scatter the sand into their eyes. Therefore their eyes are bleary."

He went and waited a while and came back and knocked on the door. He said, "Who's here? Who's here?"

Hillel wrapped himself up in his cloak and come out.

He said to him, "My son, what do you need?"

He said to him, "I need to ask a question."

He said to him, "Go ahead."

He said to him, "Why are the feet of the Africans flat?"

He said to him, "Because they live by swamps, and every day walk in water, therefore their feet are flat."

He said to him, "I have a lot of questions to ask, but I'm afraid that you'll get mad."

He said to him, "Whatever questions that you have, go and ask."

He said to him, "Are you the Hillel, whom people call the patriarch of Israel?"

He said to him, "Yup."

He said to him, "Well, if that's who you are, then I hope there won't be many in Israel like you!"

He said to him, "My son, how come?"

He said to him, "You have cost me four hundred *zuz*."

He said to him, "You should be careful of your moods! Hillel is worth your losing four hundred *zuz* without Hillel's losing his temper"

BAVLI TO MISHNAH-TRACTATE SHABBAT 2:5/30B-31A

The Impulse to Do Evil

Confronted by the question of evil, the sages do not seek to define; rather, they categorize. What is evil, what is good —these are the issues that confound and occupy them. From where does evil come? Not a natural impulse, but a dialectic. And from the struggle to come up with the right behavior emerges the fate of the world.

Said Rab, "The impulse to do evil is like a fly. It sits between the two doors of the heart, as it is said, 'Dead flies make the ointment of the perfumes fetid and putrid' (Qoh. 10:1)."

And Samuel said, "It is like a grain of wheat, as it is said, 'Sin crouches at the door' (Gen. 4:7)."

Our rabbis have taught on Tannaite authority:

Man has two kidneys, one counseling him to do good, the other counseling him to do evil.

And it is reasonable to suppose that the one for good is at the right side and for evil at the left.

For it is written, "A wise man's understanding is at his right hand, but a fool's understanding is at his left" (Qoh. 10:2).

Our rabbis have taught on Tannaite authority:

The kidneys counsel, the heart discerns, the tongue shapes [words], the mouth expresses them, the gullet admits and gives out all sorts of food, the wind-pipe produces sound, the lungs take in all sorts of liquids, the liver produces anger, the gall drops a drop into it and calms it, the milt [spleen] makes one laugh, the large intestine grinds food, the maw [mouth] induces sleep, the nose wakes one up.

If what produces wakening sleeps, or what produces sleep wakes one up, a person will pine away.

It has been taught on Tannaite authority:

If both of them produce sleep or both of them wakes one up, one forthwith dies.

It has been taught on Tannaite authority:

R. Yosé the Galilean says, "As to the righteous, the impulse to do good produces their judgments [of what to do or not to do], for it is said, 'My heart is slain within me' (Ps. 109:22).

"As to the wicked, the impulse to do evil produces their judgments [of what to do or not to do], for it is said, 'Transgression speaks to the wicked, I think, there is no fear of God before his eyes' (Ps. 36:2).

"As to people who fall in the middle, both impulses produce their judgments [of what to do or not to do], for it is said, 'Because he stands at the right hand of the needy, to save him from them that judge his soul' (Ps. 109:31)."

Said Raba, "People such as we fall in the middle."

Said Abbayye to him, "The master has not allowed anyone else to live [if so righteous a man is only middling]."

And Raba said, "The world was created only for those who are completely wicked or for those who are completely righteous."

Said Raba, "A person should know concerning himself whether he is completely righteous or not."

Said Raba, "The world was created only for Ahab son of Omri, and for R. Hanina b. Dosa, this world for Ahab son of Omri, and the world to come for R. Hanina b. Dosa."

BAVLI TO MISHNAH-TRACTATE BERAKHOT 9:5/60B-61A

Insight and Sight

This is a perplexing analogy-story, because its conclusion leaves the reader thinking that one of the two protagonists didn't get it. But the wisdom of the utterance from sage R. Sheshet is not lost. Neither, too, is the way it is said, and what he uses to support his point.

R. Sheshet was blind. Everyone was running to give a reception to the king. R. Sheshet got up and went with them. A man said to him, "Whole jugs go to the river [for water], where do broken ones go?"

He said to him, "Come and you will see that I know more than you."

The first troop came by. When a cry arose, the man said to him, "The king is coming."

R. Sheshet said to him, "He is not coming."

The second troop came by. At the outcry, the man said to him, "Now the king is coming."

Said R. Sheshet to him, "The king is not coming."

The third troop passed by. When the crowds became hushed, R. Sheshet said to him, "Now the king is assuredly coming."

The man said to him, "How do you know?"

He said to him, "Because earthly royalty is like the royalty of the firmament.

"For it is written, 'Go forth and stand upon the mount before the Lord. And behold, the Lord passed by and a great and strong wind broke the mountains and shattered the rocks before the Lord, but the Lord was not in the wind. And after the wind an earthquake, but the Lord was not in the earthquake. And after the earthquake a fire, but the Lord was not in the fire. And after the fire a still small voice' (1 Kings 19:11–12)."

When the king came by, R. Sheshet said a blessing for him.

Said the man to him, "Are you going to say a blessing for someone whom you cannot see?"

BAVLI TO MISHNAH-TRACTATE BERAKHOT 9:2

Integrity

The sages are both pragmatic and idealistic. And the following passages illustrate the manner in which they correlate the two impulses. The wisdom to know what is right—and to ignore the potential rewards of getting along—is clearly admired here. But, as we shall see, integrity, even spiritual integrity, should not cause one's death. The point is clear: do not sacrifice integrity to gain earthly riches, but do not use it to gain eternal life.

Aqabia b. Mahalalel gave testimony in four matters.

They said to him, "Aqabia, retract the four rulings which you laid down, and we shall make you patriarch of the court of Israel."

He said to them, "It is better for me to be called a fool my whole life but not be deemed a wicked person before the Omnipresent for even one minute, so that people should not say, 'Because he craved after high office, he retracted.'"

He would declare unclean residual hair [in a leprosy sign] and green blood [of a vaginal discharge].

And sages declare clean.

He would permit use of the wool which fell out in the case of a first-ling which was blemished, and which one put away in a niche, and [which firstling] one afterward slaughtered.

And sages prohibit.

He would say, "They do not administer bitter water [to test the woman accused of adultery] in the case of a proselyte woman or in the case of a freed slave girl."

And sages say, "They do administer the test."

They said to him, "Karkemit, a freed slave girl, was in Jerusalem, and Shemaiah and Abtalion administered the bitter water to her."

He said to them, "They administered it to her to make her into an example."

They excommunicated him, and he died while he was subject to the excommunication, so the court stoned his bier.

Said R. Judah, "God forbid that Aqabia was excommunicated! "For the courtyard is never locked before any Israelite of the wisdom and fear of sin of a man like Aqabia b. Mahalalel.

"But whom did they excommunicate? It was Eliezer b. Hanokh, who cast doubt on [the sages' ruling about] the cleanness of hands.

"And when he died, the court sent and put a stone on his bier."

This teaches that whoever is excommunicated and dies while he is subject to the excommunication—they stone his bier.

When he was dying, he said to his son, "My son, retract in the four rulings which I had laid down."

He said to him, "And why do you retract now?"

He said to him, "I heard the rulings in the name of the majority, and they heard them in the name of the majority, so I stood my ground on the tradition which I had heard, and they stood their ground on the tradition they had heard.

"But you have heard the matter both in the name of an individual and in the name of the majority.

"It is better to abandon the opinion of the individual and to hold with the opinion of the majority."

He said to him, "Father, give instructions concerning me to your colleagues."

He said to him, "I will give no instructions."

He said to him, "Is it possible that you have found some fault with me?"

He said to him, "No. It is your deeds which will bring you near, or your deeds which will put you off [from the others]."

MISHNAH EDUYYOT 5:6

Abba bar Zemina worked as a tailor for a certain Aramean [i.e., a gentile] in Rome.

Meat that was not properly slaughtered was brought to him [and the gentile] told him, "Eat!"

[Abba] said to him, "I will not eat [it]."

[The gentile] said to him, "Eat [it], for otherwise I will kill you!"

[Abba] said to him, "If you want to kill [me, go ahead and] kill me, but I will not eat meat that was not properly slaughtered."

[The gentile] said to him, "Since now [you have proven yourself], you should know that [in truth] if you had eaten it, I would have killed you.

"If you are a Jew, [you must act according to the customs of] the Jews.

"If you are an Aramean, [you must act according to the customs of] the Arameans."

Said R. Mana, "Had R. Abba bar Zemina known the words of the rabbis, [above, who state that, in private, one should transgress rather than be killed], he would have eaten [the unkosher meat]."

YERUSHALMI SHEBIIT TO MISHNAH 4:2/VI

Justice

In this age of litigation, the following passages comprise a simple statement of natural law. But the sages appear to anticipate the natural results of mixing law and human emotion—sympathy for the downtrodden, respect for the powerful.

Hillel saw a skull floating on the water and said to it [in Aramaic]: "Because you drowned others, they drowned you, and in the end those who drowned you will be drowned."

TRACTATE ABOT 2:6

"You shall do no injustice in judgment; [you shall not be partial to the poor or defer to the great, but in righteousness shall you judge your neighbor. You shall not go up and down as a slanderer among your people, and you shall not stand forth against the life of your neighbor: I am the Lord]" (Lev. 19:15–16):

This teaches that a judge who misjudges a case is called "unjust," "hated," "an abomination," "beyond all use," "an abhorrent."

And he causes five things to happen: he imparts uncleanness to the land, he desecrates the divine name, he makes the Presence of God depart, he impales Israel on the sword, and makes Israel go into exile from its land.

". . . you shall not be partial to the poor":
You should not say, "This man is a poor man. Since both this rich

man and I are obligated to feed him, let me decide in his favor, so that he will turn out to gain his living in an easy way."

That is why it is said, "you shall not be partial to the poor."

". . . or defer to the great":

You should not say, "This man is a rich man. He is son of important people. I shall not humiliate him and be seen through his humiliation to impose humiliation upon him."

Therefore it is said, "or defer to the great."

". . . but in righteousness shall you judge your neighbor":

This means that one party may not be permitted to speak as long as he needs, while to the other you say, "Cut it short."

One should not stand while the other sits down.

Said R. Judah, "I have heard a tradition that if they wanted to let both of them sit down, they let them sit down. What is prohibited is only that one of them should sit while the other is standing."

Another interpretation of the statement, "but in righteousness shall you judge your neighbor":

In judging everyone, give the benefit of the doubt.

SIFRA CC:I

The Justice of God

The following passage is self-explanatory.

And said R. Isaac, "Three things call to mind a person's iniquities.

"These are they: a shaky wall, testing of prayer, and requesting [divine] judgment upon one's fellow." [By walking by a teetering wall, the individual tempts fate. "Testing prayer" refers to experimenting to see if prayer produces the desired effect. The third item is explained in the following.]

For said R. Abin, "Whoever requests [divine] judgment on his fellow—he is done [that is, judged] first, as it says (Gen. 16:5): 'And Sarai said to Abram, "May the wrong done to me be on you!"'" [Sarah thus called for divine judgment of Abraham.]

"And [proving that, as a result, she herself was judged first] it is written [after that, Gen. 23:2]: 'And Abraham went in to mourn for Sarah and to weep for her.'"

And said R. Isaac, "Four things cancel the judgment against a person.

"And these are they: charity, crying out [in supplication], change of name, and change of character.

"Charity—as it is written [Prov. 10:2: 'Treasures gained by wickedness do not profit], but righteousness delivers from death.'

"Crying out [in supplication]—as it is written [Ps. 106:6]: 'And they cried out to the Lord in their trouble, and he delivered them from their distress.'

"Change of name—as it is written (Gen. 17:15): 'And God said to Abraham], "As for Sarai your wife, you shall not call her name Sarai, but Sarah shall be her name."' And [after this statement] it is written (Gen. 17:16): 'I will bless her, and moreover I will give you a son by her.'

"Change of character—as it is written (Jonah 3:10): 'When God saw what they did, [how they turned from their evil way . . . .' And [after this statement, in the continuation of the verse] it is written: 'God repented of the evil which he had said he would do to them, and he did not do it].'"

And some say also [that] changing location [cancels a person's judgment].

For it is written (Gen. 12:1): "Now the Lord said to Abram, 'Go from your country [and your kindred and your father's house to the land that I will show you].'" And it continues (Gen. 12:2): "'And I will make of you a great nation, [and I will bless you and make your name great, so that you will be a blessing].'"

Said R. Kruspedai said R. Yohanan, "Three books are opened [by God] on the New Year: one for the thoroughly wicked, one for the thoroughly righteous, and one for middling [people].

"The thoroughly righteous immediately are inscribed and sealed for [continued] life.

"The thoroughly wicked immediately are inscribed and sealed for death.

"Middling [people] are left hanging from New Year until the Day of Atonement.

"If they [are found to have] merit, they are inscribed for life.

"If they [are found] not [to have] merit, they are inscribed for death."

Said R. Abin, "What is the Scriptural [foundation for this]? [Ps. 69:29 states]: 'Let them be blotted out of the book of the living. Let them not be inscribed among the righteous.' 'Let them be blotted out of the book'—this refers to the book of the thoroughly wicked. '[. . . of the] living'—this refers to the book of the righteous. 'Let them not be inscribed among the righteous'—this refers to the book of middling [people]."

Rab Nahman bar Isaac said, "From here [Exod. 32:32, referring to Moses's entreating of God to forgive the people's sin: 'So Moses returned to the Lord and said, ". . . But now, if you will, forgive their sin]. But if not, blot me, I pray, from your book which you have written.'" 'Blot me, I pray'—this refers to the book of the thoroughly wicked. 'From your book'—this refers to the book of the righteous. 'Which you have written'—this refers to the book of middling [people]."

It has been taught on Tannaite authority:
The House of Shammai say, "[There will be] three groups on the Day of Judgment [when the dead will rise]: one comprised of the thoroughly righteous, one comprised of the thoroughly wicked, and one of middling [people].

"The thoroughly righteous immediately are inscribed and sealed for eternal life.

"The thoroughly wicked immediately are inscribed and sealed for Gehenna,

"as it is written (Dan. 12:2): 'And many of those who sleep in the dust of the earth shall awake, some to eternal life and some to shame and everlasting contempt.'

"Middling [people] go down to Gehenna, scream [in prayer], and rise [again],

"as it is written (Zech. 13:9): 'And I will put this third into the fire and refine them as one refines silver and test them as gold is tested. They will call on my name, and I will answer them.'

"And, concerning this group, Hannah said (I Sam. 2:6): 'The Lord kills and brings to life. He brings down to Sheol and raises up.'"

[The Hillelites reject the notion that the middling group initially is sent to Gehenna.] The House of Hillel say, "But [contrary to what the Shammaites hold, God] who abounds in mercy leans towards [a judgment of] mercy.

"And concerning them [that is, the middling group] David said (Ps. 116:1): 'I love the Lord, because he has heard my voice [and my supplications].'

"And [further] concerning them David stated the whole passage [which begins, Ps. 116:6]: 'The Lord preserves the simple; when I was brought low, he saved me.'"

Israelite wrongdoers [who sin] with their body and gentile wrongdoers [who sin] with their body go down to Gehenna and are judged
[i.e., punished] there for twelve months.

After twelve months their body is consumed [in fire], their soul is
burned, and a wind scatters them under the feet of the righteous.

[This is] as it says (Mal. 4:3): "And you shall tread down the wicked,
for they will be ashes under the soles of your feet [on the day when I
act, says the Lord of hosts]."

But the sectarians, the informers, and heretics, who denied the
Torah, who denied the resurrection of the dead, who separated themselves from the ways of the community, who tyrannized the land of the
living, and who sinned and caused many others to sin—such as Jeroboam
son of Nebat and his associates—[these individuals] go down to
Gehenna and are judged there for generations.

[This is] as it says (Isa. 66:24): "And they shall go forth and look
on the dead bodies of the men that have rebelled against me. [For their
worm shall not die, their fire shall not be quenched, and they shall be
an abhorrence to all flesh]."

Gehenna will be consumed [by fire], but they will not be consumed,
as it says (Ps. 49:14): "And their form shall waste away; Sheol shall
be their habitation."

Now, [as for] all of this—why?

Because they place their hands on the habitation, as it says [Ps.
49:15]: "their habitation."

And [the term] "habitation" refers only to the Temple sanctuary, as
it says [1 Kings 8:13, concerning Solomon's completion of the Temple]:
"I have built you an exalted habitation, [a place for you to dwell forever]."

And concerning those Hannah said (1 Sam. 2:10): "The adversar-
ies of the Lord shall be broken to pieces."

Said R. Isaac bar Abin, "Now, their faces shall look like the sides
of a pot [that is, black and charred]."

And said Raba, "And these are the most handsome of the people
of Mehoza, and they shall be called, 'sons of Gehenna.'"

The House of Hillel say, "But [God] who abounds in mercy leans
towards [a judgment of] mercy."

How does [God] act?

R. Eleazar says, "He presses down [on the side of the balance-
scale representing merit], as it is said (Mic. 7:19): 'He will again have
compassion upon us. He will push down our iniquities.'"

R. Yosé bar Hanina said, "He lifts [the side of the balance-scale representing wrongdoings], as it is said [Mic. 7:18: 'Who is a God like you], raising iniquity and passing over transgression.'"

It is taught on Tannaite authority in the house of R. Ishmael: He passes over the first transgression [of each type], and this is [God's] attribute [of mercy].

Said Raba, "The transgression itself is not erased, so that, if there [turns out to] be a majority of transgressions, [God] considers it with the others."

Raba said, "[As for] anyone who passes over his right [to exact punishment against another], they pass over all of his transgressions,

"as it says [Mic. 7:18: 'Who is a God like you], pardoning iniquity and passing over transgression.'

"For whom does [God] pardon iniquity? For the one who pardons transgression [in others]."

Rab Huna the son of Rab Joshua was ill. Rab Pappa entered to ask about him. He saw that he was in his final illness. [Pappa therefore] said to those [present], "Prepare a [burial] shroud for him!" In the end [however, Huna] recovered. Rab Pappa was embarrassed to see him.

[Pappa] said to him, "[When you were ill] what did you see?"

[Huna] said to him, "Indeed, it was as [you thought], but the Holy One, blessed be he, said to them [that is, to the Heavenly court], 'Since [Huna] did not [needlessly assert his rights [against others], do not assert [yourselves] against him, as it says (Mic. 7:18): "Pardoning iniquity and passing over transgression."'" For whom does [God] pardon iniquity? For the one who pardons transgression [in others]."

[We continue with an unrelated analysis of the continuation of Mic. 7:18:] "[Who is a God like you, pardoning iniquity and passing over transgression] for the remnant of his inheritance?"

Said R. Aha bar Hanina, "[This is like] a fat tail that has a thorn in it. [God passes over transgression] 'for the remnant of his inheritance,' but not for all [the people] of his inheritance!"

[The verse means that God passes over the transgression of] whoever makes himself as though he were a remnant [by humbling himself and behaving like the righteous (Rashi)].

Said R. Yohanan, "Great is [the power of] repentance, which obliterates a person's final judgment.

"[This is] as it says (Isa. 6:10): 'Make the heart of this people fat and their ears heavy and shut their eyes, lest they see with their eyes and hear with their ears and understand with their hearts and turn and be healed.'

Said Rab Pappa to Abbayye, "But perhaps [Isa. 6:10's notion that, if people 'turn' they will be 'healed,' applies only] before the final decree [is made]?" [In this view, contrary to Yohanan, once final judgment has been passed, repentance does not have the power to obliterate that judgment.]

[Abbayye] said to him, "[At Isa. 6:10] 'and be healed' is written. Which thing [leads the individual to] require healing? Let us say [it is] the final decree!" [Hence the power of repentance is as Yohanan said.]

They objected: "[We know a teaching which states that if a wrong-doer] repented between [New Year and the Day of Atonement, his transgressions] are forgiven. If he did not repent, even if he brought [as sacrifices] all of the rams of Nebayot, he will not be forgiven." [Accordingly, the efficacy of repentance is restricted to a specific period. Repentance does not have the power Yohanan ascribes to it.]

There is no contradiction. This [latter statement refers] to an individual. This [former statement refers] to a community.

They objected [on the basis of a prior teaching], "Referring to the land of Israel, Deut. 11:12 states]: 'The eyes of the Lord your God are always upon it'—[which means] sometimes for good and sometimes for evil. 'Sometimes for good'—how so? Lo, if at New Year [the people of] Israel were [in the category of people who are] thoroughly evil, so that insubstantial rains were decreed for them, [but], in the end, they turned [and changed their ways]—[for God] to supply additional rain is impossible, since the judgment already has been decreed. Rather, the Holy One, blessed be he, brings down [the rain] at the proper time, upon the land that requires it, entirely according to [the needs of the particular plot of] land. [But the amount of rain, previously decreed, does not change.] 'Sometimes for evil'—how so? Lo, if at New Year [the people of] Israel were [in the category of people who are] thoroughly righteous, so that substantial rains were decreed for them, [but], in the end, they turned [and changed their ways]— [for God] to supply less rain is impossible, since the judgment already has been decreed. Rather, the Holy One, blessed be he, brings down [the rain] at the wrong time, upon land that does not require it. [The previously decreed quantity of rain does not change. But the rain is made to fall in areas in which it is wasted.] [If, as Yohanan claims, in response to repentance, the decree will be rescinded], for [the case of individuals who changed their ways to the] good, at least, let the judgment be rescinded so as to increase for them [the quantity of rain]!" [The fact that the quantity of rain is not increased proves that repentance does not have the power Yohanan ascribes to it.]

There [in the case of a decree regarding the quantity of rain] it is different, since it is possible to [solve the problem by doing] that . [In this case actually altering the decree is not necessary and therefore is not done. This reflects the special nature of the circumstance, not a limitation of the power of repentance.]

Come and learn [a further challenge to Yohanan's position]:

[Ps. 107:23–31 states:] "Some went down to the sea in ships, doing business on the great waters. They saw the deeds of the Lord, [his wondrous works in the deep]. For he commanded and raised the stormy wind, which lifted up the waves of the sea. [They mounted up to Heaven, they went down to the depths. Their courage melted away in their evil plight]. They reeled and staggered like drunken men [and were at their wits' end]. Then they cried to the Lord in their trouble, [and he delivered them from their distress. He made the storm be still, and the waves of the sea were hushed. Then they were glad because they had quiet, and he brought them to their desired haven]. Let them thank the Lord for his steadfast love, [for his wonderful works to the sons of men]!" [The psalmist] made them signs corresponding to the "buts" and "onlys" in the Torah, so as to teach you [that if] they cried [in supplication to the Lord] prior to the passing of [their] final judgment, they were answered. [Reference is to an inverted Hebrew letter (*nun*) that appears in the Masoretic text before a number of the verses of this psalm.] But if they cried [to the Lord] after [their] final judgment was passed, they were not answered. [Accordingly, we see that repentance does not have the unmitigated power Yohanan ascribes to it.]

BAVLI TO MISHNAH-TRACTATE ROSH HASHANAH 1:2/17A-B
[*Translated by Alan J. Avery-Peck*]

Keeping One's Word

One of the primary skills in Talmudic argument is seeing beyond suffering and discerning a logical assignment of blame. So it is with the following discussions, which draw distinctions between suffering, and thus, the punishment for those responsible.

He who hires craftsmen,
and one party deceived the other—

one has no claim on the other party except a complaint [which is not subject to legal recourse].

[If] one hired an ass driver or wagon driver to bring porters and pipes for a bride or a corpse,

or workers to take his flax out of the steep,

or anything which goes to waste [if there is a delay],

and [the workers] went back on their word—

in a situation in which there is no one else [available for hire],

he hires others at their expense,

or he deceives them [by promising to pay more and then not paying up more than his originally stipulated commitment].

He who hires craftsmen and they retracted—

their hand is on the bottom.

If the householder retracts,

his hand is on the bottom.

Whoever changes [the original terms of the agreement]—

his hand is on the bottom.

And whoever retracts—

his hand is on the bottom.

He who rents out an ass to drive it through hill country but drove it through a valley,

to drive it through a valley but drove it through the hill country,

even though this route is ten miles and that route is ten miles,

and [the ass] died—

[the one who rented it is] liable.

He who rents out an ass to drive it through hill country, but he drove it through a valley.

if it slipped, is exempt.

But if it suffered heat prostration, he is liable.

[If he hired it out] to drive it through a valley, but he drove it through hill country,

if it slipped, he is liable.

And if it suffered heat prostration, he is exempt.

But if it was on account of the elevation, he is liable.

He who rents out an ass, and it went blind or was seized for royal service—

[the one who provided it has the right to] say to [the one who rented it], "Here's yours right before you" [and he need not replace it for the stated period].

[If] it died or broke a leg,

[the one who provided it out] is liable to provide him with another ass.

He who hires a cow to plough in the hill country but ploughed in the valley,

if the plough-share was broken,

is exempt.

[If he hired the cow to plough] in the valley and ploughed in the hill country,

if the plough-share was broken,

he is liable.

[If he hired a cow to] thresh pulse and he threshed grain,

[if the cow slipped and fell],

he is exempt.

[If he hired it] to thresh grain and he threshed pulse,

[if the cow slipped and fell],

he is liable,

because pulse is slippery.

Mishnah-Tractate Baba Mesia 6:1-4

Licentiousness

Just as Jesus declared adultery to be a matter of attitude as much as of action, so sages held licentiousness to extend to intentionality. They regarded obsessive staring at a woman as an act of licentiousness, and labeled positioning oneself so as to fantasize about a woman's sexuality as equivalent to pornography. Thus, they held, one should not stare at or follow a woman. How they would have regarded contemporary mores we need hardly wonder. They will certainly have concurred with the insistence of feminism that women be accorded the dignity of privacy, the right to autonomy.

Our rabbis have taught on Tannaite authority:

He who counts out coins into a woman's hand from his own in order to have a chance to stare at her, even if such a one has in hand Torah and good deeds like Moses, our master, will not be quit of the judgment of Gehenna.

For it is said, "Hand to hand, he shall not escape from evil" (Prov. 11:21). He shall not escape from the judgment of Gehenna.

Said R. Nahman, "Manoah was an ignorant man.

"For it is written, 'And Manoah went after his wife' (Judg. 13:11)."

To this statement R. Nahman bar Isaac objected, "But does the same judgment apply to Elkanah. For it is written, 'And Elkanah went after his wife' [no such verse exists], and, also, with respect to Elisha, does this judgment apply, for it is written, 'And he rose and went after her' (2 Kings 4:30)?

"Is the meaning then that he literally went after her? But what it means was that he followed her views and her counsel. Here, too, he followed her views and her counsel."

Said R. Ashi, "Now in regard to the view of R. Nahman that Manoah was an ignorant man, he had not learned as much Scripture as someone who is in the house of a master [as a beginner in Scripture studies].

"For it is said, 'And Rebecca arose and her maidens, and they rode upon the camels and followed the man' (Gen. 24:61). Thus [they went] after the man, not before him."

Longevity

The secret to a good long life is one which amuses many Western thinkers—it is often associated with physical upkeep and a certain attitude. The sages are different, and in the following discussion, detail the full extent of their ideological underpinnings.

R. Zakkai's students asked him: "Through what have you attained long life?"

He said to them: "In my [entire] life, I never urinated within four cubits of prayer; and I never called my fellow a nickname; and I never missed the daytime Qiddush [prayer of sanctification of the Sabbath day]."

R. Eleazar ben Shammua's students asked him: "Through what have you attained long life?"

He said to them: "In my [entire] lifetime, I never took a shortcut through the synagogue; and I never trod on the heads of the holy people; and I never raised my hands without [saying] a blessing."

R. Pereidah's students asked him: "Through what have you attained long life?"

He said to them: "In my [entire] lifetime, no one ever preceded me at the academy; and I never recited a blessing before a priest; and I never ate from an animal whose [priestly] gifts were not removed, for

"Said R. Isaac, said R. Yohanan: 'It is forbidden to eat from an animal from which the [priestly] gifts were not removed.'

"And said R. Isaac: 'Anyone who eats from an animal from which the [priestly] gifts were not removed is like one who eats produce from which tithes have not been removed.'"

And the halakhah is not according to him.

"And I never recited a blessing before a priest"—is that to say that this is better?

And said R. Yohanan: "Any scholar before whom anyone, even an ignorant high priest, recites a blessing, is worthy of death, as is said, 'all of my enemies loved death' (Prov. 8:36). Do not read *mesane'ai*, 'my enemies' [i.e., those who hate me], but *maseni'ai*, 'those who make me hate.'

When he said this, [it was] about equals.

R. Nehuniah ben HaQaneh's students asked him: "Through what have you attained long life?"

He said to them: "In my [entire] lifetime, (1) I was never honored through my fellow's embarrassment; (2) and my fellow's curse never followed me to bed; (3) and I was generous with my money."

"I was never honored through the embarrassment of my fellow . . ." Similarly, when Rab Huna was carrying a hoe on his shoulder, Rab Hanna bar Hanilai came along and took it from him. He [Rab Huna] said to him: "If you regularly carry [one] in your town, carry [it]; and if not, I am uncomfortable being honored through your degradation."

"And my fellow's curse never followed me to bed . . ." Similarly, when Mar Zutra climbed into his bed, he would say: "I forgive everyone who has pained me."

"And I was generous with my money," as a master said: "Job was generous with his money, since he used to leave a coin (*perutah*) for the storekeeper from his money."

R. Aqiba asked R. Nehuniah the Elder: "Through what have you attained long life?"

He said to him: "The attendants came and beat him.

He climbed and stayed on the top of a date palm."

He [Aqiba] said to him: "My master, if 'lamb' is mentioned [in Num. 28:4], why is 'one' [also] mentioned?"

He [Nehuniah] said to him: "He is a student of the rabbis; leave him alone."

He said to him [Aqiba]: "'One' [means] unique in its flock."

He [Nehuniah] said to him: "In my entire lifetime, (1) I never received gifts, (2) and I never stood on my dues [lit.: insisted on retribution]; (3) [and] I was generous with my money.

. . . "I never received gifts." Similarly R. Eleazar. When they gave him gifts from the Patriarch's house, he did not take [them]. When they invited him, he did not go. He said to them: "Are you not comfortable if I live, as is written, 'One who hates gifts will live' (Prov. 15:27)."

When they sent R. Zeira [gifts] from the Patriarch's house, he did not take [them]. When they invited him, he went. He said: "They honor themselves through me."

. . . "And I never stood on my dues," as Raba said: "Anyone who passes over (*hama'avir 'al*) his dues, they remove from him (*ma'avirim mi-*) all his sins, as is said, ". . . [who] forgives evil and passes over (`over 'al*) sin." To whom does he forgive evil? To he who passes over sin [done to him]."

A. R. asked R. Joshua ben Qorha: "Through what have you attained long life?"

He said to him: "Are you hostile to my life?" [Cf. Gen. 27:46.]

He said to him: "R., it is Torah, and I must learn [it]."

He said to him: "In my [entire] lifetime, (1) I never looked at the image of an evil man, for said R. Yohanan: 'It is forbidden for one to look at the visage of an evil man, as is said, "Were it not for the face of Jehoshafat, King of Judah, I swear I would not look at you or see you" (2 Kings 3:14).'"

R. Eleazar said: "His eyes were dim, as is said, 'And when Isaac was old, his eyes dimmed' (Gen. 27:1), because he looked at Esau, the evil one.

"And did this [really] cause it [i.e., the weakness of his eyes]?"

For, said R. Isaac: "Never take the curse of a commoner lightly, because Abimelekh cursed Sarah, and it was fulfilled through her seed, as is said, '. . . behold it is for you as a covering (*kesut*) of the eyes' (Gen. 20:16). Do not read *kesut*, 'covering,' read *kesiyat*, 'closing.'

"[Both] this and that caused it [i.e., the weakness of his eyes]."

Raba said from here: "Tolerating (*se'et*) the face of an evil person is not good" (Prov. 18:5).

At the time of his death, he said to him: "R., bless me."

He said to him: "May it be [His] will that you reach to half of my days."

He said to him: "But not to all of them?"

He said to him: "Will those who come after you herd cattle [and not have a chance to be scholars]?"

Abbahu bar Ihi and Minyamin bar Ihi: "One said: 'May it [i.e., the blessing] come to me, because I have not looked at a Kuthean [literally a Samaritan, but here probably substituted for any non-Jew].'

"And one said: 'May it [i.e., the blessing] come to me, because I have not made any partnership with a Kuthean.'"

R. Zeira's students asked him: "Through what have you attained long life?"

He said to them: "In my [entire] lifetime, (1) I never got angry in my house; (2) and I never walked in front of someone greater than myself; (3) and I never thought [holy thoughts] in unclean alleys; (4) and I never walked four cubits without Torah or without Tefillin; (5) and I never slept in the academy, neither soundly nor dozing; (6) and I never rejoiced at the misfortune of my fellow; (7) and I never addressed my fellow by his insulting nickname, some say, not even by his [regular] nickname."

BAVLI TO MISHNAH-TRACTATE MEGILLAH 4:3/27B-28A

Losing One's Wife

And R. Yohanan said, "Any man whose first wife dies is as if the Temple was destroyed in his day. For it is said, 'Son of man, behold I take away from you the desire of your eyes with a stroke, yet you shall not make lamentation nor weep, neither shall your tears run down.' And it is written, 'And I spoke to the people in the morning, and at evening my wife died.' And it is written, 'Behold I will profane my sanctuary, the pride of your power, the desire of your eyes' (Ezek. 24:16-18)."

Said R. Alexandri, "For every man whose wife dies in his lifetime the world grows dark, as it is said, 'The light shall be dark because of his tent and his lamp over him shall be put out' (Job 18:6)."

R. Yosé bar Hanina said, "His steps grew short, as it is said, 'The steps of his strength shall be straightened' (Job 18:7)."

R. Abbahu said, "His good sense fails, as it is said, 'And his own counsel shall cast him down' (Job 18:7)."

Said R. Samuel bar Nahman, "Everything can be replaced except for the wife of one's youth,

"as it is said, 'And a wife of one's youth, can she be rejected?' (Isa. 54:6)."

R. Judah repeated on Tannaite authority to his son, R. Isaac, "A man finds true serenity only with his first wife, as it is said, 'Let your fountain be blessed and have joy of the wife of your youth' (Prov. 5:18)."

He said to him, "Such as whom?"

He said to him, "Such as your mother."

Is this so? And did not R. Judah recite for R. Isaac, his son, the verse of Scripture, "And I find more bitter than death the woman whose heart is snares and nets" (Qoh. 7:26)?

And he said to him, "Such as whom?"

He said to him, "Such as your mother."

She was easy to anger but easy to appease with a good word.

Said R. Samuel bar Onia in the name of Rab, "A woman is unformed, and she makes a covenant only with him who turns her into a utensil, as it is said, 'For your maker is your husband, the Lord of hosts is his name' (Isa. 54:5)."

It has been taught on Tannaite authority:

"A man dies only for his wife, and a woman dies only for her husband.

"A man dies only for his wife, as it is said, 'And Elimelech, Naomi's husband, died' (Ruth 1:3).

"And a woman dies only for her husband, as it is said, 'And as for me, when I came from Padan, Rachel died for me' (Gen. 48:7)."

BAVLI TO MISHNAH-TRACTATE SANHEDRIN 2:5/22A-B

Love for the Other, Seeking Peace

The following passages include some of the most memorable—and quoted—sections of Talmud. The sages' deep respect for the leadership of Aaron belies their respect for the peacemaker, someone who with intellect and grace bring two warring sides together.

Hillel and Shammai received [the Torah] from them. Hillel says: "Be disciples of Aaron, loving peace and pursuing peace, loving people and drawing them near to the Torah."

He would say [in Aramaic]: "A name made great is a name destroyed, and one who does not add subtracts.

"And who does not learn is liable to death. And the one who uses the crown, passes away."

He would say: "If I am not for myself, who is for me? And when I am for myself, what am I? and if not now, when?

"Loving peace: How so?"

This teaches that a person should love peace among Israelites as Aaron did,

as it is said, "The Torah of truth was in his mouth, and unrighteousness was not found in his lips; he walked with me in peace and uprightness and did turn away many from iniquity" (Mal. 2:6).

R. Meir says, "Why does the cited verse state, did turn away many from iniquity ?

"When Aaron would go along, he might meet a bad man or a wicked one. He greeted him. The next day the same man might want to commit a transgression. But he thought to himself, 'Woe is me, how can I raise my eyes afterward and look at Aaron? I should be ashamed on his account, for he has now greeted me.' That person would then keep himself from committing a transgression.

"So too, if there were two people quarreling with one another, Aaron went and took a seat near one of them and said to him, 'My son, see your friend—what is he saying? His heart is torn, he rips his garments, saying, "Woe is me, how can I raise my eyes afterward and see my friend? I should be ashamed on his account, for I am the one who [Goldin:] treated him foully."'

"He would sit with him until he had removed the envy from his heart.

"Then Aaron would go to his fellow and take a seat near him, and say to him, 'My son, see your friend—what is he saying? His heart is torn, he rips his garments, saying, "Woe is me, how can I raise my eyes afterward and see my friend? I should be ashamed on his account, for I am the one who [Goldin:] treated him foully."'

"He would sit with him until he had removed the envy from his heart.

"Then, when the two met, they hugged and kissed one another.

"Therefore it is said, 'And every member of the house of Israel wept for Aaron for thirty days' (Num. 20:20)."

Another comment on the same verse: Why did all the Israelites mourn for Aaron for thirty days [Goldin: while only the men wept for Moses]?

Because Moses gave a strict judgment in accord with the truth, while Aaron never said to someone, "You have committed an offense," or to a woman, "You have committed an offense."

That is why every member of the house of Israel wept for Aaron for thirty days .

But of Moses, who rebuked the people with harsh words, it is said, And the sons of Israel mourned for Moses (Deut. 34:8).

And how many thousands of Israelites are called Aaron, for were it not for Aaron['s principles], this one would not have come into the world.

. . . and pursuing peace: how so?

This teaches that a person should pursue peace in Israel between one person and the next, just as Aaron pursued peace in Israel between one person and the next.

So it is said, "Depart from evil and do good, seek peace and pursue it" (Ps. 34:15).

R. Simeon b. Eleazar says, "If someone stays in his own place and keeps silent, how is he going to pursue peace in Israel between one person and the next?

"But he has to go forth from his place and circle around the world and pursue peace in Israel."

"So it is said, '. . . seek peace and pursue it' (Ps. 34:15).

"How so? Seek it in your own locale pursue it in another locale."

So too the Holy One, blessed be he, made peace on high.

What is the peace that the Holy One, blessed be he, made on high?

That he did not call ten [angels] by the name of Gabriel, ten Michaels, ten Uriels, ten Raphaels, as people may use the name Reuben for ten different people, or Simeon, or Levi, or Judah.

For if he had done things the way mortals do, if he then called one of them, all of those bearing that name would come before him and express jealousy of one another.

So he called only one angel by the name of Gabriel, one Michael, and when he calls one of them, only that one comes and stands before him, and he sends him wherever he wishes.

How, then, do we know that they fear and honor one another and exhibit greater humility than do mortals?

When they open their mouths and recite a song, this one says to his fellow, "You start, for you are greater than I am," and that one says, "You start, for you are greater than I am."

This is not the way of mortals, for this one says to his fellow, "I am greater than you are," and that one says to his fellow, "I am greater than you are."

Some say that they form groups, and one group says to its fellow, "You start, for you are greater than I am."

For so it is said, "And this calls to that" (Isa. 6:3).

Loving people: how so?

This teaches that someone should show love to others and not hate them.

For so we find of the men of the Generation of the Dispersion [who built the tower of Babel] that, because they showed love to one another, the Holy One, blessed be he, did not want to destroy them from the world, but he merely scattered them in the four corners of the world.

But the men of Sodom, because they hated one another, did the Holy One, blessed be he, destroy from this world and from the world to come.

For it is said, 'And the men of Sodom were evil, sinning greatly against the world' (Gen. 13:13).

. . . evil against one another,

. . . sinful in fornication,

. . . against the Lord in the profanation of the divine name,

. . . greatly, that they sinned through malice.

Lo, you have learned that because they hated one another, the Holy One, blessed be he, destroyed them from this world and from the world to come.

THE FATHERS ACCORDING TO RABBI NATHAN XII:I-IV:1

Love of God vs. Fear of God

It has been taught on Tannaite authority:

R. Meir says, "The words, *feared God* are used with reference to Job, and the words *feared God* are used with reference to Abraham.

"Just as *God-fearing*, stated with respect to Abraham, means that he did so out of love, so *God-fearing* stated with reference to Job means that he feared God out of love."

And how do we know that Abraham himself did so out of love?

As it is written, "The seed of Abraham, who loved me" (Isa. 41:8).

What is the difference between one who acts out of love and one who acts out of fear?

The difference is in line with that which has been taught on Tannaite authority:

R. Simeon b. Eleazar says, "Greater is [the achievement of one] who acts out of love than of one who acts out of fear.

"For the [merit attained] through fear suspends [punishment] for a thousand generations, while [the merit attained out of] love suspends [punishment] for thousands of generations.

"Here it is written, 'Unto thousands of them that love me and keep my commandments' (Exod. 20:6), while elsewhere it is written, 'And keep his commandments to a thousand generations' (Deut. 7:9)."

But as to the latter, it also is written, "With those who love him and keep his commandments to a thousand generations!"

In the former, [the word *thousand*] is joined [to "those who love me,"] and in the latter, [the word *thousand*] is attached [to "keep his commandments"]. [So in the former the motive is love, in the latter fear of punishment.]

Two disciples were in session before Raba. One of them said to him, "In my dream, the following verse of Scripture was recited to me: 'O how great is your goodness, you have laid up for those who fear you' (Ps. 31:20)."

The other said to him, "In my dream, the following verse of Scripture was recited to me: 'But let all those who put their trust in you rejoice, let them shout for joy, because you defend them, let them also who love your name be joyful in you' (Ps. 6:12)."

He said to them, "Both of you are completely righteous masters. One [does the right thing] out of love, the other out of fear. [Both are correct.]"

BAVLI TO MISHNAH-TRACTATE SOTAH 5:3

Love Work, Hate Idleness and Sloth

Shemaiah and Abtalyon received [the Torah] from them. Shemaiah says: "Love work. Hate authority. Don't get friendly with the government."

Love work: how so?

This teaches that a person should love work and not hate work.

For just as the Torah has been given as a covenant, so work has been given as a covenant.

For so it is written, "Six days will you labor and do all your work, and the seventh day is a Sabbath to the Lord your God" (Exod. 20:10).

R Simeon b. Eleazar says, "Even the first Man tasted nothing before he had performed work.

"For it is said, 'And he put him into the Garden of Eden to tend it and to keep it; of every tree of the garden you may freely eat [having worked]' (Gen. 2:15–16)."

R. Tarfon says, "Also the Holy One, blessed be he, did not bring his Presence to rest on Israel before they had carried out work.

"For it is said, 'They shall make a sanctuary for me, then I shall dwell in their midst' (Exod. 25:5)."

R. Judah b. Batera says, "If someone has no work to do, what should he do? If he has a neglected courtyard or field, he should go and keep himself busy puttering in it.

"For it is said, 'Six days will you labor and do all your work.'

"Why does Scripture say, 'all your work'?

"It means to encompass one who has a neglected courtyard or field, indicating that he should go and keep himself busy puttering in it."

R. Yosé says, "A person dies only out of idleness.

"For it is said, 'And he expired and was gathered unto his people' (Gen. 49:33).

"Lo, if someone was smitten and fell at his furrow and died, lo, he will have died only out of idleness.

"If he was standing on his roof top or on the bank of the stream and fell and died, he will have died only out of idleness."

[These cases serve to prove the case] only for men, but how may we provide examples of the same fact for women?

As it is said, "Let neither man nor woman make any more work for the offering of the sanctuary" (Exod. 36:6).

And as to children? "And the people [inclusive of children] was restrained from bringing" (Exod. 36:6).

Said R. Nathan, "When Moses was engaged in the work of the tabernacle, he did not wish to take counsel with the heads of Israel, and the heads of Israel sat silently.

"They thought, 'Now Moses is going to need us.'

"When they heard the announcement in the camp, 'The stuff they had was sufficient' (Exod. 36:7), they thought, 'Woe is us, for we do not have a share in the work of the tabernacle.'

"They went and added a major donation on their own part, as it is said, 'And the rulers brought the onyx stones' (Exod. 35:27)."

THE FATHERS ACCORDING TO RABBI NATHAN XI:I.1

Lust

Human impulses are not always at war with God and man, but in this case, they are. The sages' view towards lust is so absolute, so clear, that the discussion does not close with a solution, but a restatement of the immutable problem.

Our rabbis have taught on Tannaite authority:

So formidable is the lust to do evil that even its creator has called it evil, as it is written, "For that the desire of man's heart is evil from his youth" (Gen. 8:21).

Said R. Isaac, "The desire to do evil renews itself daily against a person: 'Every imagination of the thoughts of his heart was only evil every day' (Gen. 6:5)."

And said R. Simeon b. Levi, "A man's inclination [to do evil] prevails over him every day and seeks to kill him. For it is said, 'The wicked watches the righteous and seeks to slay him' (Ps. 37:32). And if the Holy One, blessed be he, were not there to help him, he could not withstand it. For it is said, 'The Lord will not leave him in his hand nor suffer him to be condemned when he is judged' (Ps. 37:32)."

A Tannaite statement of the household of R. Ishmael: "If that vile one meets you, drag it to the house of study. If it is a stone, it will dissolve. If it is iron, it will be pulverized. If it is a stone, it will dissolve," as it is written, "Lo, everyone who is thirsty, come to water" (Isa. 55:1). And it is written, "The water wears down stones" (Job 14:19). "If it is iron, it will be pulverized," as it is written, "Is not my word like fire, says the Lord, and like a hammer that breaks the rock into pieces" (Jer. 23:29).

BAVLI TO MISHNAH-TRACTATE QIDDUSHIN 1:7

The impulse to do evil is thirteen years older than the impulse to do good.

From the mother's womb it grows and develops with a person.

If one began to profane the Sabbath, it does not stop him. If he wanted to kill, it does not stop him. If he goes to commit a transgression [of a sexual character], it does not stop him.

After thirteen years the impulse to do good is born. When the man then violates the Sabbath, it says to him, "Empty head, lo, Scripture says, 'Those who profane it will surely die' (Exod. 31:11)."

When the man then kills, it says to him, "Empty head, lo, Scripture says, 'One who sheds man's blood by man his blood will be shed' (Gen. 9:6)."

When he goes to commit a transgression, it says to him, "Empty head, lo, Scripture says, 'The adulterer and the adulteress will surely die' (Lev. 20:10)."

When a man arouses himself and goes to commit fornication, all of his limbs obey him, because the impulse to do evil is king over the two hundred and forty-eight limbs.

But when he goes to carry out a religious duty, all his limbs [Goldin:] begin to drag, because the impulse to do evil from the womb is king over the two hundred and forty-eight limbs that are in a man.'

The impulse to do good is only like one who is imprisoned, as it is said, 'For out of prison he came forth to be king' (Qoh. 4:14), referring to the impulse to do good.

Now there are those who say that this [verse] refers to Joseph, the righteous man.

When that wicked woman [Potiphar's wife] came, she disturbed him by her words, saying to him, "I shall lock you up in prison [if you do not go to bed with me]."

He said to her, "The Lord loosens prisoners" (Ps. 146:7).

She said to him, "I shall put out your eyes."

He said to her, "The Lord opens the eyes of the blind" (Ps. 146:8).

She said to him, "I shall force you to stoop."

He said to her, "The Lord raises up those who are bowed down" (Ps. 146:8).

She said to him, "I shall make you wicked."

He said to her, "The Lord loves the righteous" (Ps. 146:8).

She said to him, "I shall make you into an Aramaean."

He said to her, "The Lord preserves strangers" (Ps. 146:9).

Finally he said, "How shall I commit this great evil" (Gen. 39:9).

And do not take as surprising the case of Joseph, the righteous man, for lo, R. Sadoq was the greatest saint of his generation. When he was taken captive in Rome, a certain noble lady took him and sent a beautiful slave-girl to him [to mate with him and produce more slaves].

When he saw her, he turned toward the wall, so as not to lay eyes on her, and he went into session repeating [Mishnah-sayings] all night long.

In the morning the girl went and complained to her mistress, say-ing to her, "I'd rather die than have you give me back to that man."

She sent and called him, saying to him, "Why did not you do with that woman what man naturally do?"

He said to her, "What can I do, for I am of the high priesthood, and I am from an important family. I thought to myself, if I have sexual rela-tions with her, I shall increase the number of *mamzer*-children in Israel."

When she heard his statement, she gave orders concerning him and freed him with great dignity.

And do not take as surprising the case of R. Sadoq, for lo, R. Aqiba was still greater than he. When he went to Rome, he was [Goldin:] slandered before an authority. He sent to him two beautiful women, washed, anointed, and outfitted like br. :es, who threw themselves at him all night long.

This one said, "Turn toward me," and that one said, "Turn toward me."

He lay between them [Goldin:] in disgust and did not turn to them.

When morning came the women went and greeted the authority, saying to him, "We'd rather die than be given to that man."

He sent and called him, saying to him, "Why did not you do with those women what man naturally do with women? Are they not pretty? Are they not ordinary folk like you? Did not the same God who made you make them?"

He said to him, "What could I do? Their odor reached me, from the meat of carrion and *terefah* [unkosher] meat and swarming things that they have eaten."

And do not take as surprising the case of R. Aqiba, for lo, there is R. Eliezer the Elder, who is still greater than he, who raised the daugh-ter of his sister for thirteen years with him in the same bed, until the puberty signs appeared.

He said to her, "Go, marry a man."

She said to him, "Am I not your slave girl, a handmaiden there to wash the feet of your disciple[s]?"

He said to her, "My daughter, I am an old man. Go and marry a youngster like yourself."

She said to him, "Have I not said to you, 'Am I not your slave girl, a handmaiden there to wash the feet of your disciple[s]?'"

When he had heard what she said, he asked permission of her, be-trothed her, and had sexual relations with her [as his bride].

R. Reuben b. Astrobuli says, "How can someone escape from the evil impulse in his guts, for the very first drop [of semen] that a man puts into a woman is the evil impulse.

"And the impulse to do evil is located only at the gates of the heart. For it is said, 'Sin couches at the door' (Gen. 4:7).

"It says to a person while still an infant in the cradle, 'Someone wants to kill you,' [and] the infant wants to pull out his hair.

"When an infant in the cradle puts its hand on a snake or a scorpion and gets bitten, is it not the impulse to do evil that is the cause?

"[If the infant] puts its hand on coals and is burned, is it not the evil impulse in his guts that is the cause?

"For the evil impulse is what [Goldin:] drives him headlong.

"But come and see the case of a kid or a lamb: when it sees a well, it jumps backward, because there is no evil impulse in a beast.

R. Simeon b. Eleazar says, "I shall draw a comparison, to what is the impulse to do evil to be likened? To iron that one tossed into the fire.

"So long as it is in the fire, people can shape it any way they want.

"So is the impulse to do evil: its remedy lies only in teachings of the Torah, which are like fire,

"For it is said, 'If your enemy is hungry, give him bread to eat, and if he is thirsty, give him water to drink, for you will heap coals of fire upon his head, and the lord will reward you' (Prov. 25:21–22).

R. Judah the Patriarch says, "I shall give you a parable. To what is the impulse to do evil to be compared? To the case of two men who went to an inn. One of them was arrested as a bandit. They said to him, 'Who is with you?'

"He could have said, 'No one is with me.'

"But he says, 'If I am going to be put to death, let my fellow be put to death with me.'

So it is with the impulse to do evil: 'Since I am going to perish in the world to come, so I shall make the entire body perish with me.'"

THE FATHERS ACCORDING TO RABBI NATHAN XVI:III–V

Marital Courtesy

Although the following passage includes a fair amount of recommendations now deemed socially inappropriate, it rests on a premise worth

*considering: even the holiest must be a part of a family. There are no
monks in Judaism, and the sages remind themselves here exactly why.*

There is the story concerning R. Hananiah b. Hakhinai and R.
Simeon b. Yohai. They went to study Torah with R. Aqiba in Bene Beraq.
They remained there thirteen years. R. Simeon b. Yohai sent to find out
what was going on in his household. R. Haninah b. Hakhinai did not
send to find out what was going on in his household.

His wife sent word to him, saying, "Your daughter has reached
maturity. Come and marry her off." Even so, he did not go.

R. Aqiba perceived through the Holy Spirit and said to [his disciples],
"Whoever has a daughter who has reached maturity should go and
marry her off." [The disciple] understood, obeyed, arose, asked permission to leave, and went his way.

He wanted to go into his house but he found that it had been moved
to a different location. What did he do? He went and sat where women
fill their jugs with water. He heard the voice of little girls saying, "Daughter of Hakhinai, it's your turn to fill your jug and go along."

What did he do? He went after her until she went into his house.
He went in after her without warning. His wife had scarcely laid eyes
on him before her soul departed.

He said before him, "Lord of the world! This poor woman—is this
her reward after thirteen years [of waiting]." At that moment her soul
returned to her body.

Said R. Simeon b. Yohai, "There are four whom the Holy One,
blessed be he, hates, and I do not love them:

"him who holds onto his penis while he urinates; him who has sexual
relations naked; him who reports intimate things of his marriage to third
parties; and him who goes into his house without warning.

"And one need hardly add, into his fellow's house."

Rab said, "Do not enter a town without warning, and do not enter
a house without warning.

"If your daughter has reached maturity, free your slave and give her to him."

LEVITICUS RABBAH XXI:VIII

Match-making

A Roman lady asked R. Yosé b. Halputa, saying to him, "In how many
days did the Holy One, blessed be he, create his world?"

He said to her, "In six days, as it is written, 'For in six days the Lord made Heaven and earth'" (Exod. 31:17).

She said to him, "What's he been doing since then?"

He said to her, "He's been sitting and making matches, assigning Mr. So-and-so's daughter to Mr. Such-and-such, the wife of Mr. So-and-so [deceased] to Mr. Such-and-such, the estate of Mr. So-and-so to Mr. Such-and-such."

She said to him, "You know I have quite a number of slave boys and slave girls, and in a brief moment I can match them up too."

He said to her, "If it's such an easy thing to you, it's a very hard thing before the Omnipresent, [as difficult] as splitting the Red Sea, as it is written, 'God brings bachelors to dwell in a home [with a wife]'" (Ps. 68:7).

R. Yosé b. Halputa went along home. What did the lady do? She sent and called a thousand slave boys and a thousand slave girls and set them up in rows. She said to them, "X marry Y, and W marry Z." [In Aramaic:] In the morning they came to her. One had a broken head, another a blind eye, a third a broken hand, a fourth a broken foot, a fifth said, "I don't want this one," and a sixth said, "I don't want that man."

She sent a message to him, "Your Torah indeed is praiseworthy."

He replied to her, "Did I not tell you, if it is such an easy thing in your eyes, it is a very hard thing before the Omnipresent, [as difficult] as splitting the Red Sea, as it is written, 'God brings bachelors to dwell in a home [with a wife]';

"'he brings out prisoners into prosperity' [Ps. 68:7].

"What is the meaning of the word for prosperity? Weeping and singing. These are weeping, and those are singing.

"What does the Holy One, blessed be he? He brings them willy-nilly and matches them up."

R. Berekhiah told the story in the following version: "R. Yosé b. Halputa answered the woman through the Holy Spirit: 'He sits and makes ladders, bringing this one down and raising that one up, lowering this one and exalting that one, as it is written, "For God is judge. This one he humbles, and that one he lifts up"'" (Ps. 75:6).

LEVITICUS RABBAH VIII:I.2

Measure for Measure: The Method of Divine Justice

Is Divine justice simple? The sages clearly do not see it that way, even though it resonates with "eye for eye" methods. Their vision of God's punishment must be understood in terms of God's rewards.

By that same measure by which a man metes out [to others], do they mete out to him:

[The wife accused of adultery] primped herself for sin, the Omnipresent made her repulsive.

She exposed herself for sin, the Omnipresent exposed her.

With the thigh she began to sin, and afterward with the belly, therefore the thigh suffers the curse first, and afterward the belly.

But the rest of the body does not escape [punishment].

Samson followed his eyes [where they led him], therefore, the Philistines put out his eyes, since it is said, And the Philistines laid hold on him and put out his eyes (Judg. 16:21).

Absalom was proud of his hair, therefore, he was hung by his hair.

And since he had sexual relations with ten concubines of his father, therefore, they thrust ten spears into his body, since it is said, And ten young men that carried Joab's armor surrounded and smote Absalom and killed him (2 Sam. 18:15).

And since he stole three hearts—his father's, the court's, and the Israelites'—since it is said, "And Absalom stole the heart of the men of Israel." Therefore, three darts were thrust into him, since it is said, "And he took three darts in his hand and thrust them through the heart of Absalom" (2 Sam. 18:14).

And so is it on the good side:

Miriam waited a while for Moses, since it is said, "And his sister stood afar off" (Exod. 2:4), therefore, Israel waited on her seven days in the wilderness, since it is said, "And the people did not travel on until Miriam was brought in again" (Num. 12:15).

Joseph had the merit of burying his father, and none of his brothers was greater than he, since it is said, "And Joseph went up to bury his father . . . and there went up with him both chariots and horsemen" (Gen. 50:7,9).

We have none so great as Joseph, for only Moses took care of his [bones]. Moses had the merit of burying the bones of Joseph, and none in Israel was greater than he, since it is said, "And Moses took the bones of Joseph with him" (Exod. 13:19).

We have none so great as Moses, for only the Holy One, blessed be he, took care of his [bones], since it is said, "And he buried him in the valley" (Deut. 34:6).

And not of Moses alone have they stated [this rule], but of all righteous people, since it is said, "And your righteousness shall go before you. The glory of the Lord shall gather you [in death]" (Isa. 58:8).

MISHNAH-TRACTATE SOTAH 1:7-9

The generation of the Flood acted arrogantly before the Omnipresent only on account of the good which he lavished on them, since it is said, "Their houses are safe from fear, neither is the rod of God upon them" (Job 21:9). "Their bull genders and fails not, their cow calves and casts not her calf" (Job 21:10). "They send forth their little ones like a pock, and their children dance" (Job 21:11). "They spend their days in prosperity and their years in pleasures" (Job 36:11).

That is what caused them to say to God, "Depart from us,for we do not desire knowledge of thy ways. What is the Almighty, that we should serve Him, and what prosperity should we have, if we pray to him" (Job 21:14).

They said, "Do we need Him for anything except a few drops of rain? But look, we have rivers and wells which are more than enough for us in the sunny season and in the rainy season, since it is said, 'And a mist rose from the earth' (Gen. 2:6)."

The Omnipresent then said to them, "By the goodness which I lavished on them they take pride before me? By that same good I shall exact punishment from them!"

What does it say? "And I, behold, I bring a pool of water upon the earth" (Gen. 6: 17).

R. Yosé b. Durmasqit says, "The men of the Flood took pride only on account of [the covetousness of] the eyeball, which is like water, as it is said, "The sons of God saw that the daughter of men were fair, and they took them wives from all which they chose" (Gen. 6:2).

"Also the Omnipresent exacted punishment from them only through water, which is like the eyeball, as it is written, "All the fountains of the great deep were broken up, and the windows of Heaven were opened" (Gen. 7:11)." 3:10 A. The men of the Tower acted arrogantly before the Omnipresent only on account of the good which he lavished on them, since it is said, "Now the whole earth had one language and few words. And as men migrated from the east, they found a plain in the land of Shinar and settled there" (Gen. 11:1–2).

And settling refers only to eating and drinking, since it is said, "And the people settled down to eat and drink and rose up to play" (Exod. 32:6).

That is what caused them to say, "Come, let us build ourselves a city, and a tower with its top in the Heavens" (Gen. 11:4).

And what does Scripture say thereafter? "From there the Lord scattered them abroad over the face of the earth" (Gen. 11:8).

The men of Sodom acted arrogantly before the Omnipresent only on account of the good which he lavished on them, since it is said, "As for the land, out of it comes bread . . . . Its stones are the place of sapphires, and it has dust of gold . . . . That path, no bird of prey knows . . . . The proud beasts have not trodden it" (Job 28:5–8).

Said the men of Sodom, "Since bread comes forth from our land, and silver and gold come forth from our land, and precious stones and pearls come forth from our land, we do not need people to come to us.

"They come to us only to take things away from us. Let us go and forget how things are usually done among us."

The Omnipresent said to them, "Because of the goodness which I have lavished upon you, you deliberately forget how things are usually done among you. I shall make you be forgotten from the world."

What does it say? "They open shafts in a valley away from where men live. They are forgotten by travelers. They hang afar from men, they swing to and fro" (Job 28:4). "In the thought of one who is at ease there is contempt for misfortune, it is ready for those whose feet slip. The tents of robbers are at peace, and those who provoke God are secure, who bring their God in their hand" (Job 12:5–6).

And so it says, "As I live, says the Lord God, your sister Sodom and her daughters have not done as you and your daughters have done. Behold, this was the guilt of your sister Sodom: she and her daughters had pride, surfeit of food, and prosperous ease, but did not aid the poor and needy. They were haughty and did abominable things before me. Therefore I removed them when I saw it" (Ezek. 16:48–50).

The Egyptians took pride before the Omnipresent, blessed be he, only on account of water, as it is said, "Then Pharaoh commanded all his people, 'Every son that is born to the Hebrews you shall cast into the Nile'" (Exod. 1:22).

So the Omnipresent, blessed be he, exacted punishment from them only by water, as it is said, "Pharaoh's chariots and his host he cast into the sea." 3:14 A. Sisera took pride before the Omnipresent, blessed be He, only on account of [his volunteer] legions which do not receive a reward [for their service to him], since it is said, "The kings came, they fought; then fought the kings of Canaan" (Judg. 5:19).

So the Omnipresent, blessed be he, exacted punishment from them only by [volunteer] legions which do not receive a reward, as it is said, "From Heaven fought the stars, from their courses they fought against Sisera" (Judg. 5:20).

And in the end they did not pay him honor or take heed of him because [he ran away by foot] like an ordinary foot-soldier.

Samson rebelled by using his eyes, as it is said, "Then Samson said to his father, I saw one of the daughters of the Philistines at Timnah, now get her for me as my wife" (Judg. 14:3).

So he was smitten through his eyes, as it is said, "And the Philistines seized him and put out his eyes" (Judg. 16:21).

Rabbi says, "The beginning of his corruption took place in Gaza, so his punishment took place only in Gaza."

Absalom rebelled through his hair, as it is said, "Now in all Israel there was no one so much to be praised for his beauty as Absalom; from the sole of his foot to the crown of his head there was no blemish in him. And when he cut the hair of his head (for at the end of every year he used to cut it, when it was heavy on him, he cut it), he weighed the hair of his head, two hundred shekels by the king's weight" (2 Sam. 4:25-26).

Therefore he was smitten through his hair.

R. Judah the Patriarch says, "Absalom was a lifelong Nazir, and he cut his hair once in twelve months, as it is said And at the end of four years Absalom said to the king, 'Pray let me go and pay my vow, which I have vowed to the Lord, in Hebron. For your servant vowed a vow while I dwelt at Geshur in Aram, saying, If the Lord will indeed bring me back to Jerusalem, then I will offer worship to the Lord'" (2 Sam. 15:7-8).

R. Nehorai says, "He cut his hair once in thirty days, as it is said, For at the end of every year" (2 Sam. 14:26).

R. Yosé says, "He cut it every Friday, for so it is the custom of kings, to cut their hair every Friday, as it is said with regard to priests, 'They shall not shave their heads or let their locks grow long, they shall only trim the hair of their heads' (Ezek. 44:20)."

He weighed the hair of his head, two hundred shekels by the king's weight (2 Sam. 14:26)—which the men of Tiberias and the men of Sepphoris do not do [cutting their hair on Fridays].

Because he had sexual relations with ten concubines of his father, therefore they thrust ten spear-heads into his body, as it is said, And ten young men that carried Joab's armor surrounded and smote Absalom and killed him (2 Sam. 18:15).

And since he stole three hearts—the heart of his father, and the heart of the court, and the heart of all Israel—

therefore three darts were thrust into him, since it is said, And he took three darts in his hand and thrust them through the heart of Absalom (2 Sam. 18:14).

Sennacherib took pride before the Omnipresent only through an agent, as it is said, By your messengers you have mocked the Lord and you have said, "With my many chariots I have gone up the heights of the mountains. . . . I dug wells and drank foreign waters, and I dried up with the sole of my foot all the streams of Egypt" (2 Kings 19:23–24).

So the Omnipresent, blessed be he, exacted punishment from him only through an agent, as it is said, "And that night the messenger of the Lord went forth and slew a hundred and eighty-five thousand in the camp of the Assyrians" (2 Kings 19:35).

And all of them were kings, with their crowns bound to their heads. 3:19 A. Nebuchadnezzar said, "The denizens of this earth are not worthy for me to dwell among them. I shall make for myself a little cloud and dwell In it," as it is said, "I will ascend above the heights of the clouds, I will make myself like the Most High" (Isa. 14:14).

Said to him the Omnipresent, blessed be he, "You said in your heart, I will ascend to Heaven, above the stars of God I will set my throne on high—I shall bring you down to the depths of the pit (Isa. 14:13, 15).

What does it say? But you are brought down to Sheol, to the depths of the pit" (Isa. 14:15).

Were you the one who said, "The denizens of this earth are not worthy for me to dwell among them"?

The king said, "Is not this great Babylon, which I have built by my mighty power as a royal residence and for the glory of my majesty? While the words were still in the king's mouth, there fell a voice from Heaven, O King Nebuchadnezzar, to you it is spoken, The kingdom has departed from you, and you shall be driven from among men, and your dwelling shall be with the beasts of the field, and you shall be made to eat grass like an ox" (Dan. 4:29–32).

"All this came upon King Nebuchadnezzar at the end of twelve months" (Dan. 4:28–29).

I know only with regard to the measure of retribution that by that same measure by which a man metes out, they mete out to him. How do I know that the same is so with the measure of goodness?

Thus do you say:

The measure of goodness is five hundred times greater than the measure of retribution.

With regard to the measure of retribution it is written, Visiting the sin of the fathers on the sons and on the grandsons to the third and fourth generation (Exod. 20:5).

And with regard to the measure of goodness it is written, "And doing mercy for thousands" (Exod. 20:6).

You must therefore conclude that the measure of goodness is five hundred times greater than the measure of retribution.

And so you find in the case of Abraham that by that same measure by which a man metes out, they mete out to him.

He ran before the ministering angels three times, as it is said, "When he saw them, he ran to meet them" (Gen. 18:2), "And Abraham hastened to the tent" (Gen. 18:6), "And Abraham ran to the herd" (Gen. 18:7).

So did the Omnipresent, blessed be he, run before his children three times, as it is said, "The Lord came from Sinai, and dawned from Seir upon us; he shone forth from Mount Paran" (Deut. 33:2).

TOSEFTA SOTAH 3:6-17

The Messiah: When Will He Come?

Strictly speaking, speculation on who the Messiah is, when the Messiah will come, and what we have to do to bring the Messiah carries us beyond the realm of wisdom and into issues of doctrine concerning history and the end of time. But our sages make use of Messianic speculation to make a point profoundly shaped by their wisdom, which is that, Israel controls its own destiny, even to the very end of days, by reason of its attitudes, the virtues of its humility, and loyalty to the Torah. The basic message that wisdom delivers through the Messianic hope is: You may bring the end by your own attitudes and actions. The Messiah is present every day, and it is for holy Israel through loyalty to the Torah and humility before God to receive, to realize, his presence: All of the "ends" have passed, and the matter now depends only on repentance and good deeds.

Once a Jew was plowing and his ox snorted once before him. An Arab who was passing and heard the sound said to him, "Jew, Jew. Loosen your ox, and loosen your plow [and stop plowing]. For today your Temple was destroyed."

The ox snorted again. He [the Arab] said to him, "Jew, Jew. Bind your ox, and bind your plow. For today the Messiah-king was born."

He said to him, "What is his name?"

[The Arab replied,] "Menahem."

He said to him, "And what is his father's name?"

He [the Arab] said to him, "Hezekiah."

He said to him, "Where is he from?"

He said to him, "From the royal capital of Bethlehem in Judea."

He [the Jew] went and sold his ox and sold his plow. And he became a peddler of infants' clothes [diapers]. And he went from place to place until he came to that very city. All of the women bought from him. But Menahem's mother did not buy from him.

He heard the women saying, "Menahem's mother, Menahem's mother, come buy for your child."

She said, "I want to choke this enemy of Israel. For on the day he was born the Temple was destroyed."

He [this Jew] said to her, "We are sure that on this day it was destroyed, and on this day [of the year] it will be rebuilt. [Do not abandon the child. Provide for him.]"

She said to him [the peddler], "I have no money."

He said to her, "It is of no matter to me. Come and buy for him and if you have no money, pay me when I return."

After a while he returned. He went up to that place.

He said to her, "What happened to the infant?"

She said to him, "Since the time you saw him a spirit came and carried him up and took him away from me."

YERUSHALMI BERAKHOT 2:4

It has been taught on Tannaite authority:

R. Nehorai says, "In the generation in which the son of David will come, children will shame elders, and elders will stand up before children. 'The daughter rises up against the mother, and the daughter-in-law against her mother-in-law' (Mic. 7:6). The face of the generation is the face of a dog, and a son is not ashamed before his father."

It has been taught on Tannaite authority:

R. Nehemiah says, "In the generation in which the son of David will come, presumption increases, and dearth increases, and the vine gives its fruit and wine at great cost. The government turns to heresy, and there is no reproof."

Our rabbis have taught on Tannaite authority:

"For the Lord shall judge his people and repent himself of his servants, when he sees that their power has gone, and there is none shut up or left" (Deut. 32:36).

The son of David will come only when traitors are many.

Another matter: Only when disciples are few.

Another matter: Only when a penny will not be found in anyone's pocket.

Another matter: Only when people will have given up hope of redemption, as it is said, "There is none shut up or left" (Deut. 32:36), as it were, when there is none [God being absent] who supports and helps Israel.

That accords with the statement of R. Zira, who, when he would find rabbis involved in [figuring out when the Messiah would come], would say to them, 'By your leave, I ask you not to put it off.

"For we have learned on Tannaite authority: Three things come on the spur of the moment, and these are they: the Messiah, a lost object, and a scorpion."

A Tannaite authority of the house of Elijah [said], "For six thousand years the world will exist.

"For two thousand it will be desolate, two thousand years [will be the time of] Torah, and two thousand years will be the days of the Messiah, but on account of our numerous sins what has been lost [of those years, in which the Messiah should have come but has not come] has been lost.

R. Hanan, son of Tahalipa, sent to R. Joseph, "I came across a man who had in hand a scroll, written in Assyrian [block] letters in the holy language.

"I said to him, 'Where did you get this?'

"He said to me, 'I was employed in the Roman armies, and I found it in the Roman archives.'

"In the scroll it is written that after 4292 years from the creation of the world, the world will be an orphan.

"[As to the years to follow] in some there will be wars of the great dragons, and in some, wars of Gog and Magog, and the rest will be the days of the Messiah.

"And the Holy One, blessed be he, will renew his world only after seven thousand years."

R. Aha, son of Raba, said, "'After five thousand years' is what is said."

Said Rab, "All of the ends have passed, and the matter now depends only on repentance and good deeds."

And Samuel said, "It is sufficient for a mourner to remain firm in his mourning."

R. Eliezer says, "If the Israelites repent, they will be redeemed, as it is said, 'Return, backsliding children, and I will heal your backslidings' (Jer. 3:22)."

Said to him R. Joshua, "And is it not written, 'You have sold yourselves for nought, and you shall be redeemed without money' (Isa. 52:3)?

"'You have sold yourselves for nought'—for idolatry.

"'But you shall be redeemed without money'—with neither repentance nor do good deeds."

Said to him R. Eliezer, "But is it not written, 'Return to me and I shall return to you' (Mal. 3:7)?"

Said to him R. Joshua, "But is it not written, 'For I am master over you, and I will take you, one from a city and two from a family and I will bring you to Zion' (Jer. 3:14)?"

Said to him R. Eliezer, "But it is written, 'In returning and rest you shall be saved' (Isa. 30:5)."

Said R. Joshua to R. Eliezer, "But is it not written, 'Thus says the Lord, the redeemer of Israel, and his Holy One, to whom man despises, to him whom the nations abhor, to a servant of rulers, kings shall see and arise, princes also shall worship' (Isa. 49:7)?"

Said to him R. Eliezer, "But is it not written, 'If you will return, O Israel, says the Lord, return to me' (Jer. 4:1)?"

Said to him R. Joshua, "But it is written elsewhere, 'And I heard the man clothed in linen, which was upon the waters of the river, when he held up his right hand and his left hand to Heaven and swore by him who lives forever that it shall be for a year, two years, and half a year and when he shall have accomplished scattering the power of the holy people, all these things shall be finished' (Dan. 12:7)."

And R. Eliezer clammed up.

R. Joshua b. Levi found Elijah standing at the door of the burial vault of R. Simeon b. Yohai. He said to him, "Am I going to come to the world to come?"

He said to him, "If this master wants."

Said R. Joshua b. Levi, "Two did I see, but a third voice did I hear."

He said to him, "When is the Messiah coming?"

He said to him, "Go and ask him."

"And where is he sitting?"

"At the gate of the city."

"And what are the marks that indicate who he is?"

"He is sitting among the poor who suffer illness, and all of them untie and tie their bandages all together, but he unties them and ties them one by one. He is thinking, 'Perhaps I may be wanted, and I do not want to be held up.'"

He went to him, saying to him, "Peace be unto you, my master and teacher."

He said to him, "Peace be unto you, son of Levi."

He said to him, "When is the master coming?"

He said to him, "Today."

He went back to Elijah, who said to him, "What did he tell you?"

He said to him, "'Peace be unto you, son of Levi.'"

He said to him, "He [thereby] promised you and your father the world to come."

He said to him, "But he lied to me. For he said to me, 'I am coming today,' but he did not come."

He said to him, "This is what he said to you, '"Today, if you will obey his voice" (Ps. 95:7).'"

His disciples asked R. Yosé b. Qisma, "When is the son of David coming?"

He said to them, "I am afraid [to answer], lest you ask an omen from me [that my answer is right]."

They said to him, "We shall not ask for an omen from you." He said to them, "When this gate falls and is rebuilt, falls and is rebuilt, and falls a third time. They will not suffice to rebuild it before the son of David will come."

They said to him, "Our master, give us an omen."

He said to them, "But did you not say to me that you would not ask for an omen from me?"

They said to him, "Even so."

He said to them, "Then let the waters of the grotto of Banias turn to blood," and they turned to blood.

When he died, he said to them, "Dig my bier deep into the ground, for there is not a palm tree in Babylonia on which a Persian horse has not been tied, nor is there a bier in the land of Israel from which a Median horse will not eat straw."

Said Ulla, "Let him come, but may I not see him."

Said Rabba, "Let him come, but may I not see him."

R. Joseph said, "May he come, and may I have the merit of sitting in the shade of the dung of his ass."

Said Abbayye to Rabbah, "What is the reason [that some do not wish to see the coming of the Messiah]? Is it because of the turmoil of the Messiah?

"And has it not been taught on Tannaite authority:

"His disciples asked R. Eliezer, 'What should someone do to save himself from the turmoil of the Messiah?'

"[He replied to them], 'Let him engage in study of the Torah and acts of loving kindness.'

"And lo, the master [at hand] practices Torah study and acts of loving kindness. [So why not want to see him?]"

He said to him, "Perhaps he fears sin will cause [him to suffer], in line with what R. Jacob bar Idi said."

For R. Jacob bar Idi contrasted two verses of Scripture, as follows: "It is written, 'And behold, I am with you and will keep you wherever you go' (Gen. 28:15), and another verse states, 'Then Jacob was greatly afraid' (Gen. 32:8).

"[Why the contrast between God's promise and Jacob's fear?] Jacob feared [and thought to himself,] 'Sin which I have done may cause [punishment for me instead].'"

That accords with what has been taught on Tannaite authority:

"'Till your people pass over, O Lord, till your people pass over, that you have acquired" (Exod. 15:16).

"'Till your people pass over" refers to the first entry into the land [in Joshua's time].

"'Till your people pass over, that you have acquired" refers to the second entry into the land [in the time of Ezra and Nehemiah. Thus a miracle was promised not only on the first occasion, but also on the second. But it did not happen the second time around. Why not?]

On the basis of this statement, sages have said, "The Israelites were worthy of having a miracle performed for them in the time of Ezra also, just as it had been performed for them in the time of Joshua b. Nun, but sin caused the miracle to be withheld."

So said R. Yohanan, "Let him come, but let me not see him."

Said R. Simeon b. Laqish to him, "What is the scriptural basis for that view? Shall we say that it is because it is written, 'As if a man fled from a lion and a bear met him, or went into the house and leaned his hand on the wall and a serpent bit him' (Amos 5:19)?

"Come and I shall show you an example of such a case in this world.

"When a man goes out to the field and bailiff meets him, it is like one whom a lion meets. He goes into town and a tax-collector meets him, it is like one whom a bear meets.

"He goes into his house and finds his sons and daughters suffering from hunger, it is like one whom a snake bit.

"Rather, it is because it is written, 'Ask you now and see whether a man travails with child? Why do I see every man with his hands on his loins, as women in travail, and all faces are turned into paleness' (Jer. 30:6)."

What is the sense of, "Why do I see every man . . ."?

Said Raba bar Isaac said Rab, "It speaks of him to whom all [manly] power belongs [God]."

And what is the sense of "all faces are turned into paleness"?

Said R. Yohanan, "[It speaks of God's] Heavenly family and his earthly family, at the moment at which God says, 'These are the creation of my hands, and those are the creation of my hands. How shall I destroy these [Gentiles] on account of [what they have done to] those [Israelites]? [to avenge the wrongs suffered by the Jews. Because the suffering would be so great that even the Almighty would lament it, Yohanan desired to be spared the Messiah's coming.]"

BAVLI TO MISHNAH-TRACTATE SANHEDRIN 11:1/B. 97A–103A

Miracles Done by God

The height of folly is to place reliance upon miracles; the depth of wisdom is to know that miracles take place. Our sages hold these two principles together, recognizing that the world is full of miracles, but we have to know exactly what they are.

On account of every sort of public trouble (may it not happen) do they sound the shofar, except for an excess of rain.

They said to Honi, the circle drawer, "Pray for rain."

He said to them, "Go and take in the clay ovens used for Passover, so that they not soften [in the rain which is coming]."

He prayed, but it did not rain.

What did he do?

He drew a circle and stood in the middle of it and said before him, "Lord of the world! Your children have turned to me, for before you I am like a member of the family. I swear by your great name—I'm simply not moving from here until you take pity on your children!"

It began to rain drop by drop.

He said, "This is not what I wanted, but rain for filling up cisterns, pits, and caverns."

It began to rain violently.

He said, "This is not what I wanted, but rain of good will, blessing, and graciousness."

Now it rained the right way, until Israelites had to flee from Jerusalem up to the Temple Mount because of the rain.

Now they came and said to him, "Just as you prayed for it to rain, now pray for it to go away."

He said to them, "Go, see whether the stone of the strayers is disappeared."

Simeon b. Shatah said to him, "If you were not Honi, I should decree a ban of excommunication against you. But what am I going to do to you?

"For you importune before the Omnipresent, so he does what you want, like a son who importunes his father, so he does what he wants.

"Concerning you Scripture says, 'Let your father and your mother be glad, and let her that bore you rejoice' (Prov. 23:25)."

MISHNAH-TRACTATE TAANIT 3:8

Miracles Done by Idols

The sages do not seem overly troubled by the apparent success of idolatry—ultimately, they chalk it up to fluke.

Zeno asked R. Aqiba, "In my heart and in your heart we both know that there is no substance whatsoever in idolatry. But lo, we see people go into a shrine crippled and come out cured. How come?"

He said to him, "I shall give you a parable. To what is the matter to be compared? To a reliable person who was in a town, and all the townsfolk would deposit their money into his care without witnesses. One man came and left a deposit in his charge with witnesses, but once he forgot and left his deposit without witnesses. The wife of the reliable man said to him, 'Come, let us deny it.' He said to her, 'Because this idiot acted improperly, shall we destroy our good name for reliability?' So it is with troubles. When they send them upon a person, they are made to take the oath, 'You shall come upon him only on such-and-such a day, and you shall depart from him only on such-and-such a day, and at such-and-such an hour, through the medium of so-and-so, with such-and-such a remedy.' When it is time for them to take their leave, it just happened that the man went to a temple of an idol. So the afflictions plea, 'It is right and proper that we not leave him and go our way, but because this fool acts as he does, are we going to break our oath?'"

That is in line with what R. Yohanan said, "What is the meaning of the verse of Scripture: 'And sore and faithful sicknesses' (Deut. 28:59)—'sore' in their mission, 'faithful' to their oath."

Raba b. R. Isaac said to R. Judah, "There is a temple to an idol in our locale. When there is need for rain, the idol appears in a dream and says to them, 'Kill someone for me and I shall bring rain.' So they kill someone for her, and she brings rain."

He said to him, "If I were dead, no one could tell you this statement which Rab said, 'What is the meaning of the verse of Scripture, ". . . which the Lord your God has divided to all the peoples under the whole Heaven" (Deut. 4:19)?' [Since the letters of the word 'divided' may be read as 'smooth,' the verse means this:] this teaches that he made them smooth talkers, so as to banish them from the world."

That is in line with what R. Simeon b. Laqish said, "What is the meaning of the verse of Scripture, 'Surely he scorns the scorners, but he gives grace to the lowly' (Prov. 3:34)? If someone comes along to make himself unclean, they open the gate for him. If he comes along to purify himself, they also help him do so."

BAVLI TO MISHNAH-TRACTATE ABODAH ZARAH 4:7

Mourning in Excess

Said R. Ishmael, "From the day on which the Temple was destroyed, it would have been reasonable not to eat meat and not to drink wine.

"But a court does not make a decree for the community concerning things which the community simply cannot bear."

He did say, "Since they are uprooting the Torah from our midst, let us make a decree against the world, that it be left desolate—

"that no one should marry a wife and produce children, or have the week of celebration for a son,

"until the seed of Abraham will die out on its own."

They said to him, "It is better for the community to behave in error and not do so deliberately."

After the last Temple was destroyed, abstainers became many in Israel, who would not eat meat or drink wine.

R. Joshua engaged them in discourse, saying to them, "My children, on what account do you not eat meat?"

They said to him, "Shall we eat meat, for every day a continual burnt-offering [of meat] was offered on the altar, and now it is no more?"

He said to them, "Then let us not eat it. And then why are you not drinking wine?"

They said to him, "Shall we drink wine, for every day wine was poured out as a drink-offering on the altar, and now it is no more."

He said to them, "Then let us not drink it."

He said to them, "But if so, we also should not eat bread, for from it they bring the Two Loaves and the Show-Bread.

"We also should not drink water, for they did pour out a water-offering on the Festival.

"We also should not eat figs and grapes, for they would bring them as First Fruits on the Festival of Aseret [Pentecost]."

They fell silent.

He said to them, "My children, to mourn too much is not possible.

"But thus have the sages said: A man puts on plaster on his house but he leaves open a small area, as a memorial to Jerusalem.

"A man prepares what is needed for a meal but leaves out some small things, as a memorial to Jerusalem.

"A woman prepares her ornaments, but leaves out some small thing, as a memorial to Jerusalem,

"since it is said, 'If I forget you, O Jerusalem, let my right hand wither! Let my tongue cleave to the roof of my mouth, if I do not remember you, if I do not set Jerusalem above my highest joy!' (Ps. 137:5–6)."

And whoever mourns for her in this world will rejoice with her in the world to come,

as it is said, "Rejoice with Jerusalem and be glad for her, all you who love her; rejoice with her in joy, all you who mourn over her" (Isa. 66:10).

TOSEFTA SOTAH 15:10-14

Not Bearing Grudges

When we bear grudges, we end up poisoned by our own venom. Nor does the pseudo-wisdom of politics—don't get mad, get even—show the way. Hatred exacts costs from the one who hates, wastes life, destroys hope. But that does not mean we cannot rebuke, correct, take the risks of expressing what we think. These define our duty: not to bear a grudge within, but to express one's views to whom they ought to concern.

"You shall not hate your brother in your heart, [but reasoning, you shall reason with your neighbor, lest you bear sin because of him. You shall not take vengeance or bear any grudge against the sons of your own people, but you shall love your neighbor as yourself: I am the Lord]" (Lev. 19:17–18).

Might one suppose that one should not curse him, set him straight, or contradict him?

Scripture says, "in your heart."

I spoke only concerning hatred that is in the heart.

And how do we know that if one has rebuked him four or five times, he should still go and rebuke him again?

Scripture says, "Reasoning, you shall reason with your neighbor."

Might one suppose that that is the case even if one rebukes him and his countenance blanches?

Scripture says, "Lest you bear sin."

Said R. Tarfon, "By the Temple service! I doubt that in this generation there is anyone who knows how to give a rebuke!"

Said to R. Eleazar b. Azariah, "By the Temple service! I doubt that in this generation there is anyone who knows how to receive a rebuke."

Said R. Aqiba, "By the Temple service! I doubt that in this generation there is anyone who knows just how a rebuke is set forth!"

Said R. Yohanan b. Nuri, "I call to testify against me Heaven and earth, if it is not so that four or five times Aqiba was given a flogging on my account on the authority of Rabban Gamaliel.

"The reason is that I complained to him about him.

"And through it all I knew that he loved me all the more on that account."

"You shall not take vengeance [or bear any grudge]":
To what extent is the force of vengeance?
If one says to him, "Lend me your sickle," and the other did not do so.
On the next day, the other says to him, "Lend me your spade."
The one then replies, "I am not going to lend it to you, because you didn't lend me your sickle."
In that context, it is said, "You shall not take vengeance."
". . . or bear any grudge":
To what extent is the force of a grudge?
If one says to him, "Lend me your spade," but he did not do so.
The next day the other one says to him, "Lend me your sickle," and the other replies, "I am not like you, for you didn't lend me your spade [but here, take the sickle]!"
In that context, it is said, "or bear any grudge."

"You shall not take vengeance or bear any grudge against the sons of your own people":
"You may take vengeance and bear a grudge against others."
". . . but you shall love your neighbor as yourself: [I am the Lord]":
R. Aqiba says, "This is the encompassing principle of the Torah."
Ben Azzai says, "'This is the book of the generations of Adam' (Gen. 5:1) is a still more encompassing principle."

SIFRA CC:III

Not Taking Oaths

Oath-taking marks us as temperamental; it is to use language to coerce the other, to express power where we have none. Our sages regard oath-taking as disreputable, but oath-breaking as still worse.

Said R. Simon, "Why do they impose an oath on a person through a Torah scroll and bring before him blown up hides? It is to indicate: Yesterday this skin was full of sinews and bones, but now it is empty of them all. So a person who takes a false oath to his fellow will end up emptied of all his money."
R. Assi said, "[That applies when a person takes an oath] falsely."
R. Jonah said, "[That applies] even if he takes the oath in truth."
R. Yannai was in session and teaching the matter in accord with the view of R. Jonah [that one should not take an oath even if it is a true oath.]

A story: There was a woman who came to knead dough with her neighbor. She had three *denars* wrapped up in her kerchief. She took them out and put them before her. When she was sitting and arranging [the dough], the coins got mixed up in the loaf. She went looking for the money and did not find it. She said to her neighbor, "Did you find my three *denars*?"

The neighbor had three sons, and she said to her, "May my son be buried if I found them." And she buried him.

Later on [the woman who lost the coins again] asked her neighbor, "Did you find the three *denars*?"

She said to her, "May I bury my second son, if I found them." And she did indeed bury him.

Yet a third time she said to her, "Did you find my three *denars*?"

She said to her, "May I bury my third son, if I found them." She buried him.

[The woman who had lost the money] said, "Should I not go and offer condolences to my neighbor?" She took a loaf of bread [with her, for the meal of consolation] and sat down. When she broke the bread, the three *denars* fell out!

This is in line with what people say: "Whether innocent or guilty, don't get involved with oaths."

LEVITICUS RABBAH VI:III

Occupations and Vocations

Here is wisdom for the young, people who at whatever age retain the power to make decisions about their future. Sages do not want us to settle for a living. They want us to seek an occupation that we may treat as a vocation, a calling, not so much work as labor that fulfils and completes our very being. But, some of them would add, no calling is degraded, but that our own attitude diminishes it, and all labor is honorable, if it is honest and sincere. Just as, they hold, better a sincere sin then hypocritical virtue, so they will insist that all work done with self-respect brings esteem; no work is beneath dignity—if we know the meaning of human dignity.

R. Meir says, "A man should always teach his son a clean and easy trade. And let him pray and ask for mercy from him to whom belong riches and possessions.

"For there is no trade that does not involve poverty or wealth.

"For poverty does not come from one's trade, nor does wealth come from one's trade.

["But all is in accord with a man's merit."]

R. Simeon b. Eleazar says, "Have you ever seen a wild beast or a bird that has a trade? Yet they get along without difficulty. and were they not created only to serve me? And I was created to serve my Master. So is it not logical that I should get along without difficulty? But I have done evil and ruined my livelihood. "

Abba Gurion of Saidon says in the name of Abba Saul, "A man should not teach his son to be an ass-driver, a camel-driver, a barber, a sailor, [a potter,] a herdsman, or a shopkeeper. For their trade is the trade of thieves."

R. Judah says in his name, "Most ass-drivers are evil, most camel-drivers are decent, most sailors are saintly, the best among physicians is going to Gehenna, and the best of butchers is a partner of Amalek."

MISHNAH-TRACTATE QIDDUSHIN 4:11P-V

R. Meir says, "A man should always teach his son a clean and easy trade.

"What should he do? Let him try to teach his son a simple trade, and let him pray and ask for mercy from him to whom belongs riches and possessions. For there is no trade that does not involve poverty or wealth. But all is in accord with a man 's merit."

[R. Simeon b. Eleazar says, "Have you ever seen a wild beast or a bird that has a trade? Yet they get along without difficulty, and were they not created only to serve me? And I was created to serve my Master. So is it not logical that I should get along without difficulty? But I have done evil and ruined my livelihood":]

R. Simeon b. Eleazar in the name of R. Meir: "In your whole life, did you ever see a lion working as a porter, a deer working as a fruit-picker, a fox working as a storekeeper, a wolf selling pots, a domestic beast or a wild beast or a bird that had a trade?

"Now these are created only to work for me, and I was made only to work for my Master.

"Now is there not an argument *a fortiori*: Now if these who were created only to work for me lo they get along without difficulty, I, who have been created to work for my Master—is it not reasonable that I too should make a living without anguish!

"But I have done evil and ruined my livelihood."

TOSEFTA QIDDUSHIN 5:15

R. Nehorai says, "I should lay aside every trade in the world and teach my son only Torah.

"For a man eats its fruits in this world, and the principal remains for the world to come.

"But other trades are not that way.

"When a man gets sick or old or has pains and cannot do his job, lo, he dies of starvation.

"But with Torah it is not that way.

"But it keeps him from all evil when he is young, and it gives him a future and a hope when he is old.

"Concerning his youth, what he does it say? 'They who wait upon the Lord shall renew their strength ' (Isa. 40: 31). And concerning his old age, what does it say? 'They shall still bring forth fruit in old age' (Ps. 92:14).

"And so it says with regard to the patriarch Abraham, may he rest in peace, 'And Abraham was old and well along in years, and the Lord blessed Abraham in all things' (Gen. 24:1).

"We find that the patriarch Abraham kept the entire Torah even before it was revealed, since it says, 'Since Abraham obeyed my voice and kept my charge, my commandments, my statutes, and my laws'" (Gen. 26:5).

MISHNAH-TRACTATE QIDDUSHIN 4:12

R. Nehorai says, "I should lay aside every trade in the world and teach my son only Torah.

"For they eat the fruit of labor in Torah in this world, but the principal remains for the world to come.

"For every sort of trade there is in the world serves a man only when he is young, when he yet has his strength

"But when he falls ill or grows old or has pains, and does not work any more, in the end does he die of starvation.

"But Torah is not so. But it honors him and keeps a man from all evil when he is young and gives him a future and a hope when he is old. When he is young, what does it say? 'They who wait upon the Lord shall renew their strength' (Isa. 40: 31). And concerning his old age, what does it say? 'They shall still bring forth fruit in old age' (Ps. 92 :14)

TOSEFTA QIDDUSHIN 5:16

Old Age

Sages portray old age in a series of evocative metaphors. They recognize its infirmities. That makes all the more striking their high appreciation for the virtues of age.

"In the day when the keeper of the house shall tremble, and the strong men shall bow themselves" (Qoh. 12:2)—

"In the day when the keeper of the house shall tremble": This refers to the sides and the ribs.

"And the strong men shall bow themselves": This refers to the legs.

"And the grinders cease"—the teeth;

"And those that look out of the windows darkened"—the eyes.

Said Caesar to R. Joshua b. Hananiah, "How come you didn't come to the celebration?"

"The mountain is snow, surrounded by ice, the dog doesn't bark, the grinders don't grind."

The household of Rab said, "What I didn't lose I'm looking for."

It has been taught on Tannaite authority: R. Yosé bar Qisma says, "Better are two than three, woe is for the one thing that goes and doesn't come back."

So what's that?

Said R. Hisda, "It's youth."

When R. Dimi came, he said, "Youth is a crown of roses, age, a crown of willow-rods."

It has been taught on Tannaite authority in the name of R. Meir, "Chew well with your teeth and you will find it in your steps: 'For then we had plenty of food and were well and saw no evil' (Jer. 44:17)."

Said Samuel to R. Judah, "Sharp wit! Open your mouth and let your food come in. Until age forty food is better, then, drink is better."

Said Rabbi to R. Simeon b. Halafta, "How come we didn't receive you on the festival in the way in which my ancestors would receive yours?"

He said to him, "You know, the rocks have gotten tall, what is near has gotten distant, two have become three, and the peacemaker of the household [sexual relations] has ceased."

"And the doors shall be shut in the streets" (Qoh. 12:4)—this refers to the holes of a man.

"And the sound of the grinding is low"—because the stomach doesn't digest things.

"And one gets up at the sound of a bird"—even a bird will wake him from sleep.

"And all the daughters of the music shall be brought low"—even the voices of male and female singers sound like a whisper.

And so said Barzillai the Gileadite say to David, "I am today four score years old, can I discern between good and bad?" (2 Sam. 19:35)—this shows that opinions of old men change.

"Can your servant taste what I eat or drink"—this shows that the lips of the old grow slack.

"Can I hear any more the voice of men and women singers?"—this shows that the ears of the old are heavy.

Said Rab, "Barzillai the Gileadite was a liar, for there was a servant in Rab's house who was ninety-two years old, and he could taste food."

Raba said, "Barzillai the Gileadite was lewd, and whoever is lewd—old age catches up with him."

It has been taught on Tannaite authority:

R. Ishmael b. R. Yosé says, "Disciples of sages, as they grow old, get more wisdom: 'With aged men is wisdom and in length of days understanding' (Job 12:12). But when the ignorant get older, they get stupider: 'He removes the speech of the reliable and takes away the understanding of elders' (Job 12:20)."

"Yes, they shall be afraid of that which is high" (Qoh. 12:5)—even a little hill looks like a high mountain.

"And terrors shall be in the way"—when he walks on the road, his heart is filled with fear.

"And the almond tree shall blossom"—that is the coccyx [Freedman: the lowest end of the vertebrae protrudes in old age].

"And the grasshopper shall be a burden"—the rump.
"And desire shall fail"—the passions.

And said R. Isaac, "What is the meaning of the verse, 'For youth and the prime of life are vanity' (Qoh. 11:10)? What a man does in his youth blackens his face in old age."

BAVLI TO MISHNAH-TRACTATE SHABBAT 23:5

Old Age, Suffering, and Sickness

The main point here is original and striking: old age, suffering, and sickness—these are gifts from God, prayed for by the founders of the world, Abraham, Isaac, and Jacob. What is natural to the human condition we must not only accept but affirm. What is part of life forms a gift that comes to us with life.

"When Isaac was old, and his eyes were dim, so that he could not see, he called Esau his older son, and said to him, 'My son,' and he answered, 'Here I am'" (Gen. 27:1):

Said R. Judah bar Simon, "Abraham sought [the physical traits of] old age [so that from one's appearance, people would know that he was old]. He said before him, 'Lord of all ages, when a man and his son come in somewhere, no one knows whom to honor. If you crown a man with the traits of old age, people will know whom to honor.'

"Said to him the Holy One, blessed be he, 'By your life, this is a good thing that you have asked for, and it will begin with you.'

"From the beginning of the book of Genesis to this passage, there is no reference to old age. But when Abraham our father came along, the traits of old age were given to him, as it is said, 'And Abraham was old' (Gen. 24:1).

"Isaac asked God for suffering. He said before him, 'Lord of the age, if someone dies without suffering, the measure of strict justice is stretched out against him. But if you bring suffering on him, the measure of strict justice will not be stretched out against him. [Suffering will help counter the man's sins, and the measure of strict justice will be mitigated through suffering by the measure of mercy.]'

"Said to him the Holy One, blessed be he, 'By your life, this is a good thing that you have asked for, and it will begin with you.'

"From the beginning of the book of Genesis to this passage, there is no reference to suffering. But when Isaac came along, suffering was given to him: his eyes were dim.

"Jacob asked for sickness. He said before him, 'Lord of all ages, if a person dies without illness, he will not settle his affairs for his children. If he is sick for two or three days, he will settle his affairs with his children.'

"Said to him the Holy One, blessed be he, 'By your life, this is a good thing that you have asked for, and it will begin with you.'

"That is in line with this verse: 'And someone said to Joseph, "Behold, your father is sick"' (Gen. 48:1)."

Said R. Levi, "Abraham introduced the innovation of old age, Isaac introduced the innovation of suffering, Jacob introduced the innovation of sickness.

"Hezekiah introduced the innovation of chronic illness. He said to him, 'You have kept a man in good condition until the day he dies. But if someone is sick and gets better, is sick and gets better, he will carry out a complete and sincere act of repentance for his sins.'

"Said to him the Holy One, blessed be he, 'By your life, this is a good thing that you have asked for, and it will begin with you.'

"'The writing of Hezekiah, king of Judah, when he had been sick and recovered of his sickness' (Isa. 38:9)."

Said R. Samuel b. Nahman, "On the basis of that verse we know that between one illness and another there was an illness more serious than either one."

GENESIS RABBAH LXV:IX

Omens

We start here with omens, but end with behavior.

Our rabbis have taught on Tannaite authority:

When the lights are in eclipse, it is a bad omen for the whole world.

It is to be compared to a mortal king who built a palace and finished it and arranged a banquet, and then brought in the guests. He got mad at them and said to the servant, "Take away the light from them," so all of them turned out to be sitting in the dark.

It has been taught on Tannaite authority: R. Meir did say, "When the lights of Heaven are in eclipse, it is a bad omen for Israel, for they are used to blows.

"It is to be compared to a teacher who came into the school house and said, 'Bring me the strap.' Now who gets worried? The one who is used to being strapped"

Our rabbis have taught on Tannaite authority:

When the sun is in eclipse, it is a bad omen for the nations of the world.

[When] the moon is in eclipse, it is a bad omen for Israel, since the Gentiles reckon their calendar by the sun, and Israel by the moon.

When it is in eclipse in the East, it is a bad omen for those who live in the East.

When it is in eclipse in the West, it is a bad omen for those who live in the West.

When it is in eclipse in-between, it is a bad omen for the whole world.

When it turns red, it is a sign that punishment by the sword is coming into the world.

When it is like sack-cloth, it is a sign that punishment by pestilence and famine are coming into the world.

If they are smitten at its entry [into sunset], the punishment will tarry. [When they are smitten] when they rise, the punishment is coming fast.

And some say matters are reversed.

You have no nation in the whole world which is smitten, the god of which is not smitten right along with it,

as it is said, 'And against all the gods of Egypt I will execute judgments' (Exod. 12:12).

When Israel do the will of the Omnipresent, they do not have to worry about all these omens,

as it is said, 'Thus says the Lord, Do not learn the way of the Gentiles, nor be dismayed at the signs of the Heavens, for the nations are dismayed at them' (Jer. 10:2)

So idolators will be dismayed, but Israelites should not be dismayed.

Our rabbis have taught on Tannaite authority:

For four reasons is the sun eclipsed:

Because a head of a court has died and has not been properly mourned,

because a betrothed girl has cried out in a town and none goes to her assistance,

because of pederasty,

and because of two brothers whose blood is spilled simultaneously.

[In Tosefta's version] And because of four reasons are the lights of Heaven eclipsed:

because of counterfeiters, perjurers, people who raise small cattle in the land of Israel and people who cut down good trees.

And because of four sorts of bad deeds in the property of Israelite householders handed over to the government:

because of holding on to writs of indebtedness which have already been paid,

because of lending on interest,

because of pledging funds to charity but not paying up, and

because of having the power to protest and not protesting [wrong-doing]

Said Rab, "For four reasons is the property of householders confiscated for taxes:

"because of those who hold back the wages of a hired hand,

"because of those who oppress a hired hand,

"because of those who remove the yoke from their shoulders and put it on their fellow,

"and because of arrogance.

"But arrogance outweighs all the others.

"And with reference to humble people, it is written, 'But the humble shall inherit the earth and delight themselves in the abundance of peace' (Ps. 37:11)."

BAVLI TO MISHNAH-TRACTATE SUKKAH 2:5/29A-B

Peace

For our sages, as for wisdom everywhere, the highest virtue is peace, in the home and in the streets, among neighbors and nations alike. "Peace" rings like a platitude, except in war and strife; then it takes on all that weight and specificity that the following sayings recognize.

Said R. Simeon b. Yohai, "The greatness of peace is shown in that all other blessings are included in it: 'The Lord will give strength to his people, the Lord will bless his people with peace'" (Ps. 29:11).

Hezekiah said two things.

Hezekiah said, "The greatness of peace is shown in the matter of

how Scripture phrases religious duties. In the case of all other commandments, Scripture states [the conditional], 'If you see' (Exod. 23:5), 'If
you meet' (Exod. 23:4), 'If it should happen' (Deut. 22:6). Accordingly,
if the opportunity to carry out a religious duty should come your way,
you are supposed to do it, but if not, you are not expected to do it.

"But in this case: 'Seek peace and pursue it [unconditionally]' [Ps.
34:15]. [Not only do you] seek peace for your own locale, [but you must]
pursue it in another."

Hezekiah made a second statement.

Hezekiah said, "The greatness of peace is shown in yet another way.
In regard to all the journeyings [of the Israelites] it is written, 'They traveled . . . and they made camp' (Num. 33:6ff.). *They* traveled in contention, and *they* made camp in contention.

"When they came before Mount Sinai, all of them became a single
camp. [How so?] 'The children of Israel made camps' is not written [in the
plural], but rather, 'And Israel made a camp [in the singular]' (Exod. 19:2).
"Said the Holy One, blessed be he, '*Now* has come the time for me to
give the Torah to my children.'"

Bar Qappara made three statements [about peace].

Bar Qappara said, "The greatness of peace is shown in that the
Scripture used misleading language in the Torah so as to bring peace
between Abraham and Sarah.

"That is in line with the following verses of Scripture: '[So Sarah
laughed to herself, saying,] After I have grown old and my husband is
old, shall I have pleasure?' (Gen. 18:12). But this was not what [God]
told Abraham. Rather: '[Why did Sarah laugh, and say, Shall I indeed
bear a child,] now that I am old?'" (Gen. 18:13).

Bar Qappara made yet another statement.

Bar Qappara said, "The greatness of peace is shown in that the Scripture used misleading language in the prophetic writings so as to bring
peace between a man and his wife.

"'[And the angel of the Lord appeared to the woman and said to
her,] Behold now, you are barren and have not borne, but you will con-
ceive and bear a son' (Judg. 13:3). But this is not what he had said to
Manoah. Rather: 'Of all that I said to the woman let her take heed'
(Judg. 13:13). [Manoah was not told that his wife was barren. Rather,
she was not barren but could be made to conceive] For all that, she
[merely] needs some medicine."

Bar Qappara made yet another statement.

Bar Qappara said, "The greatness of peace is shown in that if [Scripture says] the creatures of the upper world need peace, and they are not subject to jealousy, hatred, competition, contention, lawsuits, arguments, or even illiberality of spirit, [for] 'He makes peace in his high places' (Job 25:3),

"the creatures down here on earth, who certainly exhibit all these traits, all the more so [need peace, which then is the most important virtue]."

Said Rabban Simeon b. Gamaliel, "The greatness of peace is shown in that Scripture used misleading language in order to bring peace between Joseph and his brothers.

"That is in line with the following verse of Scripture: ['And they sent a message to Joseph, saying, "Your father commanded before he died, saying,] 'So shall you say to Joseph, Forgive, I pray you, the sin of the servants of the God of your father''" (Gen. 50:16–17).

"But we do not find in Scripture that Jacob had given any such instructions."

Said R. Yosé the Galilean, "The greatness of peace is shown in that even in times of war, one should open discourse with talk of peace.

"That is in line with the following verse of Scripture: 'When you draw near to a city to fight against it, you will offer peace to it'" (Deut. 20:10).

Said R. Yudan b. R. Joseph, "The greatness of peace is shown in that the name of the Holy One, blessed be he, is Peace.

"For it is said, 'And he called him, "Lord, Peace"'" (Judg. 6:24).

Said R. Tanhum, "On the basis of this story, [we learn that] it is forbidden for a person to greet his fellow in a filthy place."

R. Ishmael taught, "The greatness of peace is shown in that the great name [of God], which is written in a state of sanctification, did the Holy One, blessed be he, instruct to have blotted out in water, if only to bring peace between a man and his wife."

R. Meir would sit and expound [the Torah] on Sabbath nights. A certain woman would attend regularly. [Once] when his exposition ran on, she remained until he was finished. When she got home, she found that the lamp had gone out. Her husband said to her, "Where were you?"

She said to him, "I was in the session and listening to the exposition."

He said to her, "You will not come in here until you go and spit in the face of the expositor."

She stayed away [from home] one week, then a second, then a third. Her neighbors said to her, "Are you people still mad at one another? Let us go with you to the expositor."

When R. Meir saw them, he understood through the Holy Spirit [what was going on]. He said to the women, "Among you is there a woman who is knowledgeable about whispering over [treating] a sore eye?"

Her neighbors said to her, "If you go and spit in his face, you will be permitted to go back to your husband."

But when the woman sat down before him, she became afraid of him. She said to him, "My lord, I am not really an expert at whispering over a sore eye."

He said to her, "Spit in my face seven times, and I'll get better."

She spit in his face seven times. He said to her, "Go and tell your husband, 'You said to do it once, but I did it seven times.'"

His disciples said to him, "My lord, is that the way people should abuse the Torah? Could you not have told one of us to whisper [over your eye] for you?"

He said to them, "Is it not sufficient [honor] for Meir to be merely equal to his Creator?

"For R. Ishmael has taught, 'The greatness of peace is shown in that the great name [of God], which is written in a state of sanctification, did the Holy One, blessed be he, instruct to have blotted out in water, if only to bring peace between a man and his wife.'"

R. Simeon b. Haleputa said, "The greatness of peace is shown by the fact that, when the Holy One, blessed be he, created his world, he made peace between the creatures of the upper world and the ones of the lower world.

"On the first day, he created some in the upper world and some in the lower world. That is in line with the verse of Scripture: 'In the beginning God created the Heaven and the earth' (Gen. 1:1).

"On the second day he created creatures of the upper world. That is in line with the following verse of Scripture: 'And God said, Let the firmament appear in the midst of the waters' (Gen. 1:6).

"On the third day, he created creatures of the lower world, as it is said, 'And God said, Let the waters be gathered together' (Gen. 1:9).

"On the fourth day, he created creatures of the upper world, as it is said, 'And God said, Let there be lights . . . ' (Gen. 1:14).

"On the fifth day he created creatures of the lower world, as it is said, 'Let the waters teem with creeping things' (Gen. 1:20).

"On the sixth day, he came to create man. God said, 'If I make him out of materials of the upper world, lo, the creatures of the upper world exceed the creatures of the lower world by one creature. If I make him of the lower world, lo, the creatures of the lower world will exceed the creatures of the upper world by one creature.'

"So what did he do?

"He created him out of materials of both the upper world and the lower world.

"That is in line with the following verse of Scripture: 'Then the Lord God formed man of the dust of the ground' (Gen. 2:7). That is so that he would be one of the creatures of the lower world.

"'And he blew into his nostrils the breath of life' (Gen. 2:7). Lo, in this regard, he was one with the creatures of the upper world."

LEVITICUS RABBAH IX:IX

Politics and Politicians

The view from the bottom proves remarkably clear-sighted when it comes to government, politics, politicians, and power—agencies of legitimate violence. Our sages, themselves clerks in the Jewish self-governing agency that Rome and Iran permitted Israel to maintain, bore no illusions about government and viewed with little sentimentality but a measure of cynicism the promises of politicians. "We're from the government and we're here to help"—our sages would not have been taken in. And yet, they also knew, the government is better than the alternative, which is, no government. The reason that violence must at some point find legitimation derives from the very sinful nature of humanity.

Be wary of the government, for they get friendly with a person only for their own convenience. They look like friends when it is to their benefit, but they do not stand by a person when he is in need.

TRACTATE ABOT 2:3

Hananiah, Prefect of the Priests, says, "Pray for the welfare of the government. For if it were not for fear of it, one man would swallow his fellow alive."

TRACTATE ABOT 3:2

Hate authority: how so?

This teaches that a person should not place the crown on his own head, but that others should put it on his head.

So it is said, Let another person praise you and not your own mouth, a stranger and not your own lips (Prov. 27:2).

Said R. Aqiba, "Whoever raises himself over teachings of the Torah—to what is such a one to be compared? To a carcass left lying on the road.

"Whoever passes be holds his nose and steps away from it.

"For it is said, 'If you have done foolishly in lifting yourself up or if you have planned devices put your hand on your mouth' (Prov. 30:32)."

Said to him Ben Azzai, "Interpret the passage in its own context. If a person humbles himself for the sake of the teachings of the Torah, eating dried dates and wearing dirty clothing and sitting and watching at the door of sages, whoever passes by will say, 'This one is a fool,' but in the end you will find that the whole of the Torah is with him."

R. Yosé says, "Going down is going up, and going up is coming down.

"Whoever raises himself over teachings of the Torah in the end will be thrown down, and whoever lowers himself over teachings of the Torah in the end will be raised up."

THE FATHERS ACCORDING TO RABBI NATHAN XI:II

Don't get friendly with the government: how so?

This teaches that a person should not make his name known to the sovereign. Once he becomes known to the sovereign, in the end they will pay attention to him and kill him and take over his entire estate.

How [would such a thing happen]? If one's fellow sits in the market and says, "The Holy One, blessed be he, shows grace to Mr. So-and-so. Today a hundred oxen have come forth from his household, a hundred sheep, a hundred goats."

A local official may hear and go and report the matter to the local authority, who goes and surrounds the entire establishment and takes everything from the man.

Concerning such a case Scripture says, 'He who blesses his friend with a loud voice—it shall be counted a curse to him' (Prov. 27:14).

Another matter: Don't get friendly with the government:

If one's fellow sits in the market and says, "The Holy One, blessed be he, shows grace to Mr. So-and-so. Today he brought into his store-house how many kors of wheat, how many kors of barley," a bandit hears and comes and surrounds the entire household, taking from him all his wealth.

In the morning he has nothing left.

Concerning such a case Scripture says, 'He who blesses his friend with a loud voice—it shall be counted a curse to him' (Prov. 27:14).

Another matter: Don't get friendly with the government:

How so?

This teaches that someone should not imagine announcing, "I am the prince of this city" or ". . . the [Goldin:] viceroy,"

for [holders of such offices merely] rob the Israelites.

THE FATHERS ACCORDING TO RABBI NATHAN XI:III-IV

The Power of Reason

The sages here outwit God. It is a sign of their humility to make it seem like a minor victory.

There we have learned: If one cut [a clay oven] into parts and put sand between the parts,

R. Eliezer declares the oven broken down and therefore insusceptible to uncleanness.

And sages declare it susceptible.

And this is what is meant by the oven of Akhnai.

Why the oven of Akhnai?

Said R. Judah said Samuel, "It is because they surrounded it with argument as with a snake and proved it was insusceptible to uncleanness."

A Tannaite statement:

On that day R. Eliezer produced all of the arguments in the world, but they did not accept them from him. So he said to them, "If the law accords with my position, this carob tree will prove it."

The carob was uprooted from its place by a hundred cubits—and some say, four hundred cubits.

They said to him, "There is no proof from a carob tree."

So he went and said to them, "If the law accords with my position, let the stream of water prove it."

The stream of water reversed flow.

They said to him, "There is no proof from a stream of water."

So he went and said to them, "If the law accords with my position, let the walls of the school house prove it."

The walls of the school house tilted toward falling.

R. Joshua rebuked them, saying to them, "If disciples of sages are contending with one another in matters of law, what business do you have?"

They did not fall on account of the honor owing to R. Joshua, but they also did not straighten up on account of the honor owing to R. Eliezer, and to this day they are still tilted.

So he went and said to them, "If the law accords with my position, let the Heaven prove it!"

An echo came forth, saying, "What business have you with R. Eliezer, for the law accords with his position under all circumstances!"

R. Joshua stood up on his feet and said, "'It is not in Heaven' (Deut. 30:12)."

What is the sense of, "'It is not in Heaven' (Deut. 30:12)"?

Said R. Jeremiah, "[The sense of Joshua's statement is this:] For the Torah has already been given from Mount Sinai, so we do not pay attention to echoes, since you have already written in the Torah at Mount Sinai, 'After the majority you are to incline' (Exod. 23:2)."

R. Nathan came upon Elijah and said to him, "What did the Holy One, blessed be he, do at that moment?"

He said to him, "He laughed and said, 'My children have overcome me, my children have overcome me!'"

BAVLI TO MISHNAH-TRACTATE BABA MESIA 4:10/59A-B

Prayer

Prayer is both content and context. The sages describe here not only what they say—which obviously matters deeply—but how they say it.

One may stand to pray only in a solemn frame of mind.

The early pious ones used to tarry one hour [before they would] pray, so that they could direct their hearts to the Omnipresent.

[While one is praying] even if the king greets him, he may not respond.

And even if a serpent is entwined around his heel, he may not interrupt [his prayer].

MISHNAH-TRACTATE BERAKHOT 5:1

The house of R. Yannai says, "When one wakes up from his sleep, he must say, 'Blessed are you Lord who resurrects the dead. My master,

I have sinned before you. May it be thy will, Lord my God, that you give to me a good heart, a good portion, a good inclination, a good associate, a good name, a good eye, and a good soul, and a humble soul and a modest spirit. And do not allow your name to be profaned among us. And do not make us the subject of [evil] talk among your creatures. And do not lead us in the end to destruction. And [do not turn] our hope to despair. And do not make our welfare depend on gifts from other people. And do not make us depend for sustenance on other people. For the beneficence of others is small and their hatred is great. And set our portion with your Torah, with those who do your will. Rebuild your house, your [Temple] courtyard, your city, and your Temple speedily in our days."

R. Hiyya bar Abba [Wawa] prayed, "May it be thy will, Lord our God, and God of our fathers, that you put in our hearts [the ability] to repent fully before you so that we not be put to shame in the presence of our forefathers in the world to come [after our death, on account of our sins]."

R. Tanhum bar Scholasticus prayed, "And may it be thy will, Lord my God, God of my fathers, that you break the yoke of the evil inclination and vanquish it from our hearts. For you created us to do your will. And we are obligated to do your will. You desire [that we do your will]. And we desire [to do your will]. And what prevents us? That bacteria [the evil inclination] which infect us [lit.: the yeast which makes the dough rise]. It is obvious to you that we do not have the strength to resist it. So let it be thy will, Lord my God, and God of my fathers, that you vanquish it from before us, and subdue it, so that we may do thy will as our own will, with a whole heart."

R. Yohanan used to pray, "May it be thy will, Lord my God, and God of my fathers that you imbue our portion [of life] with love and brotherhood, peace and friendship. And bring [our lives] to a happy end and [fulfill] all our hopes. And fill our dominion with disciples. And grant that we may enjoy our portion in paradise [in the world to come]. And provide for us a good heart and a good associate. And grant that we may rise early and find [each day] our hearts' desires. And let our souls' yearnings come before you for [our future] good."

YERUSHALMI BERAKHOT 4:2

One who enters a town recites two prayers, one on his entry and one on his exit.

Ben Azzai says, "[He recites] four [prayers], two on his entry, and two on his exit.

"He gives thanks for the past and cries out for the future [both upon his arrival and his departure]."

MISHNAH-TRACTATE BERAKHOT 9:4

One who enters a town recites two prayers, one on his entry and one on his exit.

What does he say when he enters? "May it be thy will, Lord my God, God of my fathers, that you bring me into this town in peace."

When he exits what does he say? "I give thanks to thee, Lord my God, that you brought me into this town in peace. So may it be thy will that you bring me forth from this town in peace."

Ben Azzai says, "[He recites] four [blessings], two on his entry and two on his exit."

He says, "May it be thy will, Lord my God, God of my fathers, that you bring me into this town in peace."

Once he has entered, he says, "I give thanks to thee, Lord my God, God of my fathers, that you brought me in in peace. So may it be thy will that you bring me forth in peace."

When he is exiting he says, "May it be thy will, Lord my God, that you bring me forth in peace."

Once he has exited, he says, "I give thanks to thee, Lord my God, God of my fathers, that you brought me forth in peace. So may it be thy will to bring me to my house in peace." Or, "[That you bring me] to such and such a place in peace"

TOSEFTA BERAKHOT 6:16

When R. Eleazar finished saying his prayer, this is what he said: "May it be pleasing before you, O Lord our God, to bring to dwell within our lot love, brotherhood, peace, and friendship, and make our territories rich in disciples, and make our destiny succeed with a future and a hope, and place our portion in the Garden of Eden, and provide us with a good colleague and good impulse in your world. And may we get up in the morning and find the yearning of our heart to fear your name. And may the serenity of our souls come before you for good."

When R. Yohanan had finished saying his prayer, this is what he said: "May it be pleasing before you, O Lord our God, to look upon our shame and see our suffering, and clothe yourself in mercy, cover yourself in your strength, and cloak yourself in your loyalty, and gird yourself in your compassion, and may the attribute of goodness come before you and that of your gentleness."

When R. Zira had finished saying his prayer, this is what he said: "May it be pleasing before you, O Lord our God, that we not sin or be ashamed or disgrace ourselves more than did our fathers."

When R. Hiyya had finished saying his prayer, this is what he said: "May it be pleasing before you, O Lord our God, that your Torah will be our craft, and that our heart not get sick or our eyes grow dim."

When Rab had finished saying his prayer, this is what he said: "May it be pleasing before you, O Lord our God, to give us long life, peaceful life, good life, blessed life, abundant life, secure life, a life of fear of sin, a life not marred by shame or humiliation, a life of wealth and honor, a life of love of Torah and fear of Heaven, a life in which you fill all the desires of our hearts for good."

When Rabbi had finished saying his prayer, this is what he said: "May it be pleasing before you, O Lord our God and God of our fathers, that you save us from those who are arrogant and from arrogance, from a bad man and a bad encounter, from the evil impulse and a bad associate, from a bad neighbor and from the destructive Satan, from a bad judgment and from a difficult litigant, whether a member of the covenant or not."

When R. Safra finished saying his prayer, this is what he said, "May it be pleasing before you, O Lord our God, to make peace in the Heavenly family and in the earthly family and among the disciples who are occupied with your Torah, whether they are occupied with it for its own sake or not for its own sake.

"And as to all those who are occupied with Torah not for its own sake, may it be pleasing before you that they should be occupied with it for its own sake."

When R. Alexandri had finished saying his prayer, this is what he said: "May it be pleasing before you, O Lord our God, to set us up in a well-lit corner and not in a dark one, and may our hearts not grow sick, or our eyes dim."

And when R. Alexandri had finished saying his prayer, this is what he said: "Lord of the ages, it is perfectly obvious to you that our will is to do your will. But what prevents it? It is the leaven in the dough, the subjugation to the pagan kingdoms. May it be pleasing before you, O Lord our God, to save us from their power so that we may return to carry out the rules that please you with a whole heart."

When Raba finished saying his prayer, this is what he said: "My God, before I was created, I was unworthy, and now that I have been created, it is as if I had not been created. I am dust in my life, all the more so in my death. Lo, I am before you as a utensil filled with shame and humiliation. May it be pleasing before you, O Lord my God, that I not sin again, and as to the sins that I have committed before you, wipe them out in your great mercies. But this should not be done through suffering or painful ailments."

When Mar, son of Rabina, finished saying his prayer, this is what he said: "My God, guard my tongue from gossiping and my lips from deceit. To those who curse me, may my soul be silent, and may my soul be as dust to everyone. Open my heart to your Torah, and let my soul pursue your religious duties. Keep me from a bad encounter, a bad impulse, a bad woman, and from all sorts of bad events that may come into the world. Quickly nullify the counsel of all who plan to do me ill and frustrate their plans. May what my mouth says and what my heart reflects be pleasing before you, O Lord, my rock and redeemer."

When R. Sheshet would sit fasting, after he had said his prayer, he would say this: "Lord of the ages, it is perfectly obvious to you that, when the house of the sanctuary stood, a person who had sinned would make an offering. And of that offering the priests would offer up only the fat and blood, yet atonement would be attained for that person. Now I have sat in a fast, and so my fat and blood have become less. May it be pleasing before you that my fat and blood that have become less be received as if I had offered them up before you on the altar and so be reconciled with me."

When R. Yohanan would finish [the study of] the book of Job, this is what he said: "The destiny of a person is to die, and the destiny of a beast is to be slaughtered, so all are destined to death. Happy is the one who grows in knowledge of Torah, whose labor is in Torah, who thereby brings pleasure to his Creator, who grows in good repute, and who dies in good repute in this world. Concerning such a one Solomon said, 'A good name is better than precious oil, and the day of death than the day of one's birth' (Qoh. 7:1)."

A pearl in R. Meir's mouth: "Learn with all your heart and with all your soul to know my ways and to attend upon the entries of my Torah.

Keep my Torah in your heart and let awe of me be before your eyes. Keep your mouth from every sort of sin, purify and sanctify yourself from all guilt and transgression. Then I shall be with you everywhere."

A pearl in the mouth of rabbis of Yabneh: "I am mortal and so is my fellow. But my labor is in town, and his is in the field. I get up early to do my work and he gets up early to do his work. Just as he does not infringe upon my work, so I do not infringe upon his work. And perhaps you might suppose that I do much and he does little? We have learned to repeat: 'All the same is the one who does much and the one who does little, so long as a person directs his heart to Heaven.'"

A pearl in the mouth of Abbayye: "A person should always be subtle [in finding ways to] fear [Heaven]. 'A soft answer turns away anger' (Prov. 15:1). One should increase peace with his brethren and relatives and everyone, even with a Gentile in the marketplace, so that he may be beloved above and pleasing below and accepted by people."

A pearl in the mouth of Raba: "The concrete realization of wisdom lies in repentance and good deeds. So a person should not study Scripture and repeat Mishnah traditions but at the same time abuse his father, his mother, his master, or someone greater than himself in wisdom and in years [Simon: rank], as it is said, 'The fear of the Lord is the beginning of wisdom, a good understanding have all they who do thereafter' (Ps. 111:10). It is not said, 'To those who do,' but 'Those who do thereafter,' meaning, those who do for their own sake and not for those who do them not for their own sake. And whoever does not for its own sake would have been better off not having been created."

A pearl in the mouth of Rab: "The world to come is not like this world. In the world to come there is neither eating nor drinking nor procreating nor give and take nor envy nor hatred nor competition. But the righteous are enthroned with their crowns on their heads, enjoying the splendor of the presence of God. For it is said, 'And they beheld God and [it was that that they] ate and drank' (Exod. 24:11)."

BAVLI TO MISHNAH-TRACTATE BERAKHOT 2:6-8/16B-17A

Pride and Its Penalty

The sages, as is their fashion, do not simply castigate the proud, but demonstrate its idiocy through the experiences of others.

Another teaching concerning "for he is highly exalted":
"He is exalted above all who take pride in themselves."

For with that in which the nations of the world take pride before him he exacts punishment from them.

For so Scripture says in connection with the men of the generation of the flood, "Their bull genders . . . they send forth their little ones . . . they sing to the timbrel and harp and rejoice" (Job 21:10–12).

And what is then stated? "Depart from us, we do not desire knowledge of your ways. What is the Almighty that we should serve him" (Job 21:14–15).

They said, "Not even for a drop of rain do we need him, for 'There goes up a mist from the earth' (Gen. 2:6)."

Said to them the Holy One, blessed be he, "Total idiots! In the very act of goodness which I have done for you do you take pride before me? Through that same act I shall exact a penalty from you."

"And the rain was upon the earth forty days and forty nights" (Gen. 7:12).

R. Yosé of Damascus says, "Since they set their eyes both above and below to express their lust. So the Holy One, blessed be he, opened up against them the springs above and below so as to destroy them.

"For so it is said, 'All the fountains of the great deep were broken up and the windows of Heaven were opened' (Gen. 7:11)."

And along these same lines, you found in connection with the men of the tower [of Babel], that with that in which they took pride before him he exacts punishment from them.

"Come let us build us a city" (Gen. 11:4).

What is said in their regard? "So the Lord scattered them abroad from thence upon the face of all the earth" (Gen. 11:8).

And along these same lines, you found in connection with the men of Sodom, that with that in which they took pride before him he exacts punishment from them.

"As for the earth out of it comes bread . . . the stones of it are the place of sapphires . . . that path no bird of prey knows . . . the proud beasts have not trodden it" (Job 28:5–8).

The men of Sodom said, "We have no need for travelers to come our way. Lo, we have food near at hand, lo, we have silver and gold. precious stones and pearls, near at hand. [Let us go and] wipe out the law of [protecting] the wayfarer from our land."

Said to them the Holy One, blessed be he, "Total idiots! On account of the act of goodness that I did for you, you take pride and you want to wipe out the law of [protecting] the wayfarer from among you. I shall wipe out the memory of you yourselves from the world."

"He breaks open a shaft away from where men sojourn" (Job 28:4).

"A contemptible brand . . . the tents of robbers prosper, and they that provoke God are secure" (Job. 12:5).

That is what made them rebel, namely, "Whatsoever God brings into their hand" (Job 12:6).

And so Scripture says, "And they were haughty and committed abominations before me."

And what did it cause for them? "'As I live,' says the Lord God, 'Sodom your sister has not done . . . as you have done . . . . Behold, this was the iniquity of your sister Sodom . . . neither did she strengthen the hand of the poor and needy, and they were haughty'" (Ezek. 16:48–50).

So you find in the case of the Egyptians that with that in which they took pride before him he exacts punishment from them.

"And he took six hundred chariots" (Exod. 14:7).

Then: "Pharaoh's chariots and his host he cast into the sea, and his picked officers are sunk in the Red Sea."

So you find in the case of Sisera that with that in which he took pride before him he exacts punishment from him.

"And Sisera collected all his chariots, nine hundred chariots of iron" (Judg. 4:13).

Then: "They fought from Heaven, the stars in their courses fought against Sisera" (Judg. 5:20).

MEKHILTA 27. SHIRATA II

Pseudo-Piety And Fakery

Sages' entire lives centered upon study of the Torah and performance of acts of piety as well as grace. So they cannot be accused of holding cynical views about religion. But they recognized how a religion that comes to express in everyday actions and statements may nurture formal piety, as much as authentic faith and pure intention to serve God. For it is always easier to go through the motions than to be moved. Jesus's critique of "the Pharisees," his opponents, dismissed their piety as formal and insincere. Our sages, heirs of the Pharisees and continuators of their traditions from Sinai, criticized formality and insincerity, and did so in the same terms. They condemned not "the Pharisees," however, but only, those Pharisees who turned religion into a show and made it a travesty. And sages knew full well that those, the hypocritical Pharisees, represented not the Torah but themselves alone.

R. Joshua would say, "A foolish saint, a smart knave, an abstemious woman,

"and the blows of Pharisees (perushim)—
"lo, these wear out the world."

MISHNAH-TRACTATE SOTAH 3:4

What is meant by a foolish saint?

If one saw a child drowning in a river and said, "When I shall remove my phylactery, I shall save him,"— while this one is taking off his phylacteries, the other one gave up the ghost.

If he found a fig which was the first of the season, and said "Whomever I shall meet first, I shall give it to him [so as not to benefit from first fruits]," if he then saw a betrothed maiden and ran after her [for that purpose]—this is in line with that which we have learned: he who runs after his fellow to kill him, after a male, after a betrothed maiden.

A smart knave:

R. Zeriqan in the name of R. Huna, "This is one who applies lenient rulings to himself and strict rulings to other people."

An abstemious woman:

This is one who sits and quotes biblical phrases in a suggestive way:

"And she said, 'You must come in to me, for I have hired you with my son's mandrakes and he lay with her that night'" (Gen. 30:16).

Said R. Abbahu: "It was as if it already was in mind. In any case he knew that it was in her mind only so as to produce a founder of a tribe."

Blows of Pharisees [Pharisees]: This is the sort of person who gives advice to heirs of an estate on how to keep the widow from getting her rightful maintenance.

It is in line with the following:

The widow of R. Shobetai was wasting his estate [by supporting herself in high style from his estate].

The heirs came and complained to R. Eleazar. He said to them, "I shall tell you what to do. Pretend that your are going to sell [the land], and she will then lay claim on her portion, and thereby she will lose."

They did exactly that. In the evening she came and complained to R. Eleazar.

She said to him, "This is a case in which the blows of the Pharisees have injured me. May [terrible things] happen to me if I ever intended such a thing to happen."

A disciple of Rabbi had two hundred *zuz* less a *denar* [in which case he was permitted to accept poor man's tithe, having too little money to be deemed well-off].

Rabbi was accustomed to give over to him his poor man's tithe every third year [when it was due] as the tithe owing to those who were in need.

One time the other disciples treated the student in a mean way by making up [the *denar*, so that he had the two hundred *zuz* and was no longer eligible to receive the poor man's tithe].

[Rabbi] came and wanted to hand over to him the poor man's tithe as he had been accustomed to do.

He said to him, "Rabbi, I have the requisite sum of money, [and so I am not eligible]."

He said, "In the case of this one, the blows of the Pharisees have smitten him."

He instructed his disciples, and he took him up to a tavern and made him one *qarat* poorer.

And then Rabbi handed over to him the poor man's tithe as he had been accustomed to do.

YERUSHALMI TO MISHNAH-TRACTATE SOTAH 3:4

Our rabbis have taught on Tannaite authority:

There are seven types of "Pharisees":

The abstemious person of the Shikmi sort, the abstemious person of the Niqpi sort, the abstemious person of the Qizai sort, the abstemious person of the pestle sort, the abstemious person [who says], "What is my duty, for I shall do it," the abstemious person out of love, the abstemious person out of fear.

"The abstemious person of the Shikmi sort": this is one who does the deeds of Shechem [who circumcised himself for an improper motive, hence, one who does the right thing for the wrong reason].

"The abstemious person of the Niqpi sort": this is one who knocks his feet together ["He walks with exaggerated humility," Cohen, p. 112, n. 6].

"The abstemious person of the Qizai sort": said R. Nahman bar Isaac, "This one lets his blood flow against walls" [Cohen: "in his anxiety to avoid looking up on a woman, he dashes his face against the wall"].

"An abstemious person of the pestle sort":—said Rabbah bar Shila, "One who bows his head like a pestle."

"An abstemious person [who says], 'What is my duty, for I shall do it?'":—Is this not a virtue [and hence should not fall into the present classification]?

Rather it is one who says, "[Tell me] what is my duty beyond [what I have done], and I shall do it."

"An abstemious person out of love, an abstemious person out of fear": Said Abayye and Raba to the Tannaite authority [who repeated the tradition at hand], "Do not repeat [in your version of the teaching] 'An abstemious person out of love, an abstemious person out of fear.'"

For R. Judah said Rab said, "A person should always occupy himself in the study of Torah and in the practice of religious deeds, even not for their own sake, for, from doing them not for their own sake, he eventually will come to do them for their own sake." [Hence the final two items do not belong on the list at all.]

Said R. Nahman bar Isaac, "What is hidden is hidden, what is public is public. The great court will exact punishment from those who [pretend to be humble by] wrapping themselves in cloaks [as if they were pious people when they are not]."

Said King Jannaeus to his daughter, "Do not fear the abstemious people [or: 'Pharisees'], nor those who are not abstemious [or: 'not Pharisees'], but only the ones who are hypocrites, who appear like abstemious people, but whose deeds are the deeds of Zimri, while they seek the reward of Phineas (Num. 25:11ff.)."

BAVLI TO MISHNAH-TRACTATE SOTAH 3:4/22B

Rebuking Sinners

Our rabbis have taught on Tannaite authority:

"You shall not hate your brother in your heart" (Lev. 19:17).

Is it possible to suppose that all one should not do is not smite, slap, or curse him, [and that is what is at issue only]?

Scripture says, ". . . in your heart," thus speaking of the sort of hatred that is in the heart [as much as hatred expressed through physical means].

How do we know [from Scripture] that one who sees in his fellow an unworthy trait is liable to remonstrate with him?

It is said, "You shall surely rebuke your fellow" (Lev. 19:17).

[If] one has rebuked him, and he has not accepted rebuke, how do we know [from Scripture] that one should go and rebuke him again?

Scripture says, "You shall surely rebuke . . ." under all circumstances. [The emphatic language "surely" implies that one must do so under all circumstances.]

Is it possible to suppose that one should do so even if his face fell [in embarrassment]?

Scripture states, "You shall not bear sin on his account" (Lev. 19:17).

It has been taught [on Tannaite authority]: Said R. Tarfon, "I should be surprised if there is anyone left in this generation who accepts rebuke. If one says to someone, 'Remove the chip from your eye,' the other party responds, 'Take the beam from your eye'!"

Said R. Eleazar b. Azariah, "I should be surprised if there is anyone left in this generation who knows how to administer rebuke."

And said R. Yohanan b. Nuri, "I call to witness against me Heaven and earth [if it not be true] that many times Aqiba was flogged on account of my complaining against him before Rabban Gamaliel, and all the more so did I increase in my love for him, to carry out what is said in the following verse of Scripture: 'Do not reprove a scorner, lest he hate you, reprove a wise man, and he will love you' (Prov. 9:8)."

R. Judah, son of R. Simeon [b. Pazzi], asked [R. Simeon b. Pazzi], "Sincere reproof or hypocritical restraint [from criticism]—which is better?" ["For a man to pretend to be unworthy of administering reproof, whereas in fact it is the fear of arousing hatred that deters him from doing his duty in this respect."]

He said to him, "Will you not concede that sincere restraint is best of all?"

For a master has said, "Restraint is best of all."

But hypocritical restraint is also better.

For R. Judah said Rab said, "Under all circumstances a person should engage in study of Torah and practice of religious duties, even if it is not for its own sake, for, out of doing these things not for their own sake, one will come to do them for their own sake."

What would be a case of sincere reproof and of hypocritical restraint?

Such an instance would involve R. Huna and Hiyya bar Rab. They were in session before Samuel. Hiyya bar Rab said to him, "See, master, how [Huna] bothers me!"

[The latter] undertook not to bother him any more. After he went out, [Huna] said [to Samuel], "This is what the other fellow was doing [which was unworthy, so I criticized him.]"

He said to him, "Why did you not say so to his face?"

He said to him, "Far be it from me to embarrass the descendant of Rab through something that I did!" [Such would be Huna's hypocritical restraint.] ["The false modesty of R. Huna expressed itself in this: He would vex Hiyya, to suggest his displeasure at his unseemly behavior [whatever it was), but he would not disgrace him by direct reproach, while reporting his misbehavior in his absence."]

BAVLI TO MISHNAH-TRACTATE ARAKHIN 3:5

Reconciliation

Said R. Isaac, "Whoever offends his fellow, even if through what he says, has to reconcile with him, as it is said, 'My son, if you have become surety for your neighbor, if you have struck your hands for a stranger, you are snared by the words of your mouth . . . do this now, my son, and deliver yourself, seeing you have come into the power of your neighbor, go, humble yourself, and urge your neighbor' (Prov. 6:1-3). If it is a money claim against you, open the palm of your hand to him [and pay him off], and if not, send a lot of intermediaries to him."

Said R. Hisda, "He has to reconcile with him through three sets of three people each: 'He comes before men and says, I have sinned and perverted that which was right and it did not profit me' (Job 33:27)."

Said R. Yosé bar Hanina, "Whoever seeks reconciliation with his neighbor has to do so only three times: 'Forgive I pray you now . . . and now we pray you' (Gen. 50:17).

"And if he has died, he brings ten people and sets them up at his grave and says, 'I have sinned against the Lord the God of Israel and against this one, whom I have hurt."

R. Abba had a complaint against R. Jeremiah, [Jeremiah] went and sat at the door of R. Abba. In the interval his serving girl threw out slops. Some drops fell on his head. He said, "They've made a dung heap out of me," and about himself he cited the verse, "He raises up the poor out of the dust" (1 Sam. 2:8).

R. Abba heard and came out to him, saying, "Now I must come out to seek reconciliation with you: 'Go, humble yourself and urge your neighbor' (Prov. 6:1).

When R. Zira had a quarrel with someone, he would pass by him repeatedly, so as to show himself to him, so that the other might come forth to seek reconciliation with him.

Rab had a fight with a certain butcher. The butcher did not come to him on the eve of the Day of Atonement, so he said, "I shall go and seek reconciliation with him."

R. Huna met him. He said to him, "Where is the master going?"

He said to him, "To seek reconciliation with Mr. So-and-so."

He thought, 'Abba [Rab] is going to bring about the other's death."

[Rab] went and stood by the man. The other was sitting and chopping up a beast's head. He raised his eyes and saw him. He said to him, "You're Abba, go away, I have no business to do with you." While he was chopping the head, a bone flew off, struck his throat, and killed him.

Rab was expounding sections of Scripture for the rabbis, and R. Hiyya entered. So he started again. Then Bar Qappara came in, so he started again. Then R. Simeon b. Rabbi came in, so he started again. Then R. Hanina bar Hama came in. He said, "So much am I supposed to backtrack" So he did not go over it again.

R. Hanina was offended. Rab went to him on thirteen occasions of the eve of the Day of Atonement, but the other was not reconciled to him.

But how could he have behaved in such a way? And didn't R. Yosé bar Hanina say, "Whoever seeks pardon from his fellow should not seek it from him more than three times?"

Rab was exceptional.

And how could R. Hanina have behaved in such a way? And didn't Raba say, "Whoever is forbearing when he has a righteous claim—they bear with all of his sins."

Rather, R. Hanina saw in a dream that Rab was suspended on a palm tree, and there is a tradition that whoever is suspended from a palm tree becomes head. He said, "That implies that authority is going to be given to him," and he was not reconciled with him so that he would have to go and teach Torah in Babylonia.

BAVLI TO MISHNAH-TRACTATE YOMA 8:9/87A-B

Refined Language, Wise Euphemisms

The same sages who defined licentiousness in terms of extraordinary sensibility and refinement took seriously, as well, the character of language, its unique power. They therefore insisted that language be used with respect and treated with dignity, not abused, not diminished, not discarded for grunts and wild gestures of the hand or mouth. Sages aimed at the civilization of Israel They saw the purpose of the Torah and commandments as the purification of the heart of sinful humanity. No wonder, then, that the medium of the Torah, language, won from them a stout defense. Refinement in language, as much as refinement in relationships with the opposite sex, formed the bulwark of civilization.

It has been taught on Tannaite authority by the household of R. Ishmael: "A person should always speak in refined language, for note, in the case of the male afflicted by flux [described at Leviticus 15], the act is called 'riding,' but in connection with a woman, the same is called 'sitting' [Lev. 15:9, 20, saddle/riding for the male, everything on which she sits for the female, but the result is the same uncleanness; sitting is more modest with respect to women]. And Scripture says, 'And you shall choose the tongue of the subtle' (Job 15:5), 'and that which my lips know they shall speak purely' (Job 33:3)."

Two disciples were in session before Rab. One said, "This tradition has made us as tired as exhausted pigs."
The other said, "This tradition has made us as tired as exhausted kids."
Rab would not talk to the former of the two any more.

Two disciples were in session before Hillel, one of whom was Rabban Yohanan b. Zakkai, and some say, they were before Rabbi, and one of them was R. Yohanan. One of them said, "How come they gather grapes in a state of cultic cleanness but don't gather olives in a state of cultic cleanness?"
The other said, "How come they gather grapes in a state of cultic cleanness but gather olives in a state of cultic uncleanness?"
He said, "I'm pretty sure that this one is going to give decisions in Israel," and the days were only a few before he gave instruction in Israel.

There were three priests. One said, "I got as much as a bean of showbread."
The second: "I got as much as an olive."
The third: "I got as much as a lizard tail."
They looked into his background and found in him a trace of unfitness.
But we have learned in the Mishnah: They do not carry a genealogical inquiry backward from [proof that one's priestly ancestor has

served] at the altar, or from [proof that one's levitical ancestor has served] on the platform, and from [proof that one's learned ancestor has served] in the Sanhedrin. [It is taken for granted that at the time of the appointment, a full inquiry was undertaken.]

Don't say "a trace of unfitness" but rather, "a low character that made him unfit."

Or if you prefer, I shall say: That case is different, because he drew doubt as to his status upon himself.

R. Kahana got sick; rabbis sent R. Joshua b. R. Idi. They said to him, "Go, find out what's with him."

He came. He found him dead. He tore his garment and put the tear behind him and went along weeping.

He came. They said to him, "Has he died?"

He said to them, "I'm not the one who said it: 'For he who brings bad news is a fool' (Prov. 10:18)."

Yohanan of Hukok went to the villages. When he came back, they said to him, "Is the wheat coming along well?"

He said to them, "The barley is doing fine."

They said to him, "Go, tell the good news to the horses and asses: 'Barley also and straw for the horses and swift steeds' (1 Kings 5:8)."

What ought he to have said?

"Last year the wheat was just fine," or, "the lentil crop was just fine."

There was someone who said, "Judge my case."

They said, "That implies that he comes from the tribe of Dan: 'Dan shall judge his people as one of the tribes of Israel' (Gen. 49:16)."

There was someone who went around saying, [Freedman:] "By the sea-shore thorn bushes are fir trees."

They examined his genealogy and found that he comes from Zebulun: "Zebulun shall dwell at the haven of the sea" (Gen. 49:13).

BAVLI TO MISHNAH-TRACTATE PESAHIM 1:1/3B=4A

Repentance

Grandsons of Haman studied Torah in Bene Beraq.
Grandsons of Sisera taught children in Jerusalem.
Grandsons of Sennacherib taught Torah in public. And who were they? Shemaiah and Abtalion [teachers of Hillel and Shammai].

BAVLI GITTIN 57B

This remarkable statement from the Talmud shows that sin is not indelible either upon one's family or upon oneself. Haman then stands for Hitler now. Sisera stands for Petlura, who murdered tens of thousands of Jews in Ukraine after World War I. Sennacherib represents Nasser, who in 1967 undertook to wipe out the State of Israel. The sinner should be, and is, punished; but sin is not indelible. If the sinner repents the sin, atones, and attains reconciliation with God, the sin is wiped off the record, the sinner forgiven, the sinners' successors blameless. The mark of repentance comes to the surface when the one-time sinner gains the chance to repeat the sinful deed but does not do so; then the repentance is complete. To understand the power of this statement, we have only to say, "Hitler's grandson teaches Torah in a yeshiva of Bene Beraq." Or: "Eichmann's grandson sits in a Jerusalem Yeshiva, reciting prayers and psalms and learning Talmud." We may then go onward with Sennacherib, who can stand for Himmler, and Shemaiah and Abtalion, the greatest authorities of their generation, who can stand for the heads of the great yeshivas and theological courts of the State of Israel, Himmler's grandsons are arbiters of the Torah, that is to say, Judaism, in the State of Israel. True, Scripture says ". . . visiting the guilt of the parents upon the children, upon the third and upon the fourth generations of those who reject me" (Exod. 20:5). But the Torah—the oral Torah reading the written Torah—qualifies that judgment: if the third and fourth generations continue the tradition of the fathers in rejecting the Lord, they too suffer punishment—for their own sins. Readers familiar with Christian accounts of repentance will find themselves on familiar ground in these statements. For Judaism no such thing as "cheap grace" or unearned, indeed, unintended, atonement exists; repentance represents an act of intentionality and full articulation, joined with deeds that match the original dereliction.

For more on the subject, see Reconciliation.

He who says, "I shall sin and repent, sin and repent"—
they give him no chance to do repentance.

"I will sin and the Day of Atonement will atone,"—the Day of Atonement does not atone.

For transgressions done between man and the Omnipresent, the Day of Atonement atones.

For transgressions between man and man, the Day of Atonement atones, only if the man will regain the good will of his friend.

This exegesis did R. Eleazar b. Azariah state: "'From all your sins shall you be clean before the Lord' (Lev. 16:30)—for transgressions between man and the Omnipresent does the Day of Atonement atone. For transgressions between man and his fellow, the Day of Atonement atones, only if the man will regain the good will of his friend."

Said R. Aqiba, "Happy are you, O Israel. Before whom are you made clean, and who makes you clean? It is your Father who is in Heaven,

"as it says, 'And I will sprinkle clean water on you, and you will be clean' (Ezek. 36:25).

"And it says, 'O Lord, the hope [Miqweh = immersion pool] of Israel' (Jer. 17:13)—Just as the immersion pool cleans the unclean, so the Holy One, blessed be he, cleans Israel."

MISHNAH-TRACTATE YOMA 8:7

R. Mattiah b. Heresh asked R. Eleazar b. Azariah, "Have you heard of the four types of atonement that R. Ishmael used to expound?"

He said to him, "They are three, besides [the requirement of] an act of repentance."

[These are the three types:] One Scripture says, "Return, O faithless children, says the Lord" (Jer. 3:14). And yet another verse of Scripture says, "For on this day shall atonement be made for you, to cleanse you; from all your sins you shall be clean before the Lord" (Lev. 16:30). [So one verse recommends repentance and the other grants absolution unconditionally.]

And one verse of Scripture says, "Then I will punish their transgression with the rod and their iniquity with scourges" (Ps. 89:32). And yet another verse of Scripture says, "Surely this iniquity will not be forgiven you till you die, says the Lord God of Hosts" (Isa. 22:14).

Now how are these verses to be reconciled [which speak of punishment and forgiveness, on the one side, and the impossibility of atonement except through death on the other]?

[If] one has violated a positive commandment but repented, he does not even leave the place before he is [wholly] forgiven. Concerning such a person the verse of Scripture says, "Return, O faithless children."

[If] one has violated a negative commandment and repented forthwith, the act of repentance suspends the punishment, and the Day of Atonement affects atonement for him. In such a case the Scripture states, "For on this day shall atonement be made for you."

[If] one has violated a commandment involving extirpation or the death penalty inflicted by a court, and has done so deliberately, repentance and the Day of Atonement effect atonement in part, and suffering on other days of the year effects atonement in part. Concerning such a person, the verse of Scripture states, "Then I will punish their transgression with the rod and their iniquity with scourges."

But as to him through whose action the Name of Heaven has been disgraced, repentance has not got the power to suspend punishment, nor does the Day of Atonement have the power to effect atonement, nor does suffering have the power to wipe away the guilt. But repentance and the Day of Atonement suspend the punishment, along with suffering; the man's death wipes away the sin. Concerning such a person does Scripture make the statement: "Surely this iniquity will not be forgiven you till you die"?

Thus we have learned the fact that death wipes away [guilt and sin]

TOSEFTA YOMA 4:6-8

Said R. Hama bar Hanina, "Great is repentance, which brings healing to the world: 'I will heal their backsliding, I will love them freely' (Hos. 14:5)."

R. Hama bar Hanina contrasted verses: "'Return you backsliding children'—who to begin with were backsliding. Vs. 'I will heal your backsliding' (Jer. 3:22). There is no contradiction, in the one case, the repentance is out of love, in the other, out of fear."

R. Judah contrasted verses: "'Return you backsliding children, I will heal your backsliding' (Jer. 3:22). Vs. 'For I am lord to you, and I will take you one of a city and two of a family' (Jer. 3:14). There is no contradiction, in the one case, the repentance is out of love or fear, in the other, repentance comes as a consequence of suffering."

Said R. Levi, "Great is repentance, which reaches up to the throne of glory: 'Return, Israel, to the Lord your God' (Hos. 14:2)."

Said R. Yohanan, "Great is repentance, for it overrides a negative commandment that is in the Torah: 'If a man put away his wife and she go from him and become another man's wife, may he return to her again? Will not that land be greatly polluted? But you have played the harlot with many lovers, and would you then return to me, says the Lord' (Jer. 3:1)."

Said R. Jonathan, "Great is repentance, for it brings redemption near: 'And a redeemer shall come to Zion and to those who return from transgression in Jacob' (Isa. 59:20)—how come 'a redeemer shall come to Zion'? Because of 'those who return from transgression in Jacob.'"

Said R. Simeon b. Laqish, "Great is repentance, for by it sins that were done deliberately are transformed into those that were done inadvertently: 'And when the wicked turns from his wickedness and does that which is lawful and right, he shall live thereby' (Ezek. 33:19)—now 'wickedness' is done deliberately, and yet the prophet calls it stumbling!"

Said R. Samuel bar Nahmani said R. Jonathan, "Great is repentance, for it lengthens the years of a person: 'And when the wicked turns from his wickedness...he shall live thereby' (Ezek. 33:19)."

Said R. Isaac, [or] they say in the West in the name of Rabbah bar Mari, "Come and take note of how the characteristic of the Holy One, blessed be he, is not like the characteristic of mortals. If a mortal insults his fellow by something that he has said, the other may or may not be reconciled with him. And if you say that he is reconciled with him, he may or may not be reconciled by mere words. But with the Holy One, blessed be he, if someone commits a transgression in private, he will be reconciled with him in mere words, as it is said, 'Take with you words and return to the Lord' (Hos. 14:3). And not only so, but [God] credits it to him as goodness: 'and accept that which is good' (Hos. 14:5); and not only so, but Scripture credits it to him as if he had offered up bullocks: 'So will we render for bullocks the offerings of our lips' (Hos. 14:5). Not you might say that reference is made to obligatory bullocks, but Scripture says, 'I will heal their backsliding, I love them freely' (Hos. 14:5)."

It has been taught on Tannaite authority:

R. Meir would say, "Great is repentance, for on account of a single individual who repents, the whole world is forgiven in its entirety: 'I will heal their backsliding, I will love them freely, for my anger has turned away from him' (Hos. 14:5). What is said is not 'from them' but 'from him.'"

How is a person who has repented to be recognized?

Said R. Judah, "For example, if a transgression of the same sort comes to hand once, and second time, and the one does not repeat what he had done."

R. Judah defined matters more closely: "With the same woman, at the same season, in the same place."

BABYLONIAN TALMUD TO MISHNAH-TRACTATE YOMA 8:9/86A-B

Resurrection of the Dead

Like the matter of the Messiah, the issue of the resurrection of the dead carries us beyond the frontiers of wisdom and into the realm of theological doctrine about last things. And yet, for all wisdom traditions,

*the issue of death takes a primary place, and reflection on the meaning
of death, natural to the human condition, proves universal. Our sages
think about death only from the perspective of resurrection, and they interpret the course of a human life in the light of the hope for eternal life
in the world to come. That is why, in the setting of an account of the wisdom of Judaism, the matter of resurrection requires some attention.*

Said R. Samuel bar Nahmani said R. Jonathan, "The righteous are
destined to resurrect the dead, as it is said, 'There shall yet old men and
old women sit in the broad places of Jerusalem, every man with his staff
in his hand for very age' (Zech. 8:4), and, 'and lay my staff upon the
face of the child' (1 Kings 4:29)."

Ulla contrasted these verses: "'He will swallow up death forever'
(Isa. 25:8) and by contrast, 'for the youngest shall die a hundred years
old' (Isa. 65:20). No problem: the one speaks of Israel, the other, gentiles. And what are Gentiles doing in that context at all? 'And strangers
shall stand and feed your flocks, and aliens shall be your plowmen and
your vine dressers' (Isa. 56:5)."

R. Hisda contrasted these verses: "'Then the moon shall be con-
founded and the sun ashamed' (Isa. 24:23), and by contrast, 'Moreover the light of the moon shall be as the light of the sun, and the light
of the sun sevenfold as the light of the seven days' (Isa. 30:26). No
problem: the one speaks of the world to come, the other, the days of
the Messiah."

And from the view of Samuel, who has said, "The only difference
between this age and the days of the Messiah is Israel's subjugation to
the kingdoms alone," what is to be said?
Both speak of the world to come, but there is no problem: the one
speaks of the camp of the presence of God; the other, the camp of the
righteous.

Raba contrasted these verses: "'I kill and I make alive' (Deut. 32:39)
and 'I wound and I heal' (Deut. 32:39). [The former implies that one is
resurrected just as he was at death, thus with blemishes, and the other
implies that at the resurrection all wounds are healed.] Said the Holy
One, blessed be He, 'What I kill I bring to life,' and then, 'What I have
wounded I heal.'"

Our rabbis have taught on Tannaite authority:

"I kill and I make alive" (Deut. 32:39). Is it possible to suppose that there is death for one person and life for the other, just as the world is accustomed [now]? Scripture says, "I wound and I heal" (Deut. 32:39). Just as wounding and healing happen to one person, so death and then resurrection happen to one person. From this fact we derive an answer to those who say, "There is no evidence of the resurrection of the dead based on the teachings of the Torah."

Another matter: at the outset, what I kill I resurrect, but then, what I wound, I heal.

BAVLI TO MISHNAH-TRACTATE PESAHIM 6:1-2

Reward and Punishment in This World and in the Next: Good Things for Good People

Our sages maintain that sometimes good things happen to good people, and sometimes bad things happen to bad people. They knew full well that, at other times, matters did not work out according to the rule of reason. Bad things happen to good people, and the wicked prosper. Our sages accepted the mystery of being and understood that God did things they did not, and could not, fully grasp. Part of their worship of God lay in their capacity to acknowledge the anomalies of an unjust world and affirm that, in the end, God will do what is right and good.

Expounded R. Nahman bar Hisda, "What is the meaning of the verse of Scripture, 'There is a vanity that occurs on the earth, for there are the righteous who receive what is appropriate to the deeds of the wicked, and there are the wicked who receive what is appropriate to the deeds of the righteous' (Qoh. 8:14). Happy are the righteous, for in this world they undergo what in the world to come is assigned as recompense for the deeds of the wicked, and woe is the wicked, for in this world they enjoy the fruits of what is assigned in the world to come to the deeds of the righteous."

Said Raba, "So if the righteous enjoy both worlds, would that be so bad for them?"

Rather, said Raba, "Happy are the righteous, for in this world they get what is set aside for the deeds of the wicked in this world, and woe to the wicked, for in this world they get what is assigned for the deeds of the righteous in this world."

R. Pappa and R. Huna b. R. Joshua came before Raba. He said to them, "Have you mastered such and such tractate and such and such tractate?"

They said to him, "Yes."

"Have you gotten a bit richer?"

They said to him, "Yes, because we bought a little piece of land."

He recited in their regard, Happy are the righteous, for in this world they undergo what in the world to come is assigned as recompense for the deeds of the wicked.

Said Rabbah bar bar Hannah said R. Yohanan, "What is the meaning of the verse of Scripture, 'For the paths of the Lord are straight, that the righteous shall pass along them, but the transgressors will stumble in them' (Hos. 14:10)? The matter may be compared to the case of two men who roasted their Passover offerings. One of them ate it for the sake of performing the religious duty, and the other one ate it to stuff himself with a big meal. The one who ate it for the sake of performing a religious duty—'the righteous shall pass along them.' And as to the one who ate it to stuff himself with a big meal—'but the transgressors will stumble in them'"

Said to him R. Simeon b. Laqish, "But do you really call him a wicked person? Granted that he did not carry out a religious duty in the best possible way, still, has he not eaten his Passover offering as he is supposed to? Rather, the matter may be compared to the case of two men. This one has his wife and sister with him in the house, and that one has his wife and his sister with him in the house. One of them had a sexual encounter with his wife, while the other had a sexual encounter with his sister. The one who had the sexual encounter with his wife—'the righteous shall pass along them.' And as to the one who had a sexual encounter with his sister.— 'but the transgressors will stumble in them'"

But are the cases comparable to the verse of Scripture? Scripture speaks of a single path in which righteous and wicked walk, but here there are two paths [one being legal the other not]. Rather, the matter may be compared to the case of Lot and his two daughters. Those who had sexual relations to carry out a religious duty [to be fruitful and multiply]—"the righteous shall pass along them." And as to the one who had sexual relations in order to perform a transgression—"but the transgressors will stumble in them"

But maybe he too had in mind to fulfill the commandment?

Said R. Yohanan, "The entire verse of Scripture is formulated to express the intention of committing a transgression, as it is said, 'And Lot lifted his eyes and saw the entire plain of the Jordan that it was well watered' (Gen. 13:10).

"[The sense of 'lifted' derives from, 'And his master's wife lifted her eyes toward Joseph and said, Lay with me' (Gen. 39:7).

"'. . . his eyes . . .': 'And Samson said, Take her for me, as she is beautiful in my eyes' (Judg. 14:3).

"'And saw . . .': 'And Shekhem, son of Hamor . . . saw her and took her and lay with her and abused her' (Gen. 34:2).

"'the entire plain of the Jordan . . .': 'For a whore can be had for the price of a loaf of bread' (Prov. 6:326). [The Hebrew words for plain and loaf being the same.]

"'that it was well watered . . .': 'I will go after my lovers, who provide my bread and water, my wool and flax, my oil and my drink' (Hos. 2:7)."

But wasn't he drunk anyhow, so he really was forced into the act!

Tannaite statement in the name of R. Yosé b. R. Honi, "Why are there dots about the word 'and' in the verse, 'and when the elder daughter arose' (Gen. 19:33)? It tells you that when she lay down with him, he didn't know what was going on, but when she got up, he knew."

So what was he supposed to do? What was was.

The point is that the next night, he shouldn't have gotten drunk [to get involved with the younger daughter.

BAVLI TO MISHNAH-TRACTATE HORAYOT 3:3

Reward of Carrying Out God's Will

The reward for doing God's will is another occasion to do God's will. For the right deed done for the right reason can only multiply itself.

It has been taught on Tannaite authority:

Said R. Nathan, "You have not got even the most minor religious duty specified in the Torah, the reward of which is not enjoyed in this world, but as to the world to come, I do not even know how great it is. Go and learn that lesson from the religious duty of the show fringes [See Num. 15:37-41]."

"There was the case of a man who was meticulous about observing the religious duty of show fringes.

"He heard that there was a whore in one of the cities by the sea, who gets a fee of four hundred gold pieces for her services. He sent her four hundred gold pieces and made a date with her.

"When the date came, he came and sat down at the door of her whorehouse. Her slave girl went in and told her, 'That man who sent you the four hundred gold pieces has arrived and is sitting at the door.'

"She said, 'Let him come in.'"

"He came in. She laid out for him a pile of seven beds, six of silver, one of gold, and between each one was a silver ladder, and the top one was of gold. She went up and took her place on top of the top one, completely nude. He too came up on the ladders to take his place, completely nude, at her side. [But as he was removing his garments], the four show fringes came out and slapped his face.

"He slipped off and sat down on the ground, and she too slipped off and sat down on the ground.

"She said to him, "By the Roman capital! I am not letting you go until you tell me what flaw you saw in me!"

"He said to her," "By the Temple service! I never saw a more beautiful woman than you in my whole life. But there is a certain religious duty that the Lord, who is our God, commanded us, and it is called show fringes. And in that connection it is written, "I am the Lord your God" (Num. 15:41) two times. The meaning is, "I am the one who is going to exact punishment from you, and I am the one who is going to pay a good reward." Now these show fringes appeared to me like four witnesses [to that oath of God].'

"She said to him, "I am not letting you go until you tell me what is your name and the name of your town and the name of your master and the name of the study hall where you have learned the Torah."

"He wrote it all down and put it in her hand. She went and split up all her property, a third to the government, a third to the poor, and a third she took in hand, along with those beds." She came to the study house of R. Hiyya. She said to him, "My lord, give orders concerning me so that they will make me a proselyte."

"He said to her, "My daughter, is it possible that you have laid eyes on one of the disciples?'

"She took out the slip of paper in her hand and gave it to him.

"He said to her, 'Go and take possession of what you have purchased.'

"Those very same beds that she had spread out for him when prohibited did she now spread out for him when permitted.

"This then is the meaning of giving the reward in this world, but as to the world to come, I do not even know how great it is."

BAVLI TO MISHNAH-TRACTATE MENAHOT 4:4

Riddles

Somebody said, "I leave a barrel of dust to one of my sons, a barrel of bones to the next, a barrel of fluff to the third."

They hadn't the slightest idea what he meant, so they asked R. Benaah. He said to them, "Do you have any land?"

"Yup."

"Do you have any cattle?"

"Yup."

"Do you have any cushions?"

"Yup."

"So that's what he meant."

There was a man who heard his wife say to her daughter, "Why don't you be more discrete about your love affairs? I have ten children, and only one of them is from your father."

When he was dying, he said to them, "All of my property is to go to one son." They didn't know which one he meant, so they asked R. Benaah.

He said to them, "Go, knock at the grave of your father until he gets up and tells you which one of you he means."

So they all went to do so, but the one who really was his son did not go. R. Benaah said, "The whole estate belongs to that one."

So they went and reported him to the state, saying, "There is among the Jews someone who extorts money from people without witnesses or any other evidence."

So they took him and threw him in jail.

His wife came and said, "I had a slave, and some people have chopped off his head, skinned him, eaten the meat, filled the skin with water, and given disciples of sages water to drink from it, and they didn't pay me the price or the rent."

They didn't know what to make of such a story, so they said, "Let's get the wise men of the Jews, and he will tell us."

They called R. Benaah, and he said to them, "She means a goat skin bottle." They said, "Since he is such a wise man, let him sit in the gate at the tribunal and judge cases."

He saw an inscription over the gateway: "Any judge who is sued in court is not worthy of the name of judge."

He said to them, "If that is so, then anybody in the street come come and sue the judge and disqualify him. What it should say, obviously, is 'Any judge who is sued in court and against whom judgment is laid down is not really a judge.'"

They therefore added, "But the elders of the Jews say, 'Any judge who is sued in court and against whom judgment is laid down is not really a judge.'" He saw another inscription, "At the head of all death am I, blood; at the head of all life am I, wine."

[But, he said,] "If someone falls from a roof or date tree and is killed, is this death from too much blood? And if he is dying, do they give him wine to drink? Not at all. What it should say is this: 'At the head of all sickness am I, blood, at the head of all medicine am I, wine.'"

They amended the plaque: "But the elders of the Jews say, 'At the head of all sickness am I, blood, at the head of all medicine am I, wine. Only where there is no wine are drugs needed.'"

Bavli to Mishnah-Tractate Baba Batra 3:5

Ridiculing Sinners

R. Meir would ridicule sinners. One day Satan appeared to him on the opposite side of a canal in the form of a woman. There being no ferry, he grabbed a rope and got across. As he had reached half way down the rope, [temptation] released him, saying, "If they had not accounted in Heaven, 'Watch out for R. Meir and his Torah learning,' I would not have valued your life for two *maahs*."

R. Aqiba would ridicule sinners. One day Satan appeared to him on the top of a palm tree in the form of a woman. He was climbing up, until he got half way up the palm tree, when [temptation] released him, saying, "If they had not accounted in Heaven, 'Watch out for R. Aqiba and his Torah learning,' I would not have valued your life for two *maahs*."

Every day Pelimo would be accustomed to say, "An arrow in the eyes of Satan." One day, the eve of the Day of Atonement, Satan appeared to him in the guise of a poor man. He came and called at the door. They brought food out to him. He said to him, "On a day such as this, when everybody is inside, should I be outside?"

They brought him in and served food to him.

He said to them, "On such a day, when everybody is at the table, should I sit all by myself?"

They brought him in and seated him at the table.

While he was sitting there, his body was covered with [Freedman:] suppurating sores, and he conducted himself in a disgusting way. He said to him, "Sit nicely."

He said to him, "Give me a cup of wine."

They gave a cup of wine to him. He coughed and spit the phlegm into it. They yelled at him. He fainted and died. They heard people saying, "Pelimo has killed a man, Pelimo has killed a man."

He fled, hiding out in a privy. [Satan] followed him in and Pelimo fell before him. When he saw how troubled he was, he revealed himself to him. He said to him, "How come you go around saying this and that?"

"So how am I supposed to talk?"

He said to him, "May the All-Merciful rebuke Satan."

R. Hiyya bar Ashi was accustomed, whenever he prostrated himself to his face, to say, "May the All-Merciful save us from the Evil Impulse."

Once his wife heard this. She said, "Now how many years he has kept away from me, so how come he says this?"

One day he was studying in his garden, and she dressed up [in disguise] and walked back and forth before him. He said to her, "How are you?"

She said to him, "I'm Haruta [the famous whore], and I've come back today."

He lusted after her. She said to him, "Bring me that pomegranate from the top bough."

He climbed up and got it for her. When he went back inside his house, his wife was heating the oven, so he climbed up and sat down in it. She said to him, "So what's going on?"

He told her what had happened. She said to him, "So it was really me." But he wouldn't believe her until she gave him the pomegranate.

He said to her, "Well, anyhow, my intention was to do what is prohibited."

For the rest of the life of that righteous man he fasted [in penitence] until he died on that account.

BAVLI TO QIDDUSHIN 4:12/81A-B

The Rights of Others

Our sages deliver their wisdom not only through sayings about every-day matters but also, and especially, through the laws that they make to cover situations of conflict. Indeed, if we were to ask the sages where, in their judgment, they make their normative statements, they would point us to the law, rather than to their wisdom stories and say-ings. And they would insist that it is in the concrete and the everyday that true wisdom inheres: the wisdom that leads to a law adjudicat-ing conflict in one way, rather than in some other. Fairness and equity—legal categories—form judgments on what not only right and wrong but wise and stupid. For in the end, foresight and prudence, traits of wisdom, will be realized in concrete rulings. That is why we include the following account of how sages make concrete and specific the general principle of wisdom, in this case, the Golden Rule of Lev. 19:18 and Hillel, "What is hateful to yourself do not do to others. That is the whole Torah. All the rest is commentary. Now, go, study." Here what is hateful is the use of one's property in a manner that neighbors will find obnoxious. That is not only unfair—it also will lead to ha-tred, the disintegration of community.

One may not dig (1) a cistern near the cistern of his fellow,
nor (2) a ditch, (3) cave, (4) water channel, or (5) laundry pool,
unless one set it three handbreadths away from the wall of his fellow,
and plastered it with plaster [to retain the water].
They set (1) olive refuse, (2) manure, (3) salt, (4) lime, or (5) stones
three handbreadths from the wall of one's fellow,
and plaster it with plaster.
They set (1) seeds, (2) a plough, and (3) urine three handbreadths
from a wall.
And they set (1) a hand mill three handbreadths from the lower
millstone, which is four from the upper millstone;
and (2) the oven so that the wall is three handbreadths from the belly
of the oven, or four from the rim.

A person should not set up an oven in a room,
unless there is a space of four cubits above it.
[If] he was setting it up in the upper story, there has to be a layer of
plaster under it three handbreadths thick,
and in the case of a stove, a handbreadth thick.

And if it did damage, [the owner of the oven] has to pay for the damage.

R. Simeon says, "All of these measures have been stated only so that if [the object] inflicted damage, [the owner] is exempt from paying compensation [if the stated measures have been observed]."

A person should not open a bake shop or a dyer's shop under the granary of his fellow,

nor a cattle stall.

To be sure, in the case of wine they permitted doing so,

but not [building] a cattle stall [under the wine cellar].

As to a shop in the courtyard,

a person may object and tell [the shopkeeper], "I cannot sleep because of the noise of people coming in and the noise of people going out."

One may [however] make utensils [and] go out and sell them in the market.

Truly one has not got the power to object and to say, "I cannot sleep because of the noise of the hammer,

"the noise of the millstones,

"or the noise of the children."

MISHNAH-TRACTATE BABA BATRA 2:1-4

Say Little, Do Much

Wisdom knows the difference between boasting and actually doing, and honors those who don't promise but deliver. That is the highest virtue.

Say little and do much: How so?

This teaches that righteous people say little but do much, while wicked people say much and even a little bit they scarcely accomplish.

How do we know that righteous people say little but do much?

We find in the case of our father, Abraham, that he said to the angels, "You shall eat bread with me today," for it is said, "And I will fetch a morsel of bread and satisfy your hunger" (Gen. 18:5).

But in the end see what Abraham did for the ministering angels! He went and prepared for them three oxen and nine *seahs* of fine flour.

So too the Holy One, blessed be he, said little but did much.

For it is said, "And the Lord said to Abram, 'Know with certainty that you seed will be a stranger in a land that does not belong to them and shall serve them and they shall afflict them four hundred years and also that nation whom they shall serve will I punish and afterward they shall come out with great substance'" (Gen. 15:13f).

He said to them only [that he would punish them] by means of his name, "the Lord."

but in the end, when the Holy One, blessed be he, exacted punishment from Israel's enemies, he exacted punishment only with the name of seventy-two letters.

For it is said, "Or has God tried to go and take him a nation from the midst of another nation, by trials, by signs, and by wonders ... and by great terrors" (Deut. 4:34).

Lo we learn that when the Holy One, blessed be he, exacted punishment from Israel's enemies, he exacted punishment only with the name of seventy-two letters.

THE FATHERS ACCORDING TO RABBI NATHAN XIII:I-II

Seeing God

What, exactly, do people see when they see God? Wisdom deals with challenges to faith coming from those who seek palpable and tangible proof, to see God in a very literal way.

Said Caesar to R. Joshua b. Hananiah, "Your God is like a lion. As it is stated, 'The lion has roared; who will not fear? [The Lord God has spoken; who can but prophesy?]' (Amos 3:8)." What is exceptional about this? Any horseman can kill a lion. He [Joshua] said to him, "He is not like any lion. He is like the lion of Be Ilai."

He said to him, "You must show it to me."

He [Joshua] said to him, "You cannot see it. [That lion is too terrifying.]"

He said to him, "Really! Show it to me!"

He [Joshua] prayed.

It was uprooted from its place [and started to be transported toward them]. When it was four hundred *parasangs* away it gave out a single roar. All of the pregnant women of Rome miscarried [from fright] and all the walls fell down [from the vibrations]. When it was three hundred *parasangs* away it gave out another roar. All of the teeth of the people [of Rome] fell out [of their mouths from the impact of the sound]. And he [Caesar] himself fell from his throne to the ground.

He said to him [Joshua], "I beg you. Pray that it go back to its place."
He prayed and it went back to its place.

The Caesar said to R. Joshua b. Hananiah, "I want to see your God."

He said to him, "You cannot see Him." He said to him, "Really! Show him to me!" He went and pointed him towards the sun during the season of Tammuz [i.e., the summer]. He [Joshua] said to him, "Look at it."

He said, "I cannot."

He said, "The sun is one of the attendants that attend the Holy One, blessed be he. You say you cannot look at it. All the more [is it impossible to look at] the Divine Presence."

The Caesar said to R. Joshua b. Hananiah, "I want to make a dinner for your God."

He said to him, "You cannot."

[He asked,] "Why not?"

[He said,] "Because he has too many in his entourage." [He said,] "Really! [I insist!]"

[He said,] "Go set it up on the widest banks of the great sea." He worked for the six months of the summer [preparing the dinner]. A storm came up and washed it all into the sea. He worked for the six months of the winter. The rains came and washed it all into the sea. He said to him, "What is the meaning of this?" He [Joshua] said to him, "These [storms] are like the [workers] who sweep and wash in preparation for his arrival." He said to him, "If that is the case, then I cannot do it."

The daughter of the Caesar said [mockingly] to R. Joshua b. Hananiah, "Your God must be a carpenter. For it is written, 'Who hast laid the beams of thy chambers on the waters, [who makest the clouds thy chariot, who ridest on the wings of the wind]' (Ps. 104:3). Tell him to make a spool for me."

He said, "On my life!" He prayed and she was smitten with leprosy. They took her into the marketplace of Rome and they brought her a spool. For it was the custom that in Rome they brought a spool to anyone who was smitten with leprosy. And they sat her in the marketplace and she wound skeins of yarn so that people would see this and pray for her. One day he [Joshua] was passing there and she was sitting and winding skeins of yarn in the marketplace of Rome. He said to her, "Did my God give you a good spool?"

She said to him, "Tell your God to take back what he gave me."

He said to her, "Our God gives but does not take back."

BAVLI TO MISHNAH-TRACTATE HULLIN 3:6-7/59B-60A

Self-Celebration

It is difficult, given the sages' sharp remonstrations against pride, to find anywhere examples of self-celebration. Yet here we have two statements, one declarative and the other metaphorical, that show how humility and celebration of Torah are consistent.

R. Sadoq says, "Do not make [Torah teachings] a crown in which to glorify yourself or a spade with which to dig. So did Hillel say, 'He who uses the crown perishes.' Thus have you learned: Whoever derives worldly benefit from teachings of the Torah takes his life out of this world."

R. Yosé says, "Whoever honors the Torah himself is honored by people. And whoever disgraces the Torah himself is disgraced by people."

TRACTATE ABOT 4:5-6

The people of Simonia came before Rabbi. They said to him, "We want you to give us a man to serve as preacher, judge, reader [of Scripture], teacher [of tradition], and to do all the things we need." He gave them Levi bar Sisi.

They set up a great stage and seated him on it. They came and asked him, "A woman without arms—with what does she remove the shoe?" And he did not answer.

If she spit blood...?

And he did not answer.

They said, "Perhaps he is not a master of the law. Let us ask him something about lore."

They came and asked him, "What is the meaning of the following verse, as it is written, 'But I will tell you what is inscribed in the book, in truth' (Dan. 10:21). If it is truth, why is it described as inscribed? And if it is inscribed, why is it described as truth?"

He did not answer them.

They came back to Rabbi and said to him, "Is this a mason of your mason's guild [a pupil of your school] ?"

He said to them, "By your lives! I gave you someone who is as good as I am."

He sent and summoned him and asked him. He said to him, "If the woman spit blood, what is the law?"

He answered him, "If there is a drop of spit in it, it is valid."

"A woman without arms—how does she remove the shoe?"

He said to him, "She removes the shoe with her teeth."

He said to him, "What is the meaning of the following verse, as it is written, 'But I will tell you what is inscribed in the book, in truth' (Dan. 10:21). If it is truth, why is it described as inscribed, and if it is inscribed, why is it described as truth?"

He said to him, "Before a decree is sealed, it is described as inscribed. Once it is sealed, it is described as truth."

He said to him, "And why did you not answer the people when they asked you these same questions?"

He said to him, "They made a great stage and seated me on it, and my spirit became exalted."

He recited concerning him the following verse of Scripture: "'If you have been foolish, exalting yourself, or if you have been de–vising evil, put your hand on your mouth' (Prov. 30:32).

"What caused you to make a fool of yourself in regard to teachings of Torah? It was because you exalted yourself through them."

YERUSHALMI YEBAMOT 12:6

Self-Respect

What follows is the single most famous saying in the entire corpus of Rabbinic wisdom writings. Hillel captures all of the paradox of virtue: what we owe ourselves, what we owe others, and when we must pay up.

Hillel would say: "If I am not for myself, who is for me? And when I am for myself, what am I? And if not now, when?"

TRACTATE ABOT 1:14

Sharing

Wisdom finds solutions to conflict, such that all parties are treated in a fair and equitable manner. Here is another case in which wisdom spells over into law, so that moral norms are recast into legal rulings.

Two [terraced] gardens, one above the other, and vegetables between them—

R. Meir says, "[They belong to the garden] on top."

R. Judah says, "[They belong to the garden] below."

Said R. Meir, "If the one on top wants to take away his dirt, there will not be any vegetables there."

R Said R. Judah, "If the one on the bottom wants to fill up his garden with dirt, there won't be any vegetables there."

Said R. Meir, "Since each party can stop the other, they consider from whence the vegetables derive sustenance [which is from the dirt (E)]."

Said R. Simeon, "Any [vegetables] which the one on top can reach out and pick—lo, these are his. And the rest belong to the one down below."

MISHNAH-TRACTATE BABA MESIA 10:6

Sin Because of Prosperity

Sin comes about for diverse reasons, both private and public, but the single most common cause of sin is prosperity. That is when we regard ourselves as invincible and do what we like, rather than what God commands and wisdom counsels.

". . . and thus you shall eat your fill. Take care not to be lured away to serve other gods and bow to them. [For the Lord's anger will flare up against you, and he will shut up the skies so that there be no rain and the ground will not yield its produce; and you will soon perish from the good land that the Lord is assigning to you]" (Deut. 11:13–17):

He said to them, "Take care lest you rebel against the Omnipresent. For a person rebels against the Omnipresent only in prosperity."

For so it is said, "Lest when you have eaten and are satisfied and have built large houses and lived in them, and when your herds and your flocks multiply, and your silver and your gold (Deut. 8:12–13).

What then? "Then your heart be lifted up and you forget the Lord your God" (Deut. 8:14).

Along these same lines: "For when I shall have brought them into the land which I swore to their fathers, flowing with milk and honey" (Deut. 31:20).

What then? "And turned to other gods and served them" (Deut. 31:20).

Along these same lines: "And the people sat down to eat and to drink" (Exod. 32:6).

What then? "They have made a molten calf" (Exod. 32:8).

Along these same lines in connection with the men of the generation of the flood, they rebelled against the Omnipresent only in prosperity.

What is said in their regard? "Their houses are safe, without fear . . . their bull genders, they send forth their little ones like a flock . . . they spend their days in prosperity" (Job. 21:9–13).

This is what made them act as they did: "Depart from us, we do not desire knowledge of your ways. What is the almighty that we should serve him" (Job 21:14–15).

They said, "Not even for a drop of rain do we need him, for 'There goes up a mist from the earth' (Gen. 2:6)."

Said to them the Omnipresent, "In the very act of goodness which I have done for you, you take pride before me? Through that same act I shall exact a penalty from you."

"And the rain was upon the earth forty days and forty nights" (Gen. 7:12).

R. Yosé of Damascus says, "Since they set their eyes both above and below to express their lust. So the Omnipresent opened up against them the springs above and below so as to destroy them.

"For so it is said, 'All the fountains of the great deep were broken up and the windows of Heaven were opened' (Gen. 7:11)."

And along these same lines, you found in connection with the men of the tower [of Babel], that they rebelled against the Omnipresent only in prosperity.

What is said in their regard? "And the whole earth was of one language and one speech, and it came to pass, as they journeyed east, they found a plain in the land of Shinar, and they dwelt there" (Gen. 11:1–3).

And the sense of "dwelling" used here is solely eating and drinking, along the lines of this usage: "And the people sat down to eat and drink and arose to play" (Exod. 32:6).

That is what made them say, "Come let us build us a city" (Gen. 11:4).

What is said in their regard? "So the Lord scattered them abroad from thence upon the face of all the earth" (Gen. 11:8).

And along these same lines, you found in connection with the men of Sodom, that they rebelled against the Omnipresent only in prosperity.

What is said in their regard? "As for the earth out of it comes bread . . . the stones of it are the place of sapphires . . . that path no bird of prey knows . . . the proud beasts have not trodden it" (Job 28:5–8).

The men of Sodom said, "Lo, we have food near at hand, lo, we have silver and gold near and hand. Let us go and wipe out the law of [protecting] the wayfarer from our land."

Said to them the Omnipresent, "On account of the act of goodness that I did for you, you want to wipe out the law of [protecting] the way-farer from among you. I shall wipe out the memory of you yourselves from the world."

What is said in their regard? "He breaks open a shaft away from where men sojourn" (Job 28:4).

"A contemptible brand . . . the tents of robbers prosper, and they that provoke God are secure" (Job. 12:5).

That is what made them rebel, namely, "Whatsoever God brings into their hand" (Job 12:6).

And so Scripture says, "'As I live,' says the Lord God, 'Sodom your sister has not done . . . as you have done . . . . Behold, this was the in-iquity of your sister Sodom . . . neither did she strengthen the hand of the poor and needy, and they were haughty'" (Ezek. 16:48–50).

Along these same lines, Scripture says, "[And Lot lifted up his eyes and behold, all the plain of the Jordan,] well-watered everywhere" (Gen. 13:10).

What is the meaning of the verse, "And they made their father drink wine" (Gen. 19:33)?

Where did they get wine in the cave?

They just happened to find it, in line with this verse: "And it shall come to pass on that day that the mountains shall drip sweet wine" (Joel 4:18).

If that is how he provides for those who anger him, all the more so for those who carry out his will.

SIFRÉ TO DEUTERONOMY XLIII:III

A Single Action Counts

Whoever does a single commandment—they do well for him and lengthen his days and his years and he inherits the Land.

And whoever commits a single transgression—they do ill to him and cut off his days, and he does not inherit the Land.

(And concerning such a person it is said, "One sinner destroys much good" (Qoh. 9: 18).

By a single sin this one destroys many good things.

A person should always see himself as if he is half meritorious and half guilty.

[If] he did a single commandment, happy is he, for he has inclined the balance for himself to the side of merit.

[If] he committed a single transgression, woe is he, for he has inclined the balance to the side of guilt.

Concerning this one it is said, One sinner destroys much good.

By a single sin this one has destroyed many good things.

R. Simeon b. Eleazar says in the name of R. Meir, "Because the individual is judged by his majority [of deeds], the world is judged by its majority.

"And [if] one did one commandment, happy is he, for he has inclined the balance for himself and for the world to the side of merit.

"[If] he committed one transgression, woe is he, for he has inclined the balance for himself and for the world to the side of guilt.

"And concerning such a person it is said, One sinner destroys much good—

"By the single sin which this one committed, he destroyed for himself and for the world many good things."

R. Simeon says, "[If] a man was righteous his entire life but at the end he rebelled, he loses the whole, since it is said, The righteousness of the righteous shall not deliver him when he transgresses (Ezek. 33:12).

"[If] a man was evil his entire life but at the end he repented, the Omnipresent accepts him,

"as it is said, 'And as for the wickedness of the wicked, he shall not fall by it when he turns from his wickedness land the righteous shall not be able to live by his righteousness when he sins' (Ezek. 33:12)."

Whoever occupies himself with all three of them, with Scripture, Mishnah, and good conduct,

concerning such a person it is said, And a threefold cord is not quickly broken (Qoh. 5:12).

TOSEFTA QIDDUSHIN 1:10

Slander

Slander is gossip in its most malevolent form—out-and-out lies about the other. If gossip tears down the defenses of society, the protections for the individual and his or her good name, slander obliterates them. That is why slander is tantamount to murder.

Said R. Samuel bar Nahman, "They said to the snake, 'On what account are you commonly found among fences?'

"He said to them, 'Because I broke down the fence of the world [causing man to sin].'

"'On what account do you go along with your tongue on the ground?'

"He said to them, 'Because my tongue made it happen to me.'

"They said to him, 'Now what pleasure do you have from it all? A lion tramples but also devours the prey, a wolf tears but also devours, while you bite and kill but do not devour what you kill.'

"He said to them, '"Does the snake bite without a charm" (Qoh. 10:11)? Is it possible that I do anything that was not commanded to me from on high?

"'And on what account do you bite a single limb, while all the limbs feel it?'

"He said to them, 'Now are you saying that to me? Speak to the slanderer, who says something here and kills his victim in Rome, says something in Rome and kills his victim at the other end of the world.'"

And why is the slanderer called "the third party"?
Because he kills three: the one who speaks slander, the one who receives it, and the one about whom it is said.
But in the time of Saul, slander killed four: Doeg, who said it, Saul, who received it, Abimelech, about whom it was said, and Abner.

And why was Abner killed?
R. Joshua b. Levi said, "Because he made a joke out of the shedding of the blood of young men.
"That is in line with this verse of Scripture: 'And Abner said to Joab, "let the young men get up and play before us"' (1 Sam. 2:14)."
R. Simeon b. Laqish said, "Because he put his name before David's name.
"That is in line with this verse of Scripture: 'And Abner sent messengers to David right away, saying, "Whose is the land"' (1 Sam. 3:12).
"He wrote, 'From Abner to David.'"
Rabbis say, "It was because he did not wait for Saul to become reconciled with David.
"That is in line with the following verse of Scripture: 'Moreover, my father, see, yes, see the skirt of your robe in my hand' (1 Sam. 24:112). Abner said to him, 'What do you want of this man's boasting! The cloth was caught in a thorn-bush.'

"When they came within the barricade, he said to him, 'Will you not answer, Abner (1 Sam. 26:14).'"

And there are those who say, "It was because he had had the power to protest against Saul in regard to Nob, the city of priests, and he did not do so."

PESIQTA DERAB KAHANA IV:II

Sloth

Laziness wastes life. It is a form of self-indulgence, and in the end ruins all ambition and denies all hope.

R. Dosa b. Harkinas says, Sleeping late in the morning, drinking wine at noon, chatting with children, and attending the synagogues of the ignorant drive a man out of the world.

Sleeping late in the morning: how so?

This teaches that a person should not intend to sleep until the time of reciting the Shema has passed.

For when someone sleeps until the time for reciting the Shema has passed, he turns out to waste time that should be spent studying the Torah.

As it is said, "The lazy one says, There is a lion in the way, yes, a lion is in the streets. The door is turning on its hinges and the lazy man is still in bed" (Prov. 26:13–14).

Drinking wine at noon: how so?

This teaches that someone should not plan to drink wine at night.

For when someone drinks wine at noon, he turns out to waste time that should be spent studying the Torah.

As it is said, "Woe to you, O land, when your king is a boy and your princes feast in the morning" (Qoh. 10:16).

And further: "Happy are you, O land, when your king is a free man, and your princes eat in due season, in strength and not in drunkenness" (Qoh. 10:17).

What is the meaning of in due season ? One must say, this refers to the coming age, as it is said, "I the Lord will hasten it in its time" (Isa. 60:22).

And further: "After a lapse of time like this shall it be said of Jacob and of Israel, O what God has done" (Num. 23:23).

So did the Holy One, blessed be he, say to the wicked Balaam, "After a period of time like this—but not now, not while you are standing among them, but at the time that I am going to carry out redemption for Israel [Goldin: will their king be free and prophecy be restored]."

Chatting with children: how so?

This teaches that a person should not plan to sit by himself and repeat traditions at home.

For if someone sits by himself and repeats traditions at home, he chats with his children and dependents and turns out to waste time that should be spend in the study of the Torah.

For it is said, This book of the Torah shall not depart out of your mouth, but you shall meditate in it day and night (Josh. 1:8).

And attending the synagogues of the ignorant drive a man out of the world: how so?

This teaches that a person should not plan to join with the idle in the corners of the marketplace.

For if someone sits around with the idle in the corners of the marketplace, he turns out to waste time that he should spend in studying the Torah.

For so it is said, "Happy is the one who has not walked in the counsel of the wicked, stood in the way of the sinners, or sat in the seat of the scornful . . . But his delight is in the Torah of the Lord" (Ps. 1:1–2).

R. Meir says, "What is the meaning of the statement, sat in the seat of the scornful ?

"This refers to the theaters and circuses of the Gentiles, in which people are sentenced to death,

"as it is said, 'I hate the gathering of evil doers and will not sit with the wicked' (Ps. 26:5).

"The word evil doers refers only to the wicked, as it is said, "For the evil doers shall be cut off, and yet a little while and the wicked is no more" (Ps. 37:9–10).

"And what will be the form of the punishment that is coming to them in time to come?

"For behold the day comes, it burns as a furnace, and all the proud and all that do wickedness shall be stubble (Mal. 3:19).

"And the proud are only the scorners, as it is said, A proud and haughty man—scorner is his name (Prov. 21:24)."

There was the case of R. Aqiba who was in session and repeating teachings for his disciples. He remembered something that he had done in his youth.

He said, "I give thanks for you, O Lord my God, that you have placed my portion among those who sit in the house of study and have not placed my portion with those who sit idly in the marketplace."

THE FATHERS ACCORDING TO RABBI NATHAN XXI:I-V

The Soul

Definition by analogy—a common logical step taken by the sages—is here used at its most compelling levels. Discussing a weighty subject, the sages make clear their point not once, but several times.

Why did the soul of David praise the Holy One, blessed be he?

David said, "Just as the soul fills the body, so the Holy One, blessed be he, fills the whole world, as it is written, 'Do I not fill the entire Heaven and earth? says the Lord' (Jer. 23:24). So let the soul, which fills the body, come and praise the Holy One, blessed be he, who fills the world.

"The soul supports the body, the Holy One [blessed be he] supports the world, for it is written, 'Even to your old age I am he, and to gray hairs [I will carry you]' (Isa. 46:4). So let the soul, which supports the body, come and praise the Holy One, blessed be he, who supports the world.

"The soul outlasts the body, and the Holy One, blessed be he, outlasts the world: 'They will perish, but you do endure, they will all wear out like a garment. [You change them like a garment and they pass away, but you are the same, and your years have no end]' (Ps. 102:26–27). So let the soul, which outlasts the body, come and praise the Holy One, blessed be he, who outlasts the world.

"The soul in the body does not eat, and as to the Holy One, blessed be he, there is no eating so far as he is concerned, as it is written, 'If I were hungry, I would not tell you, for the world and all that is in it is mine' (Ps. 50:12). Let the soul in the body, which does not eat, come and praise the Holy One, blessed be he, before whom there is no eating.

"The soul is singular in the body, and the Holy One, blessed be he, is singular in his world, as it is said, 'Hear, O Israel, the Lord our God is a singular Lord' (Deut. 6:4). Let the soul, which is singular in the body, come and praise the Holy One, blessed be he, who is singular in his world.

"The soul is pure in the body, and the Holy One, blessed be he, is pure in his world: 'You who are of eyes too pure to behold evil' (Hab. 1:13). Let the soul, which is pure in the body, come and praise the Holy One, blessed be he, which is pure in his world.

"The soul sees but is not seen, and the Holy One, blessed be he, sees but is not seen, as it is written, '[Am I a God at hand says the Lord, and not a God afar off?] Can a man hide himself in secret places so that I cannot see him? says the Lord. Do I not fill Heaven [and earth? says the Lord]' (Jer. 23:23–24). Let the soul, which sees but is not seen, come and praise the Holy One, blessed be he, who sees but is not seen.

"The soul does not sleep in the body, and the Holy One, blessed be he, is not subject to sleep, as it is said, 'Lo, the Guardian of Israel neither slumbers nor sleeps' (Ps. 121:4). Let the soul, which does not sleep in the body, come and praise the Holy One, blessed be he, who is not subject to sleep: 'Lo, he slumbers not nor sleeps.'"

LEVITICUS RABBAH IV:VIII

Our rabbis have taught on Tannaite authority:
"And the dust return to the earth as it was and the spirit returns to God" (Qoh. 12:7)—
Give it back to him: Just as it was given to you, in purity, so give it back to him in purity.
The matter may be compared to the case of a mortal king who divided up royal garments among his staff. The intelligent ones among them folded them up and laid them away in a chest. The stupid ones went and did their daily work in them. Some time later the king wanted his garments back. The intelligent ones among them returned them to him immaculate. The stupid ones returned them dirty. The king was pleased to greet the intelligent ones but angry with the stupid ones. To the intelligent ones he said, "Let the garments be sent back to storage, and they will go home in peace." On the stupid ones he said, "Let the garments be sent to the laundry, and let them be sent to prison."
So the Holy One, blessed be He, concerning the bodies of the righteous, says, "He enters into peace, they rest in their beds" (Isa. 57:2). Concerning their souls, he says, "Yet the soul of my lord shall be bound up in the bundle of life with the Lord your God" (1 Sam. 25:29). But of the bodies of the wicked he says, "There is no peace, says the Lord, for the wicked" (Isa. 58:22), and of their souls: "And the souls of your enemies, them shall he sling out, as from the hollow of a sling" (1 Sam. 25:29).

It has been taught on Tannaite authority:

R. Eliezer says, "The souls of the righteous are hidden away under the throne of glory: 'Yet the soul of my lord shall be bound up in the bundle of life with the Lord your God' (1 Sam. 25:29). And those of the wicked are kept in prison. One angel stands at one end of the world, and another angel stands at the other end of the world, and they sling their souls from one to the other: 'And the souls of your enemies, them shall he sling out, as from the hollow of a sling' (1 Sam. 25:29)."

Said Rabbah to R. Nahman, "So what about the middling ones?"

He said to him, "If I'd not died, I couldn't have told you this fact: This is what Samuel said, 'These and those [the souls of the middling and of the wicked] are handed over to Dumah. These get rest, those get no rest."

Said R. Mari, "The righteous are destined to be dust: 'And the dust return to the earth as it was' (Qoh. 12:7)."

Some grave-diggers were digging in the earth at R. Nahman's. R. Ahai bar Josiah snorted at them. They came and told R. Nahman, "Somebody snorted at us." He came and said to him, "Who are you?"

He said to him, "I am Ahai bar Josiah."

He said to him, "Well, didn't R. Mari say, 'The righteous are destined to be dust'?"

He said to him, "So who's Mari? I know nothing of him!"

He said to him, "But there is a verse of Scripture that makes the point: 'And the dust return to the earth as it was' (Qoh. 12:7)."

He said to him, "So whoever taught you the Scriptures of Qohelet didn't teach you the Scriptures of Proverbs, where it is written, 'but envy is the rottenness of the bones' (Prov. 14:30): Whoever has envy in his heart—his bones rot. Whoever has no envy in his heart—his bones don't rot."

[Nahman] touched him and saw that he was substantial. He said to him, "May the master rise and come to my house?"

He said to him, "You've shown that you haven't even studied the prophets: 'And you shall know that I am the Lord when I open your graves' (Ezek. 37:13)."

He said to him, "But isn't it also written, 'for dust you are and to dust you shall return' (Gen. 3:19)?"

He said to him, "That applies a moment before the resurrection of the dead."

Said a Sadducee to R. Abbahu, "You people say, the souls of the righteous are hidden under the throne of glory. Then how did the necromancer working with bones bring up Samuel through his necromancy (1 Sam. 28:7)?"

He said to him, "It was done within twelve months of death."

For it has been taught on Tannaite authority:

For the full twelve months after death, the body still endures, and the soul goes up and goes down. After twelve months, the body is null, and the soul goes up but doesn't go down again.

Said R. Judah b. R. Samuel bar Shila in the name of Rab, "On the basis of the funeral eulogy of a person, it is known whether he is destined to the world to come or not."

Well, now, is that so? But didn't Rab say to R. Samuel bar Shila, "Be enthusiastic in my eulogy, for I'll be standing right there on the spot!"

No problem, in the one case a warm-hearted eulogy is given and is found moving, in the other, a warm-hearted eulogy is given and is not found moving.

Said Abbayye, "For instance, the master, whom everybody in Pumbedita loathes—who in the world is going to give a moving eulogy for you?"

He said to him, "You and Rabbah bar R. Hanan will be quite sufficient, thank you very much."

R. Eleazar asked Rab, "Who is a person destined for the world to come?"

He said to him, "'And your ears shall hear a word behind you, saying, This is the way, walk in it; when you turn to the right hand and when you turn to the left' (Isa. 30:21)."

R. Hanina said, "It is any one with whom our masters are pleased."

BAVLI TO MISHNAH-TRACTATE SHABBAT 23:5/152A-153A

Status

Sages deemed all persons created equally responsible before God, but different in standing and achievement. They viewed society as a hierarchy, certain inherited, sacred tasks marking out one class of persons as higher than another. But at the same time, they insisted, the marks of status give way before the achievements of intellect, so that mastery of the Torah raises a person of low status and ignorance lowers a person of high status. In the end, therefore, status is not conferred, for instance by noble ancestry, but it is achieved by solid work in learning in the Torah.

A priest takes precedence over a Levite, a Levite over an Israelite, an Israelite over a *mamzer* [a person whose parents may not legally ever marry, e.g., brother and sister], a *mamzer* over a Netin [a descendant of the cast of Temple servants], a Netin over a proselyte, a proselyte over a freed slave.

Under what circumstances?

When all of them are equivalent.

But if the *mamzer* was a disciple of a sage and a high priest was an *am haares* [in context: ignorant of the Torah], the *mamzer* who is a disciple of a sage takes precedence over a high priest who is an *am haares*.

MISHNAH-TRACTATE HORAYOT 3:5

A sage takes precedence over a king; a king takes precedence over a high priest; a high priest takes precedence over a prophet; a prophet takes precedence over a priest anointed for war; a priest anointed for war takes precedence over the head of a priestly watch; the head of a priestly watch takes precedence over the head of a household [of priests]; the head of a household of priests takes precedence over the superintendent of the cashiers; the superintendent of the cashiers takes precedence over the Temple treasurer; the Temple treasurer takes precedence over an ordinary priest; an ordinary priest takes precedence over a Levite; a Levite takes precedence over an Israelite; an Israelite takes precedence over a *mamzer*; a *mamzer* takes precedence over a Netin; a Netin takes precedence over a proselyte; a proselyte takes precedence over a freed slave.

Under what circumstances? When all of them are equivalent.

But if the *mamzer* was a disciple of a sage, and a high priest was an ignoramus,

the *mamzer* who is the disciple of a sage takes precedence over a high priest who is an ignoramus.

A sage takes precedence over a king.

[For if a sage dies, we have none who is like him.

[If] a king dies, any Israelite is suitable to mount the throne.

TOSEFTA HORAYOT 2:8

The Straight Path in Life

No one loves correction, and the tough, demanding teacher is not seldom called "mean," though that is the teacher that asks most of the students and treats them with the highest expectations. The hard (not harsh) teacher is the one who gives the most and pays the highest compliment. And so in every other relationship in life.

It has been taught on Tannaite authority: Rabbi says, "What is the straight path that a person should choose? Love correction, for when correction comes into the world, serenity comes into the world, goodness and blessing come into the world, and evil takes its leave of the world, as it is said, 'Those who are corrected will be comforted, a good blessing shall come upon them' (Prov. 24:25)."

Some say, "One should strengthen himself with even an excess of faith, as it is said, 'My eyes are upon the faithful of the land so that they may sit with me' (Ps. 101:6)."

Said R. Samuel bar Nahmani said R. Jonathan, "Whoever corrects his fellow for the sake of Heaven gains the grace of a share with the Holy One, blessed be he, as it is said, 'One who corrects someone follows after me' (Prov. 28:23)."

"And, furthermore, a thread of mercy is tied to him: 'He who reproves someone will in the end find more flavor than a flatterer' (Prov. 28:23)."

BAVLI TO MISHNAH-TRACTATE TAMID 1:1

Rabbi says: "What is the straight path which a person should choose for himself? Whatever is an ornament to the one who follows it, and an ornament in the view of others. Be meticulous in a small religious duty as in a large one, for you do not know what sort of reward is coming for any of the various religious duties. And reckon with the loss [required] in carrying our a religious duty against the reward for doing it; and the reward for committing a transgression against the loss for doing it. And keep your eye on three things, so you will not come into the clutches of transgression. Know what is above you. An eye which sees, and an ear which hears, and all your actions are written down in a book."

TRACTATE ABOT 2:1

Rabban Yohanan ben Zakkai said to his disciples: "Go and see what is the straight path to which someone should stick."

Rabbi Eliezer says: "A generous spirit." Rabbi Joshua says: "A good friend." Rabbi Yosé says: "A good neighbor." Rabbi Simeon says: "Foresight." Rabbi Eleazar says: "Good will."

He said to them: "I prefer the opinion of Rabbi Eleazar ben Arakh, because in what he says is included everything you say."

He said to them: "Go out and see what is the bad road, which someone should avoid." Rabbi Eliezer says: "Envy." Rabbi Joshua says: "A bad friend." Rabbi Yosé says: "A bad neighbor." Rabbi Simeon says: "A loan." (All the same is a loan owed to a human being and a loan owed to the Omnipresent, the blessed, as it is said, "The wicked borrows and does not pay back, but the righteous person deals graciously and hands over [what is owed]." Ps. 37:21.)

Rabbi Eleazar says: "Ill will."

He said to them: "I prefer the opinion of Rabbi Eleazar ben Arakh, because in what he says is included everything you say."

TRACTATE ABOT 2:8-9

Suffering Is Beloved: God Tries the Righteous

Wisdom time and again returns to the subject of suffering and seeks sense and meaning in what violates the natural condition of comfort and long life. Suffering never comes to final solution, and no one in the end resolves the conflict between faith and fate, virtue and an easy path through life. But, wisdom maintains, when suffering comes, it is not necessarily a mark of disfavor or even of punishment for sin. It can be received as a sign of God's confidence and favor, and one may offer suffering upon the altar of God's service.

"The Lord tries the righteous, [but the wicked and him who loves violence his soul hates" (Ps. 11:5)]:

Said R. Jonathan, "A potter does not test a weak utensil, for if he hits it just once, he will break it. So the Holy One, blessed be he, does not test the wicked but the righteous: 'The Lord tries the righteous' (Ps. 11:5)."

Said R. Yosé bar Haninah, "When a flax maker knows that the flax is in good shape, then the more he beats it, the more it will improve and glisten. When it is not of good quality, if he beats it just once, he will split it. So the Holy One, blessed be he, does not try the wicked but the righteous: 'The Lord tries the righteous' (Ps. 11:5). "

Said R. Eleazar, "The matter may be compared to a householder who has two heifers, one strong, one weak. On whom does he place the yoke? It is on the one that is strong. So the Holy One, blessed be he, does not try the wicked but the righteous: 'The Lord tries the righteous' (Ps. 11:5).

Genesis Rabbah XXXIV:II

So does Job say, "The Lord gave and the Lord has taken away. Blessed be the name of the Lord" (Job 1:21).

That is the case for the measure of goodness.

As to the measure of punishment, what does his wife say to him? "Do you still hold fast your integrity? Blaspheme God and die" (Job 2:9).

And what does he say to her? "You speak as one of the impious women speaks. Shall we receive good at the hand of God and shall we not receive evil?" (Job 2:10).

"The men of the generation of the flood were churlish as to the good, and when punishment came upon them, they took it willy-nilly.

"The men of Sodom The men of the generation of the flood were churlish as to the good, and when punishment came upon them, they took it willy-nilly.

"And as to us, [is it not an argument *a fortiori*: if one who was churlish as to the good behaved with dignity in a time of punishment,] we who behave with dignity in response to good should surely behave with dignity in a time of trouble.

"And so did he said to her, 'You speak as one of the impious women speaks. Shall we receive good at the hand of God and shall we not receive evil?' (Job 2:10).

"And, furthermore, a person should rejoice in suffering more than in good times. For if someone lives in good times his entire life, he will not be forgiven for such sin as may be in his hand.

"And how shall he attain forgiveness? Through suffering."

R. Eliezer b. Jacob says, "Lo, Scripture says, 'For whom the Lord loves he corrects, even as a father corrects the son in whom he delights' (Prov. 3:12).

"What made the son be pleasing to the father? You must say it was suffering [on account of correction]."

R. Meir says, "'And you shall consider in your heart, that as a man chasten his son, so the Lord your God chastens you' (Deut. 8:5).

"'You know in your heart the deeds that you did, and also the suffering that I brought upon you, which was not in accord with the deeds that you did at all.'"

R. Yosé b. R. Judah says, "Beloved is suffering, for the name of the Omnipresent rests upon the one upon whom suffering comes,

"as it is said, 'So the Lord your God chastens you' (Deut. 8:5)."

R. Jonathan says, "Beloved is suffering, for just as a covenant is made through the land, so a covenant is made through suffering, as it is said, 'The Lord, your God" chastens you' (Deut. 8:7).

"And it says, 'For the Lord your God brings you into a good land' (Deut. 8:7)."

R. Simeon b. Yohai says, "Suffering is precious. For through suffering three good gifts were given to Israel, which the nations of the world desire, and these are they: the Torah, the land of Israel, and the world to come.

"How do we know that that is the case for the Torah? As it is said, 'To know wisdom and chastisement' (Prov. 1:2). And it is said, 'Happy is the man whom you chastise O Lord and teach out of your Torah" (Ps. 94:12).

"How do we know that that is the case for the land of Israel? 'The Lord your God chastens you . . . for the Lord your God brings you into a good land' (Deut. 8:5, 7).

"How do we know that that is the case for the world to come? 'For the commandment is a lamp and the Torah is a light, and reproofs of chastisement are the way of life' (Prov. 6:23). What is the way that brings a person to the world to come? One must say it is suffering."

R. Nehemiah says, "Beloved is suffering, for just as offerings appease, so does suffering appease.

"In the case of offerings, Scripture says, 'And it shall be accepted for him to make atonement for him' (Lev. 1:4).

"And in the case of suffering: 'And they shall be paid the punishment for their iniquity' (Lev. 26:43).

"And not only so, but suffering appeases more than do offerings. For offerings are a matter of property, but suffering, of one's own body.

"And so Scripture says, 'Skin for skin, yes, all that a man has will he give for his life' (Job 2:4)."

Now when R. Eliezer was sick, four sages, R. Tarfon, R. Joshua, R. Eleazar b. Azariah, and R. Aqiba, came to visit him.

Responded and said to him R. Tarfon, "My lord, you are more precious to Israel than the sun's orb. For the sun's orb gives light to this world, but you give light to us in this world and the world to come."

Responded and said to him R. Joshua, "My lord, you are more precious to Israel than the gift of rain, for rain gives life in this world, but you give life to us in this world and the world to come."

Responded and said to him R. Eleazar b. Azariah, "My lord, you are more precious to Israel than a father or a mother. For a father or mother bring one into this world, but you bring us into this world and the world to come."

Responded and said to him R. Aqiba, "My lord, suffering is precious."

R. Eliezer said to his disciples, "Lift me up."

R. Eliezer went into session, saying to him, "Speak, Aqiba."

He said to him, "Lo, Scripture says, 'Manasseh was twelve years old when he began to reign, and he reigned for fifty-five years in Jerusalem. And he did what was evil in the eyes of the Lord' (2 Chron. 33:1). And it further says, 'These are the proverbs of Solomon, which the men of Hezekiah, king of Judah, copied out' (Prov. 25:1).

"Now can anyone imagine that Hezekiah taught Torah to all Israel, while his son, Manasseh, he did not teach Torah?

"But one must conclude that, despite all of the learning that his father taught him, and all the work that he put into him, nothing worked for him except suffering.

"For it is said, 'And the Lord spoke to Manasseh and to his people, but they gave no heed. Therefore the Lord brought upon them the captains of the host of the king of Assyria, who took Manasseh with hooks and bound him with fetters and carried him to Babylonia. And when he was in distress, he besought the Lord, his God, and humbled himself greatly before the God of his fathers and prayed to him, and he was entreated of him and heard his supplication and brought him back to Jerusalem into his kingdom' (2 Chron. 33:10–13).

"That proves that suffering is precious."

MEKHILTA ATTRIBUTED TO R. ISHMAEL LVI:3

Suffering, Sin, and Atonement

Said Raba, and some say, R. Hisda, "If a person sees that sufferings afflict him, let him examine his deeds.

"For it is said, 'Let us search and try our ways and return to the Lord' (Lam. 3:40).

"If he examined his ways and found no cause [for his suffering], let him blame the matter on his wasting [time better spent in studying] the Torah.

"For it is said, 'Happy is the man whom you chastise, O Lord, and teach out of your Torah' (Ps. 94:12).

"If he blamed it on something and found [after correcting the fault] that that had not, in fact, been the cause at all, he may be sure that he suffers the afflictions that come from God's love.

"For it is said, 'For the one whom the Lord loves he corrects' (Prov. 3:12)."

Said Raba said R. Sehorah said R. Huna [said], "Whomever the Holy One, blessed be he, prefers he crushes with suffering.

"For it is said, 'The Lord was pleased with him, hence he crushed him with disease' (Isa. 53:10).

"Is it possible that even if the victim did not accept the suffering with love, the same is so?

"Scripture states, 'To see if his soul would offer itself in restitution' (Isa. 53:10).

"Just as the offering must be offered with the knowledge and consent [of the sacrifier—the one who gains the benefit of the offering], so sufferings must be accepted with knowledge and consent.

"If one accepted them in that way, what is his reward?

"'He will see his seed, prolong his days' (Isa. 53:10).

"Not only so, but his learning will remain with him, as it is said, 'The purpose of the Lord will prosper in his hand' (Isa. 53:10)."

R. Jacob bar Idi and R. Aha bar Hanina differed. One of them said, "What are sufferings brought on by God's love? They are any form of suffering which does not involve one's having to give up studying Torah.

"For it is said, 'Happy is the man whom you chasten, O Lord, and yet teach out of your Torah' (Ps. 94:12)."

The other said, "What are sufferings brought on by God's love? They are any form of suffering which does not involve having to give up praying.

"For it is said, 'Blessed be God, who has not turned away my prayer nor his mercy from me' (Ps. 66:20)."

Said to them R. Abba, son of R. Hiyya bar Abba, "This is what R. Hiyya bar Abba said R. Yohanan said, 'Both constitute forms of suffering brought on by God's love.

"'For it is said, "For him whom the Lord loves he corrects" (Prov. 3:12).

"'What is the sense of the Scripture's statement, 'And you teach him out of your Torah"? Do not read it as "You teach him," but "You teach us."

"'This matter you teach us out of your law, namely, the argument [concerning the meaning of the suffering brought on by God's love] *a fortiori* resting on the traits of the tooth and the eye:

"'Now if, on account of an injury done to the slave's tooth or eye, which are only one of a person's limbs, a slave goes forth to freedom, sufferings, which drain away the whole of a person's body, how much the more so [should a person find true freedom on their account].'"

This furthermore accords with what R. Simeon b. Laqish said. For R. Simeon b. Laqish said, "A 'covenant' is stated in respect to salt, and a covenant is mentioned with respect to suffering.

"With respect to a covenant with salt: 'Neither shall you allow the salt of the covenant of your God to be lacking' (Lev. 2:13).

"With respect to a covenant with suffering: 'These are the words of the covenant' (Deut. 28:69) [followed by discourse on Israel's suffering].

"Just as the covenant noted with salt indicates that salt sweetens meat, so the covenant noted with suffering indicates that suffering wipes away all of a person's sins."

It has been taught on Tannaite authority:

R. Simeon b. Yohai says, "Three good gifts did the Holy One, blessed be he, give to Israel, and all of them he gave only through suffering.

"These are they: Torah, the Land of Israel, and the world to come.

"How do we know that that is the case for Torah? As it is said, 'Happy is the man whom you chasten, O Lord, and teach out of your Torah' (Ps. 94:12).

"The Land of Israel? 'As a man chastens his son, so the Lord your God chastens you,' (Deut. 8:5), after which it is said, 'For the Lord your God brings you into a good land' (Deut. 8:7).

"The world to come? 'For the commandment is a lamp and the teaching is light, and reproofs of sufferings are the way of life' (Prov. 6:23)."

A Tannaite authority repeated the following statement before R. Yohanan: "Whoever devotes himself to study of the Torah or acts of loving kindness, or who buries his children, is forgiven all his sins."

Said to him R. Yohanan, "Now there is no issue with regard to study of the Torah or practice of deeds of loving kindness, for it is written, 'By mercy and truth iniquity is expiated' (Prov. 16:6).

"'Mercy' refers to acts of loving kindness, for it is said, 'He who follows after righteousness and mercy finds life, prosperity, and honor' (Prov. 21:21).

"'Truth' of course refers to Torah, for it is said, 'Buy the truth and do not sell it' (Prov. 23:23).

"But how do we know that that is the case for one who buries his children?"

An elder repeated for him on Tannaite authority the following statement in the name of R. Simeon b. Yohai, "We draw an analogy to the sense of the word 'sin' used in several passages.

"Here it is written, 'By mercy and truth iniquity is expiated' (Prov. 16:6), and elsewhere, 'And who repays the iniquity of the fathers into the bosom of their children' (Jer. 32:18)."

Said R. Yohanan, "The suffering brought by skin-ailments [such as are listed at Lev. 13-14] and by the burial of one's children are not sufferings that are brought by God's love."

Is it really the case that the sufferings brought by the skin ailments are not [sufferings of love]?

And has it not been taught on Tannaite authority:

"Whoever has any one of the four skin-traits that indicate the presence of the skin-ailment may know that these serve solely as an altar for atonement [of his sins]"?

To be sure, they serve as an altar for atonement, but they are not sufferings that come on account of God's love.

If you prefer, I shall explain that the one teaching belongs to us [in Babylonia], the other to them [in the Land of Israel].

If you wish, I shall propose that the one teaching [that they are sufferings brought on by God's love] applies when the skin-ailment appears on hidden places of the body, the other, when it appears on parts of the body that people see.

And with respect to burying one's children is it not [a sign of suffering brought on by God's love]?

Now what sort of case can be in hand? If I say that one actually had the children but they died,

did not R. Yohanan say, "This is the bone of my tenth son [whom I buried]"? [Yohanan then regarded the death of the child as suffering brought on by God's love.]

Rather, the one case involves someone who never had any children at all, the other, to someone who had children who died.

R. Hiyya bar Abba got sick. R. Yohanan came to him. He said to him, "Are these sufferings precious to you?"

He said to him, "I don't want them, I don't want their reward."

He said to him, "Give me your hand."

He gave him his hand, and [Yohanan] raised him up [out of his sickness].

R. Yohanan got sick. R. Hanina came to him. He said to him, "Are these sufferings precious to you?"

He said to him, "I don't want them. I don't want their reward."
He said to him, "Give me your hand."

He gave him his hand and [Hanina] raised him up [out of his sickness].

Why so? R. Yohanan should have raised himself up?

They say, "A prisoner cannot get himself out of jail."

R. Eliezer got sick. R. Yohanan came to see him and found him lying in a dark room. [The dying man] uncovered his arm, and light fell [through the room]. [Yohanan] saw that R. Eliezer was weeping. He said to him, "Why are you crying? Is it because of the Torah that you did not learn sufficiently? We have learned: 'All the same are the ones who do much and do little, so long as each person will do it for the sake of Heaven.'

"If it is because of insufficient income? Not everyone has the merit of seeing two tables [Torah and riches, as you have. You have been a master of Torah and also have enjoyed wealth].

"Is it because of children? Here is the bone of my tenth son [whom I buried, so it was no great loss not to have children, since you might have had to bury them]."

He said to him, "I am crying because of this beauty of mine which will be rotting in the ground."

He said to him, "For that it certainly is worth crying," and the two of them wept together.

In the course of time, he said to him, "Are these sufferings precious to you?"

He said to him, "I don't want them, I don't want their reward."

He said to him, "Give me your hand."

He gave him his hand, and [Yohanan] raised him up [out of his sickness].

BAVLI TO MISHNAH-TRACTATE BERAKHOT 1:1/5A-B

Supporting the Poor

The sages' approach to poverty is characteristic of their logic: that is, they see a method to everything, and in that method one discovers a world view extending far beyond the case at hand.

Our rabbis have taught on Tannaite authority:

An orphan boy or an orphan girl who seek to be supported—they support the orphan girl first, then they support the orphan boy, for the boy can make the rounds of household doors, but the girl would not ordinarily make the rounds.

An orphan boy and an orphan girl who came for money to get married—they marry off the orphan girl first, and then they marry off the orphan boy, for the shame of a girl is greater than that of the boy.

Our rabbis have taught on Tannaite authority:

An orphan boy who seeks to marry—they rent a room for him, then they lay out a bed, and afterward they marry off a girl to him, as it is said, "But you shall open your hand to him and lend him sufficient for his need, whatever it may be" (Deut. 15:8)—"sufficient for his need" refers to a room, "whatever it may be" refers to a bed and a table," "he" refers to as a wife: "I will make him a help meet for him" (Gen. 2:18).

Our rabbis have taught on Tannaite authority:

"Sufficient for his need" you are commanded to provide for him, but you are not commanded to enrich him.

"Whatever it may be"—even a horse to ride on, even a slave to run before him.

They say of Hillel the Elder that for a certain poor man of good parents he bought a horse to ride on and a slave to run before him.

Once he couldn't find a slave to run before him, so he ran before him for three *mils*.

Our rabbis have taught on Tannaite authority:

There was the case involving the people of Upper Galilee, who bought for a poor member of good parents in Sepphoris a pound of meat every day.

A pound of meat . . . ? So what's the big deal?

It was chicken.

And if you wish, I will say, "It was ordinary meat for a *litra* of money per *litra* of meat."

R. Ashi said, "It was a little village. Every day it would involve the loss of a beast for his sake."

Someone once came to R. Nehemiah for support. He said to him, "What do you usually eat?"

He said to him, "Fat meat and old wine."

"How would you like to share my lot and eat lentils?"

He shared his lot and ate lentils and died.

He said, "Woe is this man, whom Nehemiah killed!"

To the contrary—"Woe is Nehemiah, who killed this man" is what he should have said!

But it was the man himself who was responsible, for he ought not to have indulged himself so much.

Someone once came to R. Nehemiah for support. He said to him, "What do you usually eat?"

He said to him, "Fat chicken and old wine."

He said to him, "Aren't you concerned about being a burden on the community?"

He said to him, "So am I eating what belongs to them? I'm eating what belongs to the All-Merciful, for it has been taught as a Tannaite statement: 'The eyes of all wait for you, and you give them their food in his season' (Ps. 145:15)—what is said is not "in their season" but "in his season," which teaches that to everyone the Holy One, blessed be he, gives his food in accord his season."

In the meanwhile Raba's sister, whom he had not seen for thirteen years, came along, and she brought him a fat chicken and old wine. He said, "What a surprise." He said to him, "I apologize to you. Get up and eat."

Our rabbis have taught on Tannaite authority:

If someone hasn't got anything but doesn't want to be supported from public money, "they give him money as a loan, and then they turn it into a gift," the words of R. Meir.

And sages say, "They give it to him as a gift, and then they go and turn it into a loan".

As a gift? But he doesn't take gifts!

Said Raba, "To begin with they present it to him as a gift."

If he has means and doesn't want to support himself, they give money to him as a gift, but then they go and collect it from him.

But then he won't take it!

Said R. Pappa, "This is after he dies [when the money is taken out of his estate]."

R. Simeon says, "If he has means and doesn't want to support himself, they simply pay no attention to him. If someone hasn't got anything but doesn't want to be supported from public money, they say to him, 'Well, give a pledge and take what you need,' so as to encourage him."

Our rabbis have taught on Tannaite authority:

"'And lending him, you shall surely lend him sufficient for his need' (Deut. 15:8):

"This refers to one who has nothing and does not want to support himself from charity, that Scripture makes explicit that the donation must be deemed only a loan but then it is transformed into a gift.

"'You shall surely lend him': This refers to someone who does have property and does not want to support himself from it [that is, by consuming his capital], to whom the support payment is given as a gift, and then repaid by his estate," the words of R. Judah.

Sages say, "If he has means and doesn't want to support himself, they simply pay no attention to him. And what is the sense of the duplication in, And lending him, you shall surely lend him sufficient for his need (Deut. 15:8)? In this case Scripture used language in an ordinary way."

There was a poor man in Mar Uqba's neighborhood, to whom he was used to sending four hundred *zuz* every year on the eve of the Day of Atonement. One year he sent the money to him through his son, who came home and said to him, "He doesn't need you."

He said to him, "What did you see?"

"I saw them sprinkling vintage wine before him."

He said, "So is he so effete?" He doubled the money and sent it to him.

When Mar Uqba was dying, he said, "Bring me my account books for charity." He found written, "Seven thousand gold *dinars* of Sianaq." He said, "The provisions are scanty and the way is long." He went and donated half of his entire estate to the poor.

But how could he act in such a way? And did not R. Ilai say, "In Usha they ordained: He who distributes his wealth to the poor should not give away more than a fifth of his estate"?

That is the case when one is alive, lest he lose his money, but after death, there is no objection to one's doing so with his estate.

R. Abba would bind up money in his scarf, sling it over his back, and make himself available to the poor [who would take the money quietly]. But he kept a sharp eye out for frauds.

There was a poor man near R. Hanina, to whom he would regularly send four *zuz* every Friday. One day he sent the money through his wife, who came home and said to him, "He doesn't need you."

He said to her, "What did you see?"

She said, "I heard that people said to him, 'On what do you want to eat, on silver cloth or gold cloth?'"

He said, "That's in line with what R. Eleazar said, 'We have to be grateful to frauds, for if it weren't for them, we would sin every day: "And he cry unto the Lord against you and it be sin unto you" (Deut. 15:9).'"

R. Hiyya bar Rab of Difti set forth as a Tannaite statement: "R. Joshua b. Qorhah says, 'Whoever hides his eyes from the needs of philanthropy is as though he worships idols. Here it is written, "Beware that there not be a base thought in your heart and your eye will be evil against your poor brother" (Deut. 14:9), and with regard to idolatry, "Certain base fellows are gone out" (Deut. 13:14). Just as there, the ultimate sin is idolatry, so here, idolatry is involved.'"

Our rabbis have taught on Tannaite authority:

He who pretends to be blind or pretends to have a swollen belly or a shrunken leg will not leave this world before he actually has such a thing. He who accepts charity but does not need it in the end will not leave this world before he needs it.

BAVLI TO MISHNAH-TRACTATE KETUBOT 6:5/67A-B

Taking Responsibility for What
Happens in the Community

*Wisdom insists that we live in community: "Give me community or give
me death," cries a lonely man in the Talmud. But to build community
we must take responsibility for one another and above all for what happens beyond the small circle of our affairs.*

Rab, R. Hanina, R. Yohanan, and R. Habiba repeated the following Tannaite statement: In the whole of the Division of Appointed
Times, in any case in which this set appears together, the name of R.
Jonathan may be substituted for the name of R. Yohanan: "Whoever
has the power to prevent his household from doing a certain improper
deed but doesn't do so is held responsible for the sins of the members
of his household. If he can stop his townsfolk, he is held responsible
along with them; if he can stop the whole world, he is responsible for
the whole world."

Said R. Pappa, "The members of the household of the exilarch are
seized on account of the whole world."

That is in line with what R. Hanina said, "Why is it written, 'The
Lord will enter into judgment with the elders of his people and the
princes thereof' (Isa. 3:14)? If the princes sinned, what sin did the elders do? But say: Punishment comes on the elders, because they didn't
stop the princes [from sinning]."

Said R. Zira to R. Simon, "Let the master rebuke the members of
the house of the exilarch."

He said to him, "They won't take it from me."

He said to him, "Even though they won't take it from you, yet the
master should rebuke them. For said R. Aha bar Hanina, 'Never did a
good ruling go forth from the mouth of the Holy One, blessed be he,
on which he went back in favor of a bad one, except for this one thing,
of which it is written, "And the Lord said to him, Go through the midst
of the city, through the midst of Jerusalem, and set a mark on the foreheads of the men that sigh and cry for all the abominations that are
committed in the midst thereof" (Ezek. 9:4).'"

[With reference to the verse, "And the Lord said to him, Go through
the midst of the city, through the midst of Jerusalem, and set a mark on

the foreheads of the men that sigh and cry for all the abominations that are committed in the midst thereof" (Ezek. 9:4)]": Said the Holy One, blessed be he, to Gabriel, "Go, make a mark on the foreheads of the righteous, a letter *tav* written in ink, so that the destructive angels won't have power over them, and make a mark of a *tav* on the foreheads of the wicked, a *tav* written in blood, so that the destructive angels will have power over them."

Said the Attribute of Justice before the Holy One, blessed be he, "Lord of the world, how are these different from those?"

He said to it, "These are utterly righteous, those are utterly wicked."

It said before the Holy One, blessed be he, "They had the power to protest but didn't protest."

He said to it, "It is quite obvious to me that if they had objected, the others would not have taken it from them."

It said before him, "Lord of the world, if it was so obvious to you, was it all that obvious to them?"

That is in line with the verse, "Slay utterly the old man, the young and the maiden and little children and women, but don't come near any man on whom is the mark, and begin at my sanctuary; then they began at the elders that were before the house" (Ezek. 9:6).

BAVLI TO MISHNAH-TRACTATE SHABBAT 5:4/54B-55A

Temper

As with other temporal emotions, the sages have little patience for anything that causes a loss of control over the mind. The mark of wisdom is temperance.

Said R. Samuel bar Nahman said R. Yohanan, "Whoever loses his temper—all the torments of Hell rule over him: 'Therefore remove anger from your heart, thus will you put away evil from your flesh' (Qoh. 11:10), and the meaning of 'evil' is only Hell: 'The Lord has made all things for himself, yes, even the wicked for the day of evil' (Prov. 16:4). Moreover, he will get a bellyache: 'But the Lord shall give you there a trembling heart and failing of eyes and sorrow of mind' (Deut. 28:65). And what causes weak eyes and depression? Stomachaches."

Ulla went up to the Land of Israel, accompanied by two men from Khuzistan. One of them went and killed the other. He said to Ulla, "So didn't I do the right thing?"

He said to him, "Yessirree! And now cut his throat right across."

When he came before R. Yohanan, he said to him, "Maybe—God forbid—I have encouraged sinners?"

He said to him, "You saved your life."

R. Yohanan expressed surprise: "It is written, 'There the Lord will give them a temperamental heart' (Deut. 28:65)—this speaks of Babylonia—so how could such a thing have happened in the Land of Israel, where people are patient with one another?]"

Ulla said to him, "At that moment we had not yet crossed the Jordan."

Said Rabbah bar R. Huna, "Whoever loses his temper—even the presence of God is not important to him: 'The wicked, through the pride of his countenance, will not seek God; God is not in all his thoughts' (Ps. 10:4)."

R. Jeremiah of Difti said, "[Whoever loses his temper]—he forgets what he has learned and increases foolishness: 'For anger rests in the heart of fools' (Qoh. 7:9), and 'But the fool lays open his folly' (Prov. 13:16)."

R. Nahman bar Isaac said, "One may be sure that his sins outnumber his merits: 'And a furious man abounds in transgressions' (Prov. 29:22)."

MISHNAH-TRACTATE NEDARIM 3:1/22A-B

Thanksgiving

It is a gift to bear the quality of gratitude, and thanksgiving is the most esteemed virtue; it is what separates us from pigs.

Said R. Judah said Rab, "Four sorts of people have to give thanks: those who go down to the sea, those who wander far in the deserts, he who was sick and got better, and he who was in prison and came forth."

How do we know that that is the case for those who go down to the sea? As it is written, "They who go down to the sea in ships . . . . These saw the works of the Lord . . . . He raised the stormy wind . . . . They mounted up to the Heaven, they went down to the deeps . . . . They reeled to and fro and staggered like a drunken man . . . . They cried to the Lord in their trouble, and he brought them out of their distress. He made the storm a calm . . . then were they glad because they were quiet . . . . Let them give thanks to the Lord for his mercy and for his wonderful works to the children of men" (Ps. 107:23–31).

How do we know that that is the case for those who wander far in the deserts? As it is written, "They wandered in the wilderness in a desert way; they found no city of habitation . . . . Then they cried to the Lord . . . and he led them by a straight way . . . . Let them give thanks to the Lord for his mercy" (Ps. 107:4–8).

How do we know that that is the case for someone who was sick and got better? As it is written, "Crazed because of the way of their transgression and afflicted because of their iniquities, their soul abhorred all manner of food . . . . They cried to the Lord in their trouble. He sent his word to them . . . . Let them give thanks to the Lord for his mercy" (Ps. 107:17–21).

How do we know that that is the case for him who was in prison and came forth? As it is said, "Such as sat in darkness and in the shadow of death . . . . Because they rebelled against the words of God . . . . Therefore he humbled their heart with travail . . . . They cried to the Lord in their trouble . . . . He brought them out of darkness and the shadow of death . . . . Let them give thanks to the Lord for his mercy" (Ps. 107:10–15).

What blessing does one say?

Said R. Judah, "Blessed is he who bestows acts of loving kindness."

BAVLI TO MISHNAH-TRACTATE BERAKHOT 9:1

True Blessings

Blessings are what we hear, not always what is said. In their remarkable capacity for interpretation, the sages here explain what a blessing really means, and how it should be received.

R. Jonathan b. Asemai and R. Judah, son of proselytes, repeated the Tannaite presentation of the laws of vows at the household of R. Simeon b. Yohai and took their leave of him by night, but the next morning they came, and again they took their leave of him. He said to them, "But did you not take leave of me last night?"

They said to him, "But did you not take leave of me last night?"

They said to him, "You have taught us, our lord: 'A disciple who takes leave of his master but spends the night in that town has to take leave from him once again, in line with this verse: "On the eighth day he sent the people home and they blessed the king and went to their own tents joyful and glad of heart for all the goodness that the Lord had shown to David his servant and to Israel his people" (1 Kings 8:66); and then it is written, "And on the twenty-third day of the seventh month he sent the people away" (2 Chron. 7:10). Thus we learn that a disciple who takes leave of his master but spends the night in that town has to take leave from him once again.'"

He said to his son, "My son, these men are men of standing. Go to them so that they will bestow their blessing on you."

He went and found them contrasting verses one against the next, in the following way: "It is written, 'Balance the path of your feet and let all your ways be established' (Prov. 4:26), and, by contrast, 'Lest you should balance the path of life' (Prov. 5:5). But there is no conflict between the advice of these two verses. The one speaks to a case in which a religious obligation can be carried out through someone else, the latter, a case in which the religious obligation can be carried out only by oneself."

They again went into session and raised questions along these lines: "It is written, 'Wisdom is more precious than rubies, and all things you can desire are not to be compared to her' (Prov. 3:10), meaning that what Heaven wants of you are comparable to Wisdom [Lazarus: your own affairs and wishes are not comparable to the study of the Torah, but such pursuits as please Heaven are comparable to it], but it is written, 'And all things desirable are not to be compared with Wisdom' (Prov. 8:11), which means that what Heaven demands of you is comparable with her. And again, 'And all things desirable are not to be compared to her' (Prov. 8:12), meaning that even things that Heaven wants of you are not comparable to her [so study of Torah is supreme over all]. But there is no conflict between the advice of these two verses. The one speaks to a case in which a religious obligation can be carried out through someone else, the latter, a case in which the religious obligation can be carried out only by oneself."

They said to him, "What did you want here?"

He said to them, "Father said to me, 'Go to them so that they may bestow their blessing on you.'"

They said to him, "May it please God that you sow and not harvest, go in but not go out, go out but not go in; that your house be empty but your inn filled; that your table be upset and you not see a new year."

When he got home, he said to his father, he said to him, "Not only did they not bless me, but they called down troubles upon me!"

He said to him, "So what did they say to you?"

"Thus and so did they say to me!"

He said to him, "But all of their statements were blessings:

"'that you sow and not harvest:' that you father children and they not die;

"'go in but not go out:' that you bring home daughters-in-law and your sons not die so that the wives do not have to depart from you;

"'go out but not go in:' that you give your daughters in marriage and their husbands not die so that your daughters do not have to come back;

"'that your house be empty but your inn filled:' this world is your inn, the other world is home, 'Their grave is their house for ever' (Ps. 49:12), reading not 'their inward thought' but 'their grave is their house for ever, and their dwelling places be for generations.'

"'that your table be upset:' by sons and daughters;

"'and you not see a new year:' your wife should not die so you do not have to take a new wife."

R. Simeon b. Halapta took his leave of Rabbi. Said Rabbi to his son, "Go to him that he may bless you."

He said to him, "May it please God that you not put anybody to shame nor feel ashamed."

He came back to his father, who said to him, "What did he say to you?"

He said to him, "Oh, nothing out of the ordinary."

He said to him, "What he gave to you was the blessing that the Holy One, blessed be he, bestowed upon Israel two times: 'And you shall eat in plenty and be satisfied and shall praise the name of the Lord your God . . . and my people shall never be ashamed. And you shall know that I am in the midst of Israel, and that I am the Lord your God, and there is none else, and my people shall never be ashamed' (Joel 2:26-27)."

BAVLI TO MISHNAH-TRACTATE BABA QAMMA 1:8/9A-B

True Faith in God's Providence

Optimism is not meant to blind from reality, but it is a useful tool here for Aqiba, who finds solace in seeing things at their very worst as a mere prelude to better things. This is a Talmudic version of the "darkness before the dawn."

Rabban Gamaliel, R. Joshua, R. Eleazar b. Azariah, and R. Aqiba were going toward Rome. They heard the sound of the city's traffic from as far away as Puteoli, a hundred and twenty miles away. They began to cry, while R. Aqiba laughed.

They said to him, "Aqiba, why are we crying while you are laughing?"

He said to them, "Why are you crying?"

They said to him, "Should we not cry, since Gentiles, idolators, sacrifice to their idols and bow down to icons, but dwell securely in prosperity, serenely, while the house of the footstool of our God has been put to the torch and left [Hammer:] a lair for beasts of the field?"

He said to them, "That is precisely why I was laughing. If this is how he has rewarded those he anger him, all the more so [will he reward] those who do his will."

Another time they went up to Jerusalem and go to Mount Scopus. They tore their garments.

They came to the mountain of the house [of the temple] and saw a fox go forth from the house of the holy of holies. They began to cry, while R. Aqiba laughed.

They said to him, "You are always giving surprises. We are crying when you laugh!"

He said to them, "But why are you crying?"

They said to him, "Should we not cry over the place concerning which it is written, And the common person who draws near shall be put to death' (Num. 1:51)? Now lo, a fox comes out of it.

"In our connection the following verse of Scripture has been carried out: 'For this our heart is faint, for these things our eyes are dim, for the mountain of Zion which is desolate, the foxes walk upon it' (Lam. 5:17-18)."

He said to them, "That is the very reason I have laughed. For lo, it is written, 'And I will take for me faithful witnesses to record, Uriah the priest and Zechariah the son of Jeberechiah' (Isa. 8:2).

"And what has Uriah got to do with Zechariah? What is it that Uriah said? 'Zion shall be plowed as a field and Jerusalem shall become heaps and the mountain of the Lord's house as the high places of a forest' (Jer. 26:18).

"What is it that Zechariah said? 'Thus says the Lord of hosts, "Old men and women shall yet sit in the broad places of Jerusalem"' (Zech. 8:4).

"Said the Omnipresent, 'Lo, I have these two witnesses. If the words of Uriah have been carried out, then the words of Zechariah will be carried out. If the words of Uriah are nullified, then the words of Zechariah will be nullified.

"Therefore I was happy that the words of Uriah have been carried out, so that in the end the words of Zechariah will come about."

In this language they replied to him: "Aqiba, you have given us comfort."

SIFRÉ TO DEUTERONOMY XLIII:III

True Gratitude

One who sees a crowd says, "Blessed [art Thou, O Lord, our God, King of the Universe,] who knows the secrets. Just as their faces are different one from the other, so are their opinions different one from the other."

When Ben Zoma saw crowds in Jerusalem [on the Temple Mount] he would say, "Blessed is he who created all these people to serve me. How hard did Adam have to toil, before eating even a morsel. He first plowed, seeded, weeded, irrigated, reaped, made sheaves, threshed, winnowed, separated, ground, sifted, kneaded, baked and only then could he eat a morsel. But I arise in the morning and find all this prepared before me.

"See how hard Adam toiled before he had a shirt to wear. He sheared, bleached, separated, dyed, spun, wove, washed, sewed and only then did he have a shirt to wear. But I arise in the morning and find all this prepared for me. How many craftsmen must rise early and retire late [to prepare my food and clothing]. And I arise in the morning and find all this before me."

And so Ben Zoma would say, "What does an ungrateful guest say? 'What did I take from this householder to eat or drink? I ate just one slice of his bread and drank just one cup of his wine. He expended his energies [to prepare the meal] only on behalf of his wife and children.'

"But the grateful guest says, 'Blessed be this householder. May this householder be remembered for good. How much wine did he bring before me! How many slices [of bread, meat and cake] did he bring before me! How much energy did he expend on my behalf. He expended his energies only for me. And so he says, 'Remember to extol his work, of which men have sung' (Job 36:24)."

YERUSHALMI BERAKHOT 9:1

True Love

There was a case in Sidon of one who married a woman and remained with her for ten years while she did not give birth.

They came to R. Simeon b. Yohai to arrange for the divorce. He said to her, "Any thing which I have in my house take and now go, return to your father's household."

Said to them R. Simeon b. Yohai, "Just as when you got married, it was in eating and drinking, so you may not separate from one another without eating and drinking."

What did the woman do? She made a splendid meal and gave the husband too much to drink and then gave a sign to her slave girl and said to her, "Bring him to my father's house."

At midnight the man woke up. He said to them, "Where am I?"

She said to him, "Did you not say to me, 'Anything which I have in my house, take and now go, return to your father's household.' And that is how it is: I have nothing more precious than you."

When R. Simeon b. Yohai heard this, he said a prayer for them, and they were visited [with a pregnancy].

The Holy One, blessed be he, visits barren women, and the righteous have the same power.

"And is it not an argument *a fortiori*: if in the case of a mortal, to whom rejoicing comes, the person rejoices and gives joy to everyone, when the Holy One, blessed be he, comes to give joy to Jerusalem, all the more so! And when Israel looks forward to the salvation of the Holy One, blessed be he, all the more so!

"I will greatly rejoice in the Lord, [my soul shall exult in my God; for he has clothed me with the garments of salvation, he has covered me with the robe of righteousness, as a bridegroom decks himself with a garland, and as a bride adorns herself with her jewels. For as the earth brings forth its shoots, and as a garden causes what is sown in it to spring up, so the Lord God will cause righteousness and praise to spring forth before all the nations] (Isa. 61:10–11)."

PESIQTA DERAB KAHANA XXII:II.4

True Religion

With the Hebrew letters assigned a numerical value, it was easy for the sages to see words in ways not otherwise intended—deconstructionism before its time. And yet here the sages seek to strip down faith to a single dictum, not multiply it.

R. Simelai expounded, "Six hundred and thirteen commandments were given to Moses, three hundred and sixty-five negative ones, corresponding to the number of the days of the solar year, and two hundred forty-eight positive commandments, corresponding to the parts of man's body."

Said R. Hamnuna, "What verse of Scripture indicates that fact? 'Moses commanded us Torah, an inheritance of the congregation of Jacob' (Deut. 33:4). The numerical value assigned to the letters of the word Torah is six hundred and eleven, not counting, 'I am' and 'you shall have no other gods,' since these have come to us from the mouth of the Almighty."

[Simelai continues:] "David came and reduced them to eleven: 'A Psalm of David: Lord, who shall sojourn in thy tabernacle, and who shall dwell in thy holy mountain? (1) He who walks uprightly and (2) works righteousness and (3) speaks truth in his heart and (4) has no slander on his tongue and (5) does no evil to his fellow and (6) does not take up a reproach against his neighbor, (7) in whose eyes a vile person is despised but (8) honors those who fear the Lord. (9) He swears to his own hurt and changes not. (10) He does not lend on interest. (11) He does not take a bribe against the innocent' (Psalm 15)."

"He who walks uprightly": this is Abraham: "Walk before me and be wholehearted" (Gen. 17:1).

"and works righteousness": this is Abba Hilqiahu.

"speaks truth in his heart": for instance R. Safra.

"has no slander on his tongue": this is our father, Jacob: "My father might feel me and I shall seem to him as a deceiver" (Gen. 27:12).

"does no evil to his fellow": he does not go into competition with his fellow craftsman.

"does not take up a reproach against his neighbor": this is someone who befriends his relatives.

"in whose eyes a vile person is despised": this is Hezekiah, king of Judah, who dragged his father's bones on a rope bed.

"honors those who fear the Lord": this is Jehoshaphat, king of Judah, who, whenever he would see a disciple of a sage, would rise from his throne and embrace and kiss him and call him, "My father, my father, my lord, my lord, my master, my master."

"He swears to his own hurt and changes not": this is R. Yohanan.

"He does not lend on interest": not even interest from a gentile.

"He does not take a bribe against the innocent": such as R. Ishmael b. R. Yosé.

"He who does these things shall never be moved."

"Isaiah came and reduced them to six: '(1) He who walks righteously and (2) speaks uprightly, (3) he who despises the gain of oppressions,

(4) shakes his hand from holding bribes, (5) stops his ear from hearing of blood (6) and shuts his eyes from looking upon evil, he shall dwell on high' (Isa. 33:25–26)."

"He who walks righteously": this is our father, Abraham: "For I have known him so that he may command his children and his household after him" (Gen. 18:19).

"speaks uprightly": this is one who does not belittle his fellow in public.

"he who despises the gain of oppressions": for example, R. Ishmael b. Elisha.

"shakes his hand from holding bribes": for example, R. Ishmael b. R. Yosé.

"stops his ear from hearing of blood": who will not listen to demeaning talk about a disciple of rabbis and remain silent.

"Micah came and reduced them to three: 'It has been told you, man, what is good, and what the Lord demands from you, (1) only to do justly and (2) to love mercy, and (3) to walk humbly before God' (Micah 6:8)."

"only to do justly": this refers to justice.

"to love mercy": this refers to doing acts of loving kindness.

"to walk humbly before God": this refers to accompanying a corpse to the grave and welcoming the bread.

"Isaiah again came and reduced them to two : 'Thus says the Lord, (1) Keep justice and (2) do righteousness' (Isa. 56:1).

"Amos came and reduced them to a single one, as it is said, 'For thus says the Lord to the house of Israel. Seek me and live.'"

Objected R. Nahman bar Isaac, "Maybe the sense is, 'seek me' through the whole of the Torah?"

Rather, [Simelai continues:] "Habakkuk further came and based them on one, as it is said, 'But the righteous shall live by his faith' (Hab. 2:4)."

BAVLI TO MISHNAH-TRACTATE MAKKOT 3:16/23B-24A

The Ubiquity of God

And R. Oshaia takes the view that the presence of God is in every place, for said R. Oshaia, "What is the meaning of the verse of Scripture, 'You are the Lord, even you alone, you made Heaven, the highest Heaven' (Neh. 9:6)? Your messengers are not like mortal messengers. Mortal messengers come back and report to the place from which they are sent forth, but your messengers report to the place to which they are sent: 'Can you send forth your lightnings that they may go and say to you, here we are' (Job 38:35). What is said is not, 'that they may come and say,' but, 'that they may go and say,' and that shows that the Presence of God is in every place."

And so, too, R. Ishmael takes the view that the presence of God is in every place, for it has been taught by a Tannaite authority of the household of R. Ishmael: "How on the basis of Scripture do we know that the presence of God is everywhere? 'And behold the angel that talked with me went forth and another angel went out to meet him' (Zech. 2:7). What is said is not, 'went out after him,' but, 'went out to meet him,' and that shows that the presence of God is in every place."

Bavli to Mishnah-Tractate Baba Batra 2:9-10/25A-B

The Unborn Child: The Character of the Foetus

"Judaism" is commonly represented these days as "pro-life," but in fact the wisdom of Judaism finds in the Torah exactly the position concerning the foetus and foeticide that pro-life Christians and Muslims espouse. The foetus becomes a person, with a soul, on the fortieth day after conception. It has a right to life, and only saving the life of the mother takes precedence. That position is explicit not only in teachings about virtue but in normative statements of law.

The woman who is in hard labor—they chop up the child in her womb and they remove it limb by limb, because her life takes precedence over his life.

[If] its greater part has gone forth, they do not touch him, for they do not set aside one life on account of another life.

Mishnah-Tractate Ohalot 7:6

R. Simlai gave the following exposition: "To what may the foetus be likened in the mother's womb? To a writing tablet that is folded up. Its hands are resting on its two temples, its two elbows on its two legs, its two heels against its buttocks. Its head lies between its knees. Its mouth is shut. Its navel is open. It eats what the mother eats and drinks what the mother drinks but does not excrete, for it if did, it would kill the mother. When it comes forth to the world's breathing space, what is closed is opened, and what is open is closed, for otherwise it could not live for even a single hour.

"A light flickers above its head, and it gazes and perceives from one end of the world to the other, as it is said, 'When his lamp shined above my head, and by his light I walked through darkness' (Job 29:3).

"And do not be surprised , for lo, someone can sleep in one place here [in the Land of Israel] and dream about what is happening in Spain.

"And you have no time in a person's life so full of well-being as those days: 'O that I were as the months of old, as in the days when God watched over me' (Job 29:2). Now what are 'the days' that make up 'months' but not years' They are, of course, the months of pregnancy.

"And the foetus is taught the entire Torah, as it is said, 'And he taught me and said to me, Let your heart hold fast my words, keep my commandments and live' (Prov. 4:4), and it is said, 'When the converse of God was upon my tent' (Job 29:4).

"As soon as the foetus comes out into the world's air, an angel comes and slaps it on the mouth and makes it forget the entire Torah: 'Sin crouches at the door' (Gen. 4:7).

"But it does not leave [the womb] before it is made to take an oath: 'To me every knee shall bow and every tongue shall swear' (Isa. 45:23).

"'every knee shall bow': this refers to the day of death: 'All those who go down to the dust shall kneel before him' (Ps. 22:30).

"'and every tongue shall swear': this refers to the day of birth: 'He who has clean hands and a pure heart, who has not taken my name in vain [that is, by swearing a false oath] and has not sworn deceitfully' (Ps. 24:4).

"And what is the nature of the oath that is imposed [on each infant when it emerges from the womb]? 'Be a righteous person and do not be a wicked person. And even if the entire world say to you, "You are righteous," in your own eyes be as a wicked person. And know that the Holy One, blessed be he, is pure, and those who minister to him are pure, and the soul that he has placed in you is pure. If you keep it in its purity, well and good, and if not, lo, I shall take it from you.'"

Our rabbis have taught on Tannaite authority:
Three form a partnership in the creation of a human being, the Holy One, blessed be he, one's father and one's mother. The father contributes the semen, from which the bones and sinews and nails and brain and white of the eyes come; the mother provides the red [blood] from which the skin, flesh, hair, blood, and dark of the eye come; and the Holy One, blessed be he, supplies the breath of life and the soul, the identifying features, eyesight, power to hear, ability to speak, and walk, understand, and discern.

And when one's time comes along to take leave of the world, the Holy One, blessed be he, takes back his share, and the share of the father and mother he leaves with them.

BAVLI TO MISHNAH-TRACTATE NIDDAH 3:7/30B-31A

Usury

Usury in our context means excessive interest, but in the setting of our sages, all interest was classified as usury. Not only so, but the prohibition against usury extended to intangibles and to actions that are not to be translated into dollars and cents. Thus an exchange, whether of money or of labor, must be exact, with each party giving as much as he got, and no participant ending up wealthier than before.

A man [may] say to his fellow, "Weed with me, and I'll weed with you,"

"Hoe with me, and I'll hoe with you."

But he [may] not say to him, "Weed with me, and I'll hoe with you,"

"Hoe with me, and I'll weed with you."

All the days of the dry season are deemed equivalent to one another.

All the days of the rainy season are deemed equivalent to one another.

One should not say to him, "Plough with me in the dry season, and I'll plough with you in the rainy season."

Rabban Gamaliel says, "There is usury paid in advance, and there is usury paid at the end.

"How so?

"[If] one wanted to take a loan from someone and so sent him [a present] and said, 'This is so that you'll make a loan to me,'—

"this is usury paid in advance.

"[If] one took a loan from someone and paid him back the money and [then] sent [a gift] to him and said, 'This is for your money, which was useless [to you] when it was in my hands,'—

"this is usury paid afterward."

R. Simeon says, "There is usury paid in words.

"One may not say to him, 'You should know that so-and-so from such-and-such a place is on his way.'"

These [who participate in a loan on interest] violate a negative commandment:

(1) the lender, (2) borrower, (3) guarantor, and (4) witnesses.

Sages say, "Also (5) the scribe."

(1) They violate the negative commandment, "You will not give [him] your money upon usury" (Lev. 25:37).

(2) And [they violate the negative command], "You will not take usury from him" (Lev. 25:36).

(3) And [they violate the negative command], "You shall not be a creditor to him" (Exod. 22:25).

(4) And [they violate the negative command], "Nor shall you lay upon him usury" (Exod. 22:25).

(5) And they violate the negative command, "You shall not put a stumbling block before the blind, but you shall fear your God. I am the Lord" (Lev. 19:14)

Said R. Yosé, "Come and see how blind are the eyes of those who lend at usurious rates.

"A man calls his fellow an idol-worshipper, one who has unlawful sexual relations, a shedder of blood,

"and hounds him to deprive him of a livelihood.

"Then this one brings a scribe, pen, ink, document, and witnesses,

"and says to them, 'Come and write concerning him that he has denied the Omnipresent [and has no share in the One who commanded concerning usury].'

"And he writes the document and registers it in the archives [of the gentiles]

"and so denies Him who spoke and thereby brought the world into being, blessed be He.]

"Thus you have learned that those who lend at usurious rates deny the principle [of divine authority]."

R. Simeon b. Eleazar says, "More than denying the principle do they deny.

"For they make the Torah into a fraud,

"and Moses into a fool.

"They say, 'Now if Moses knew how much we would make, he would never have written the prohibition of usury!'"

R. Aqiba says, "Usury is hard, for even a favor may be usury.

"Lo, if he decided to buy vegetables from him in the marketplace [to whom he owed money], even though he paid him the money which was owing, lo, this favor constitutes usury."

R. Simeon says, "Usury is hard,

"for even a very greeting is a matter of usury.

"How so?

"This one never greeted the other in his entire life, until he had to borrow money from him. Now he rushes to greet him.

"So this is a greeting which is usury."

And so did Simeon b. Eleazar say, "Whoever has money and does not put it out at usurious rates—

"concerning him does Scripture say, '. . . who does not put out his money at interest, and does not take a bribe against the innocent. He who does these things shall never be moved' (Ps. 15:5).

[Y. lacks: "Thus you have learned that those who lend money at usurious rates tremble and pass away from the world."]

Said R. Samuel bar Immi,] "Now just what this trembling is I do not know."

[But Solomon came and explained,] "But it is along the lines of that which is said, 'Rescue those who are being taken away to death; hold back those who are stumbling to the slaughter'" (Prov 24:11).

YERUSHALMI TO MISHNAH-TRACTATE BABA MESIA 5:8

Virtue

The sages know what they like based on what they don't like. It is a pervasive element of their wisdom that they show what they mean in each case here, providing characterization of virtue and of piety when there was none.

There are four sorts of people. (1) He who says, "What's mine is mine and what's your is yours"—this is the average sort. (And some say, "This is the sort of Sodom.") (2) "What's mine is yours and what's yours is mine"—this is a boor. (3) "What's mine is yours and what's yours is yours"—this is a truly pious man. (4) "What's mine is mine and what's yours is mine"—this is a truly wicked man.

There are four sorts of personality: (1) easily angered, easily calmed—he loses what he gains; (2) hard to anger, hard to calm—what he loses he gains; (3) hard to anger and easy to calm—a truly pious man; (4) easy to anger and hard to calm—a truly wicked man.

There are four types of disciples: (1) quick to grasp, quick to forget—he loses what he gains; (2) slow to grasp, slow to forget—what he loses he gains; (3) quick to grasp, slow to forget—a sage; (4) slow to grasp, quick to forget—a bad lot indeed.

There are four traits among people who give charity: (1) he who wants to give, but does not want others to give—he begrudges what belongs to others; (2) he wants others to give, but he does not want to give—he begrudges what belongs to himself; (3) he will give and he wants others to give—he is truly pious; (4) he will not give and he does not want others to give—he is truly wicked.

[In] any loving relationship which depends upon something, [when] that thing is gone, the love is gone. But any which does not depend upon something will never come to an end. What is a loving relationship which depends upon something? That is the love of Amnon and Tamar [2 Sam. 13:15]. And one which does not depend upon something: That is the love of David and Jonathan.

Any dispute which is for the sake of Heaven will in the end yield results, and any which is not for the sake of Heaven will in the end not yield results. What is a dispute for the sake of Heaven? This is the sort of dispute between Hillel and Shammai. And what is one which is not for the sake of Heaven? It is the dispute of Korach and all his party.

TRACTATE ABOT 5:10-17

Virtue and Its Reward

A certain man came before one of the relatives of R. Yannai. He said to him, "Rabbi, attain merit through me [by giving me charity]."

He said to him, "And didn't your father leave you money?"

He said to him, "No."

He said to him, "Go and collect what your father left in deposit with others."

He said to him, "I have heard concerning property my father deposited with others that it was gained unlawfully [so I don't want it]."

He said to him, "You are worthy of praying and having your prayers answered."

A certain ass-driver appeared before the rabbis [in a dream] and prayed, and rain came. The rabbis sent and brought him and said to him, "What is your trade?"

He said to them, "I am an ass-driver."

They said to him, "What good deed have you done?"

He said to them, "One time I rented my ass to a certain woman, and she was weeping on the way, and I said to her, 'What troubles you?' She said to me, 'The husband of that woman [me] is in prison [for debt], and I wanted to see what I can do to free him.' So I sold my ass and I gave her the proceeds, and I said to her, 'Here is your money, free your husband, but do not sin [by becoming a prostitute to raise the necessary funds].'"

They said to him, "You are worthy of praying and having your prayers answered."

In a dream that appeared to R. Abbahu Mr. Pentakaka ["Five sins"] prayed that rain would come, and it rained. R. Abbahu summoned him. He said to him, "What is your trade?"

He said to him, "Five sins does that man [I] do every day: hiring whores, cleaning up the theater, bringing home their garments for washing, dancing, and banging cymbals before them."

He said to him, "And what good deed have you done?"

He said to him, "One day that man [I] was cleaning the theater, and a woman came and stood behind a pillar and cried. I said to her, 'What troubles you?' And she said to me, 'That woman's [my] husband is in prison, and I wanted to see what I can do to free him,' so I sold my bed and cover, and I gave the proceeds to her. I said to her, 'Here is your money, free your husband, but do not sin.'"

He said to him, "You are worthy of praying and having your prayers answered."

A pious man from Kepar Immi appeared [in a dream] to the rabbis. He prayed for rain and it rained. The rabbis went up to him. His householders told them that he was sitting on a hill. They went out to him, saying to him, "Greetings," but he did not answer them.

He was sitting and eating, and he did not say to them, "You break bread too."

When he went back home, he made a bundle of faggots and put his cloak on top of the bundle [instead of on his shoulder].

When he came in, he said to his household [wife], "These rabbis are here [because] they want me to pray for rain. If I pray and it rains, it is a disgrace for them, and if not, it is a profanation of the name of Heaven. But come, you and I will go up [to the roof] and pray. If it rains, we shall tell them, 'Heaven has done a miracle [for you],' and if not, we shall tell them, 'We are not worthy to pray and have our prayers answered.'"

They went up and prayed and it rained.

They came down to them [and asked], "Why have the rabbis troubled themselves to come here today?"

They said to him, "We want you to pray so that it would rain."

He said to them, "Now do you really need my prayers? Heaven already has done its miracle."

They said to him, "Why, when you were on the hill, did we say hello to you, and you did not reply?"

He said to them, "I was then doing my job. Should I then interrupt my concentration [on my work]?"

They said to him, "And why, when you sat down to eat, did you not say to us, 'You break bread too'?"

He said to them, "Because I had only my small ration [of food]. Why should I have invited you to eat by way of mere flattery [when I knew I could not give you anything at all]?"

They said to him, "And why when you came to leave, did you put your cloak on top of the bundle?"

He said to them, "Because the cloak was not mine. It was borrowed for use at prayer. I did not want to tear it."

They said to him, "And why, when you were on the hill, did your wife wear dirty clothes, but when you came down from the mountain, did she put on clean clothes?"

He said to them, "When I was on the hill, she put on dirty clothes, so that no one would gaze at her. But when I came home from the hill, she put on clean clothes, so that I would not gaze at any other woman."

They said to him, "It is well that you pray and have your prayers answered."

YERUSHALMI TAANIT 1:4

Wealth

People understand by "wealth" the material things of the world. But wisdom defines wealth differently. Specifically, the story that follows has one sage identify wealth with silver and gold and especially real estate, while the other explains that true wealth is learning—specifically in this setting, study of the Torah.

"And your ancient ruins shall be rebuilt" (Isa. 58:12).

R. Tarfon gave to R. Aqiba six silver *centenarii*, saying to him, "Go, buy us a piece of land, so we can get a living from it and labor in the study of Torah together."

He took the money and handed it out to scribes, Mishnah teachers, and those who study Torah.

After some time R. Tarfon met him and said to him, "Did you buy the land that I mentioned to you?"

He said to him, "Yes."

He said to him, "Is it any good?"

He said to him, "Yes."

He said to him, "And do you not want to show it to me?"

He took him and showed him the scribes, Mishnah teachers, and people who were studying Torah, and the Torah that they had acquired. He said to him, "Is there anyone who works for nothing? Where is the deed covering the field?"

He said to him, "It is with King David, concerning whom it is written, 'He has scattered, he has given to the poor, his righteousness endures for ever'" (Ps. 112:9).

LEVITICUS RABBAH XXXIV:XVI

Our rabbis have taught on Tannaite authority:

Rich in property, rich in pomp—this is a master of lore.

Rich in cash, rich in oil—that is a master of analytical reasoning.

Rich in products, rich in stores—that is a master of traditions.

Everyone, however, is in need of the one who has wheat—solid analytical study of Tannaite traditions.

Said R. Zira said Rab, " What is the meaning of the verse of Scripture, 'All the days of the afflicted are evil' (Prov. 15:15)?

"This refers to masters of Talmud.

"'But he that is of a good heart has a continuous banquet' (Prov. 15:15)? This refers to masters of the Mishnah."

Raba said, "Matters are just the opposite."

And that is in line with what R. Mesharshayya said in the name of Raba, "What is the meaning of the verse of Scripture: 'Whoever removes stones shall be hurt with them' (Qoh. 10:9)?

"This refers to masters of the Mishnah.

"'But he who cleaves wood shall be warmed by it' (Qoh. 10:9)?

"This refers to masters of Talmud."

R. Hanina says, "'All of the days of the afflicted are evil' (Prov. 15:15) refers to a man who has a bad wife.

"'But he that is of a good heart has a continuous banquet' (Prov. 15:15) refers to a man who has a good wife.

R. Yannai says, "'All the days of the afflicted are evil' (Prov. 15:15) refers to one who is fastidious.

"'But he that is of a good heart has a continuous banquet (Prov. 15:15) refers to one who is easy to please."

R. Yohanan said, "'All the days of the afflicted are evil' (Prov. 15:15) refers to a merciful person.

"'But he that is of a good heart has a continuous banquet' (Prov. 15:15) refers to someone who is cruel by nature [so nothing bothers him]."

R. Joshua b. Levi said, "'All the days of the afflicted are evil' (Prov. 15:15) refers to someone who is worrisome.

"'But he that is of a good heart has a continuous banquet' (Prov. 15:15) refers to one who is serene."

R. Joshua b. Levi said, "'All the days of the afflicted are evil' (Prov. 15:1)—but [not] there are Sabbaths and festival days [on which the afflicted gets some pleasure]?"

The matter accords with what Samuel said. For Samuel said, "The change in diet [for festival meals] is the beginning of stomachache."

"'All the days of the poor are evil" (Prov. 15:15). It is written in the book of Ben Sira: "So too his nights. His roof is the lowest in town, his vineyard on the topmost mountain. Rain flows from other roofs onto his and from his vineyard onto other vineyards."

BAVLI TO MISHNAH-TRACTATE BABA BATRA 9:4D-J

Welcoming Strangers

The wisdom of holy Israel greatly values hospitality and the welcoming of strangers, because Israel begins in the experience of being a stranger in a foreign country. Those who have lived overseas know how much appreciated is an act of friendship, generosity, or hospitality done for an outsider, who cannot repay. Some countries are famous for inhospitable conduct (contemporary Germany comes to mind, its universities being famous for their large helpings of cold shoulder), and others become known for their cordiality to the outsider: Ireland, Italy, and, as a matter of fact, the State of Israel as well.

"You shall not wrong a stranger or oppress him, for you were strangers in the land of Egypt":

"You shall not wrong him" in words.

"or oppress him" in property.

You may not say to him, "Yesterday you worshipped Bel, Kores, and

Nebo. Up to now, lo, there was pig-meat sticking out from between your teeth, and now you stand and contradict me."

And how do we know that if you have wronged him, he may also wrong you?

Scripture says, "You shall not wrong a stranger or oppress him, for you were strangers in the land of Egypt."

In this regard R. Nathan would say, "Don't label your fellow with your own faults."

Beloved are strangers [meaning, converts]. For in every passage Scripture admonishes concerning them:

"You shall not wrong a stranger or oppress him, for you were strangers in the land of Egypt."

"Love you therefore the stranger" (Deut. 10:19).

"For you know the heart of a stranger" (Exod. 23:9).

R. Eliezer says, "As to a stranger, because there is a bad streak in him, therefore Scripture admonishes concerning him in many passages."

R. Simeon b. Yohai says, "Lo, Scripture says, 'But they who love him are as the sun when it goes forth in his might' (Judg. 5:31).

"Now who is the greater, the one who loves the king or the one whom the king loves?

"One must say that it is the one whom the king loves.

"And it is written, 'You shall not wrong a stranger or oppress him, for you were strangers in the land of Egypt.' 'Love you therefore the stranger' (Deut. 10:19). 'For you know the heart of a stranger' (Exod. 23:9)".

Beloved are strangers. For in numerous passages Scripture calls them by the same names as it uses for Israel.

Israel it called "slaves," as it is said, "For the children of Israel are to me as slaves" (Lev. 25:55), and strangers are called "slaves," as it is said, "And to love the name of the Lord, to be his slaves" (Isa. 56:6).

The Israelites are called "ministers": "But you shall be named the priests of the Lord, people shall call you the ministers of our God" (Isa. 61:6), and strangers are called "ministers": "Also the strangers, who join themselves to the Lord, to minister to him" (Isa. 56:6).

The Israelites are called "friends:" "But you, Israel, my servant, Jacob whom I 'have chosen, the seed of Abraham, my friend" (Isa. 41:8), and strangers are called "friends": "and loves the stranger" (Deut. 10:18).

A covenant is noted with regard to Israel: "And my covenant shall be in your flesh" (Gen. 17:13), and a covenant is noted with regard to strangers: "and holds fast by my covenant" (Isa. 56:6).

"Acceptance" is noted in regard to Israel: "That they may be accepted before the Lord" (Exod. 28:38), and "acceptance" is noted in regard to strangers: "Their burnt-offerings and sacrifices shall be acceptable upon my altar" (Isa. 56:7).

Guarding is noted in regard to Israel: "Behold, he who guards Israel neither slumbers nor sleeps" (Ps. 121:4), and guarding is noted in regard to strangers: "The Lord guards the strangers" (Ps. 146:9).

Abraham called himself a stranger: "I am a stranger and a sojourner with you" (Gen. 23:4).

David called himself a stranger: "I am a stranger in the earth" (Ps. 119:19); "For we are strangers before you and sojourners, as all our fathers were; our days on the earth are as a shadow and there is no abiding" (1 Chron. 29:15); "For I am a stranger with you, a sojourner, as all my fathers were" (Ps. 39:13).

Beloved are strangers. For Abraham our father circumcised himself only at ninety-nine years of age, for had he circumcised himself at the age of twenty or thirty, no stranger could have been able to convert to Judaism unless he was under the age of thirty.

Therefore the Omnipresent bore with him until he reached the age of ninety-nine years, so as not to slam the door before strangers [who wish to convert].

This was also to provide a reward in accord with the days and years, so increasing the reward for the one who does his will.

That carries out the following verse of Scripture: "The Lord was pleased, for his righteousness' sake, to make the Torah great and glorious" (Isa. 42:21).

And so too you find [strangers/proselytes] in the four groups who respond and speak before the One who spoke and brought the world into being:

"One shall say, 'I am the Lord's'" (Isa. 44:5), meaning, "All of me belongs to the Lord, with no mixture of sin in me."

"Another shall call himself by the name of Jacob" (Isa. 44:5): this refers to righteous proselytes.

"And another shall subscribe with his hand to the Lord" (Isa. 44:5): this refers to sinners who repent.

"And surname himself by the name of Israel" (Isa. 44:5): this refers to those who fear Heaven [proselytes].

MEKHILTA LXXV:I.1

Whence Do We Come, Whither Do We Go

Here, the sages give advice, but they back into it. They set up a statement that could stand on its own as wisdom, but then fill in the blanks, providing a new level of wisdom that supersedes the original statement.

Aqabiah b. Mehallalel says, "Reflect upon three things and you will not fall into the clutches of transgression: "Know (1) from whence you come, (2) whither you are going, and (3) before whom you are going to have to give a full account of yourself.

"From whence do you come? From a putrid drop. Whither are you going? To a place of dust, worms, and maggots.

"And before whom you are going to give a full account of yourself? Before the King of kings of kings, the Holy One, blessed be he."

TRACTATE ABOT 3:1

When Punishment and Misfortune Come into the World

Our sages saw the drama in ordinary things. To them punishment and misfortune happen not by chance but by choice. The evil people bring evil upon the world, but, alas, the righteous suffer first of all. For our sages, "the angel of death" is not a metaphor but a palpable being. And since no one should die before the fullness of years, people should do what they can to avoid the angel of death. For them that meant avoiding him; for us it can mean, not smoking.

Said R. Simeon bar Nahmani said R. Jonathan, "Punishment comes into the world only when there are wicked people in the world, but it begins only with the righteous first of all, as it is said, 'If fire breaks out and catches in thorns . . . .' (Exod. 22:6). When does fire break out? Only when there are thorns. But it begins only with the righteous: 'so that the sheaves of wheat or the standing grain or the field be consumed . . . .' What is said is not 'it consumes the sheaves of wheat,' but, 'sheaves of wheat are consumed'—meaning, it has already been consumed [before the thorns are touched]."

R. Joseph repeated as a Tannaite statement: "What is the meaning of the verse of Scripture: 'And none of you shall go out at the door of his house until the morning' (Exod. 12:22)? Once permission is given to the destructive angel to do his work, he does not distinguish between righteous and wicked.

"And not only so, but so far as he is concerned, he begins with the righteous first: 'And I will cut off from you the righteous and the wicked' (Ezek. 21:8)."

Now when R. Joseph said this, he wept, "So much are the righteous compared to nothing?"

Said to him Abbayye, "It is in fact an act of kindness to them: 'That the righteous is taken away from the evil to come' (Isa. 57:1)."

Said R. Judah said Rab, "One should always enter a town with 'it was good' [that is, in daylight] and leave with 'it was good' [in light]: 'And none of you shall go out at the door of his house until the morning' (Exod. 12:22)."

Our rabbis have taught on Tannaite authority:

If there is an epidemic in town, stay indoors: "And none of you shall go out at the door of his house until the morning" (Exod. 12:22). And further: "Come my people, enter you into your chambers and shut your doors about you" (Isa. 26:20). And further: "The sword without, the terror within shall destroy" (Deut. 32:25).

Why the other two proof-texts?

Should you say that the counsel given here applies only at night but not to day: "Come my people, enter you into your chambers and shut your doors about you" (Isa. 26:20).

And should you say that that pertains only where there is nothing to be afraid of inside, but if there is something to be afraid of inside, it is better to go out and sit among people all together: "The sword without, the terror within shall destroy" (Deut. 32:25). Even the terror is within, the sword will destroy more without.

In a time of epidemic, Raba would close the windows: "For death has come up into our windows" (Jer. 9:20)

Our rabbis have taught on Tannaite authority:

If there is an epidemic in town, stay indoors: "And there was a famine in the land, and Abram went down into Egypt to sojourn there" (Gen. 12:10). And further: "If we say, we will enter into the city, then the famine is in the city and we shall die there" (2 Kings 7:4).

Why the other proof-text?

Should you say that the counsel given here applies only where there is no danger to life, but where there is a danger to life, don't do it, so come and hear: "Now therefore come and let us fall into the host of the Aramaeans, if they save us alive, we shall live" (2 Kings 7:4).

Our rabbis have taught on Tannaite authority:

If there is an epidemic in town, a person should not walk down the middle of the road, for the angel of death walks down the middle of the road.

Once he has been given permission to do his work, he does it quite openly.

If there is peace in town, a person should not walk down the side of the road.

If the angel of death has not got permission to do his work, he hides and slinks along the sides of the road.

Our rabbis have taught on Tannaite authority:

If there is an epidemic in town, a person should not enter the house of assembly by himself, for the angel of death deposits his utensils there.

That rule applies only if no children are reciting Scripture there or ten people are not praying there.

Our rabbis have taught on Tannaite authority:

When dogs howl, it means the angel of death is coming to town.

When dogs romp, it means Elijah the prophet is coming to town.

But that rule applies only if there is not among them a bitch in heat.

BAVLI TO MISHNAH-TRACTATE BABA QAMMA 6:4G-H/60A-B

The Wisdom of Jerusalem and the Wisdom of Athens

The following parables illustrate a certain bravado of the sages.

Ten questions did Alexander of Macedonia ask the elders of the South.

He said to them, "Is the distance from Heaven to earth greater than the distance from east to west?"

They said to him, "From east to west. You may know that that is the fact, since lo, when the sun is in the east, everybody can see it, and when the sun is in the west, everybody can see it, but when it is in the center [at high noon], no one can look at it [since it is too close at hand]."

But sages say, "This distance and that distance are equal, since it is said, 'As the Heavens are high above the earth . . . as the distance from east to west' (Ps. 103:11, 12). Now if one of the distances were greater than the other, Scripture should refer to one distance as greater than the other." [since both examples are used, they must be the same.]

Then how come no one can look at the sun at high noon?

Because it stands alone, and nothing obscures its radiance.

He said to them, "Was Heaven created first, or was earth?"

They said, "Heaven was created first, as it is said, 'In the beginning God created the Heaven and the earth' (Gen. 1:1)."

He said to them, "Was light created first, or darkness?"

They said to him, "That is a matter that has no solution."

But why not say to him that the darkness was created first, since it is written, "And the earth was unformed and voice, and darkness . . . ." followed by "And God said, 'Let there be light,' and there was light'" (Gen. 1:2)?

They were concerned that he might proceed to investigate what is above and what is below, what is before and what is after.

Well, then, they shouldn't have taken up his questions about Heaven either.

They supposed that he just stumbled on that question. When they saw that he went and asked further, they determined not to say anything to him, lest he proceed to investigate what is above and what is below, what is before and what is after.

He said to them, "Who is called wise?"

They said to him, "Who is wise? He who sees what is going to happen."

He said to them, "Who is called mighty?"

They said to him, "Who is mighty? He who overcomes his impulses."

He said to them, "Who is called rich?"

They said to him, "Who is rich? He who takes pleasure in his lot."

He said to them, "What should a person do to live?"

They said to him, "He should kill his 'self.'" [He should be humble so as to gain eternal life.]

"What should someone do to die?"

"He should resurrect his 'self.'" [He should indulge himself and so merit eternal death.]

"What should someone do to be accepted by others?"

"They said, "Let him hate the king and the ruler."

He said to him, "My answer is better than yours: 'Let him love the king and the ruler and do good for others.'"

He said to him, "Is it better to live in the sea or on dry land?"

They said to him, "On dry land it is better to live, for lo, everyone who sets out at sea has no peace of mind until returning home to land."

He said to them, "Who is the wisest among you?"

They said to him, "We're all the same, for lo, to every question that you posed to us, we gave the same answer."

He said to them, "How come you refuse to accept me?"

They said, "Satan is victorious [through you]."

He said to him, "Look, I'm going to kill you by royal decree."

They said to him, "Power is in the hand of the king, and it is hardly appropriate for the king to dissimulate."

On the spot he dressed them in purple garments and put golden chains around their necks.

He said to them, "I am planning to go to a city in Africa."

They said to him, "You won't be able to go there, because the mountains of darkness block the way."

He said to them, "That won't stop me. This is what I'm asking you: what do I need to do to get there?"

They said to him, "Get yourself some Libyan asses that can travel in the dark and get some coils of rope. Tie the rope along the sides of the road, so when you come back, you will follow the rope and get home."

He did it and went. He came to a place that was populated solely by women. He wanted to do battle with them. They said to him, "If you kill us, people will say he killed women, and if we kill you, they'll say, he was the king whom women killed."

He said to them, "Bring me bread."

They brought him gold bread on gold plates.

He said to them, "Do people eat gold bread?"

They said to him, "Well, now, if you wanted real bread to eat, then don't you have break to eat where you come from, that you have gone and made the trip here?"

When he left, he wrote on the gate of the city, "I, Alexander of Macedonia, was a fool until I came to this African town made up of women and learned wisdom from women."

As he was going along, he encamped by a well to eat bread. He had in hand salted fish, and, as he was washing off the salt, a fragrance wafted. He said, "From that fact we may conclude that the well flows from the Garden of Eden."

Some say that he took some of the water and washed his face [and then smelled the scent of it].

Some say that he took all of the water out of the well until he got to the gates of the Garden of Eden, whereupon he said in a loud voice, "Open the gates.": They responded, "This is the gate of the Lord" (Ps. 118:20).

He said to them, "I too am a king, I too possess dignity. Give me something."

They gave him an eyeball.

He went and weighed in the balance against it all his silver and gold, but they did not outweigh it. He said to our rabbis, "What's going on?"

They said to him, "It is the eyeball of a mortal, which is never satisfied."

He said to them, "How so?"

They took some dirt and covered it, and on the spot, it was outweighed in the balance: "As death and destruction are never satisfied, so people are never satisfied" (Prov. 27:20).

BAVLI TO MISHNAH-TRACTATE TAMID 4:3/31B-32B

Four Jerusalemites went to Athens and were received by someone there. In the evening he made a meal for them. After they had eaten and drunk, he set four beds for them, one of them damaged [and supported by the next].

After they had eaten and drunk, he said, "I'm going to listen, for the Jerusalemites are very smart. I'll go and lie down near them to know what they are saying."

One of them woke up, the one sleeping in the damaged bed, and said, "Do you think that I am sleeping on a bed? I am sleeping only on the ground."

The second woke up and said, "Are you surprised at that? The meat that we were eating tasted of dog."

The third woke up and said, "Are you surprised at that? The wine that we drank tasted like the grave."

The fourth awoke and said, "Are you surprised at that? The householder here is not the father of his son."

At that moment the man said, "One of them spoke the truth, and three told lies."

He got up in the morning and went to the butcher, saying to him, "Here is some money, and give me the same meat that you gave me yesterday."

He said to him, "I don't have any left."

He said, "What was there special about it?"

He said to him, "I had one lamb which was sucking, but its dam died, and I had a bitch, so the lamb sucked from her. When you came in the evening, I was out of meat when you came to buy some, and I had nothing else so I gave you some of this."

He said to himself "Two of them told the truth and two lied."

He went to the wine-dealer and said to him, "Give me some of the wine that you sold me last night."

He said to him, "I don't have any left."

He said to him, "What was there special about it?"

He said to him, "I had one vine, planted over my father's grave. I pressed the grapes and poured the wine into casks. I was running out of wine when you came to buy some, and I had no choice but to give you some of that."

He said to himself "Three of them told the truth and one lied."

He said, "I'm going to go and ask mother."

He went to his mother and said to her, "Whose son am I?"

She said to him, "Your father's son."

He said to her, "Tell me the truth, whose son am I? And if you don't tell me the truth, I'll cut off your head."

She said to him, "Your father was infertile. Did I do wrong by going and playing the whore so as to bring you all this property [that you have inherited from your putative father], so that it would not go to a third party?"

Then he said, "And are the Jerusalemites going to come to us and declare us all to be illegitimate?"

They made an agreement among themselves not to receive Jerusalemites [as guests].

A Jerusalemite came to Athens, but no one wanted to extend him hospitality, so he went to a stall.

After they had eaten and drank, he wanted to sleep there.

The owner of the stall said to him, "We have made an agreement among us that no one from Jerusalem will sleep among us until he has jumped three jumps."

He said to him, "I don't know how you people jump. You jump first, and I'll follow you."

He took one jump, then another, and a third, and ended up outside the stall. The Jerusalemite went and locked the door after him.

He said to him, "What's this?"

He said to him, "What you wanted to do to me, I have done to you."

An Athenian came to Jerusalem and went to the school house and found youngsters there, but their master was not present.

He asked them questions, and they answered him.

They said to him, "Let us make a deal that whoever is asked a question and cannot answer it will lose a piece of clothing."

They agreed.

They said to him, "You go first, for you are a sage."

He said to them, "You ask first, because you are locals."

They said to him, "Explain the following: Nine go out but eight come in, two pour out but one drinks, and twenty-four serve."

He could not explain these things to them. They took away his clothes.

He went to R. Yohanan, saying to him, "Is this how you act in your place? They strip guests naked."

He said to him, "Who stripped you?"

He said to him, "School children!"

He said to them, "Did they ask you something that you did not answer?"

He repeated the story to him.

He said to him, "Go and tell them: [Cohen, p. 78:] the nine which go in are the nine months of gestation, and the eight that come out are the eight days of circumcision,

"the two that pour are the two breasts that give milk, and the one that drinks is the baby,

"and the twenty-four that serve are the twenty-four months of nursing."

He went and told them all this and they returned his clothing, and they recited in his regard, "If you had not plowed with my heifer, you would not have solved my riddle" (Judg. 14:18).

An Athenian came to Jerusalem and came upon a child and gave him some money, saying to him, "Go, buy me cheese and eggs.

When he came back, he said to him, "Tell me, as to these eggs, whence do they come, from a white chicken or a black one?"

The child said to him, "You tell me, as to this cheese, where does it come from, white goats or black?

An Athenian came to Jerusalem and came upon a child and gave him some money, saying to him, "Go, buy me figs."

He said to him, "Many thanks."

He said to him, "Was it for nothing?"

He said to him, "What do you want?"

He said to him, "You with your month and I with my legs."

He said to him, "Go and divide."

There was an inferior portion, which the boy set before himself, and a better portion, before the visitor.

He said to him, "Many thanks, well do people say that the Jerusalemites are very clever. Since the child knew that the money was mine, he chose the better portion and set it before me."

When he was going, he said to him, "By your life! Let's cast lots. If yours comes up, you will take what's mine and if mine comes up, I'll take yours."

They agreed, so the child got the man's portion.

An Athenian came to Jerusalem and came upon a child and gave him some money, saying to him, "Take this money and bring me something to eat now, with something left over for the way."

He went and brought him salt.

He said to him, "Did I tell you to bring me salt?"

He said to him, "Something to eat and be satisfied, with something left over.

"By your life, in this you will find something of which you can eat and be satisfied and leave something over for your trip."

An Athenian came to Jerusalem and came upon a broken mortar. He took it and went to a tailor, saying to him, "Sew this broken mortar for me."

He took out a handful of sand, saying to him, "Twist this into thread for me, and I'll sew the mortar."

An Athenian came to Jerusalem and came upon a priest, saying to him, "How much of that load of wood will turn into smoke?"

He said to him, "When it is damp, all of it, when it is dry, a third is smoke, a third ash, and a third fire."

Where had the priest learned this?

From the wood on the temple altar.

An Athenian came to Jerusalem and wanted to learn wisdom.

He worked for three and a half years and had learned nothing.

When he came to leave, he bought a slave, blind in one eye. The one who had sold the slave said to him, "By your life, he is very clever and can see at a distance."

When they had come out of the gate, the slave said to him, "Make haste, so we may overtake the caravan."

He said to him, "Is there a caravan before us?"

He said to him, "Yes, and there is a she-camel in front of us, blind in one eye; it has twins in its womb; it is carrying two skin bottles, one with wine, the other, vinegar; it is four miles away, and the camel-driver is a Gentile."

He said to him, "How do you know that it is blind in one eye?"

"Because one side of the path has been grazed by the camel, but not the other."

"How do you know that it has twins in the womb?"

"It lay down, and I saw the graces of two."

"How do you know that it is carrying two skin bottles, one with wine, the other, vinegar":

"From the drippings. The ones of wine are absorbed in the ground, those of vinegar ferment."

"How do you know that the camel-driver is a Gentile?"

"He pissed in the middle of the road. A Jew would go off to one side."

"And how do you know that it is four miles away?"

"Up to four miles you can make out the mark of the camel's hoof, but not beyond."

Someone from Athens was making fun of the locals of Jerusalem. They said, "Who will go and bring him to us?"

One of them said, "I'll bring him to you, with his head shaved."

He went to Athens and stayed with him.

He was walking in the marketplace, and one of his sandals broke. He gave it to a workman, saying, "Take this *tremis* [a sizable sum of money] and fix this sandal."

He said to him, "Are sandals so costly where you live?"

He said to him, "When they are expensive, they cost ten *denars*, and when cheap, eight."

He said to him, "If I come with you there bringing a stock of sandals, could you sell them?"

He said to him, "Yes, but do not enter the place without me."

He did so. When he got outside the gates, he sent word and called the other, who came out to him, receiving him and greeting him.

He said to him, "What can we do for you, for we have agreed among ourselves not to let a stranger come in here to sell anything unless his head is shaven [and his face blackened]."

He said to him, "What difference does shaving my head make to me if I sell my goods."

He went and shaved his head, entered and took his seat in the middle of the market place, spreading out his sandals before him.

Someone came by and said, "How much is this sandal?"

He said to him, "They cost ten *denars*."

He said to him, "Show me a sandal for ten *denars*!" He hit him on the head with it and went away.

Whoever came by did the same to him, until his head was broken.

Afterward he came to him and said to him, "Did I pay you off so badly?"

He said, "Don't ridicule the locals of Jerusalem any more."

LAMENTATIONS RABBATI XXXV:VII.4

The Wisdom of Jerusalem and the Wisdom of Egypt

Our rabbis have taught on Tannaite authority:

On the twenty-four of Nisan the tax-farmers were dismissed from Judea and Jerusalem.

When the Africans came to trial with Israel before Alexander of Macedonia, they said to him, "The land of Canaan belongs to us, for it is written, 'The land of Canaan, with the coasts thereof' (Num. 34:2), and Canaan was the father of these men."

Said Gebiha, son of Pasisa, to sages, "Give me permission, and I shall go and defend the case with them before Alexander of Macedonia. If they should win out over me, say, 'You won over a perfectly common person of our group,' and if I should win out over them, say to them, 'It is the Torah of Moses that overcame you.'"

They gave him permission, and he went and engaged in debate with them. He said to them, "From whence do you bring proof?"

They said to him, "From the Torah."

He said to them, "I too shall bring you proof only from the Torah, for it is said, 'And he said, Cursed be Canaan, a servant of servants shall he be to his brothers' (Gen. 9:25).

"Now if a slave acquires property, for whom does he acquire it? And to whom is the property assigned?

"And not only so, but it is quite a number of years since you have served us."

Said King Alexander to them, "Give him an answer."

They said to him, "Give us a span of three days time." He gave them time.

They searched and did not find an answer. They forthwith fled, leaving their fields fully sown and their vineyards laden with fruit, and that year was the Sabbatical Year. [So the Israelites could enjoy the produce in a time in which they most needed it.]

There was another time, [and] the Egyptians came to lay claim against Israel before Alexander of Macedonia. They said to him, "Lo, Scripture says, 'And the Lord gave the people favor in the sight of the Egyptians, and they lent them gold and precious stones' (Exod. 12:36). Give us back the silver and gold that you took from us."

Said Gebiha, son of Pasisa, to sages, "Give me permission, and I shall go and defend the case with them before Alexander of Macedonia. If they should win out over me, say, 'You won over a perfectly common person of our group,' and if I should win out over them, say to them, 'It is the Torah of Moses, our master, that overcame you.'"

They gave him permission, and he went and engaged in debate with them. He said to them, "From whence do you bring proof?"

They said to him, "From the Torah."

He said to them , "I too shall bring you proof only from the Torah, for it is said, 'Now the sojourning of the children of Israel, who dwelt in Egypt, was four hundred and thirty years' (Exod. 12:40).

"Now pay us the salary of six hundred thousand people whom you enslaved in Egypt for 430 years."

Said Alexander of Macedonia to them, "Give him an answer."

They said to him, "Give us time, a span of three days."

He gave them time. They searched and found no answer. They forthwith fled, leaving their fields sown and their vineyards laden with fruit, and that year was the Sabbatical Year.

There was another time, [and] the children of Ishmael and the children of Keturah came to trial with the Israelites before Alexander of Macedonia. They said to him, "The land of Canaan belongs to us as well as to you, for it is written, 'Now these are the generations of Ishmael, son of Abraham' (Gen. 25:12), and it is written, 'And these are the generations of Isaac, Abraham's son' (Gen. 25:19). [Both Ishmael and Isaac have an equal claim on the land, hence so too their descendants]."

Said Gebiha, son of Pasisa, to sages, "Give me permission, and I shall go and defend the case with them before Alexander of Macedonia. If they should win out over me, say, 'You won over a perfectly common person of our group,' and if I should win out over them, say to them, 'It is the Torah of Moses, our master, that overcame you.'"

They gave him permission, and he went and engaged in debate with them. He said to them, "From whence do you bring proof?'

They said to him, "From the Torah."

He said to them, "I too shall bring you proof only from the Torah, for it is said, 'And Abraham gave all that he had to Isaac. But to the sons of the concubines which Abraham had Abraham gave gifts' (Gen. 25:5-6).

"In the case of a father who gave a bequest to his sons while he was yet alive and sent them away from one another, does any one of them have a claim on the other? [Certainly not.]"

What were the gifts [that he gave]?

Said R. Jeremiah bar Abba, "This teaches that he gave them [the power of utilizing the divine] Name [for] unclean [purposes]."

BAVLI TO MISHNAH-TRACTATE SHABBAT 11:1

The Wise Man and the Fool

There are seven traits that characterize an unformed clod, and seven a sage. (1) A sage does not speak before someone greater than he in wisdom. (2) And he does not interrupt his fellow. (3) And he is not at a loss for an answer. (4) He asks a relevant question and answers properly. (5) And he addresses each matter in its proper sequence, first, then second. (6) And concerning something he has not heard, he says, "I have not heard the answer." (7) And he concedes the truth [when the other party demonstrates it]. And the opposite of these traits apply to a clod.

A sage does not speak before someone greater than he in wisdom:
This refers to Moses, for it is said, "And Aaron spoke all the words
which the Lord has spoken to Moses and did the signs in the sight of
the people" (Exod. 4:30).

Now who was the more worthy to speak, Moses or Aaron?

One has to say it was Moses.

For Moses had heard the message from the mouth of the Almighty,
while Aaron heard it from Moses.

But this is what Moses said: "Is it possible for me to speak in a situation in which my elder brother is standing?"

Therefore he said to Aaron, "Speak."

Thus it is said, "And Aaron spoke all the words which the Lord had
spoken to Moses" (Exod. 4:30).

And he does not interrupt his fellow:
This refers to Aaron.

For it is said, "Then Aaron spoke . . . . Behold, this day have they
offered their sin-offering and their burnt offering . . . and such things
as these have happened to me" (Lev. 10:19).

He kept silence until Moses had finished speaking and did not say
to him, "Cut it short."

But afterward he said to Moses, "Then Aaron spoke . . . . Behold,
this day have they offered their sin-offering and their burnt offering . . .
and such things as these have happened to me .

"And we are in mourning."

Some say that Aaron drew Moses apart from the group and said to
him, "My brother, if of tithes, which are of lesser sanctity, it is forbidden for one who has yet to bury his deceased to eat, a sin offering, of
greater sanctity, all the more so should be forbidden as a meal to a person who has yet to bury his deceased."

Moses immediately agreed with him, as it is said, "And when Moses
heard it, it was well-pleasing in his sight" (Lev. 10:20),

and in the view of the Almighty as well.

He is not at a loss for an answer.
This is exemplified by Elihu ben Barachel the Buzite.

For it is said, "I am young and you are very old, which is why I held
back and did not tell you my opinion. I said, Days should speak, and
the multitude of years should teach wisdom" (Job 32:6).

This teaches that they remained seated in silence before Job. When he stood up, they stood up. When he sat down, they sat down. When he ate, they ate. When he drank, they drank. Then he took permission from them and cursed his day:

After this Job opened his mouth and cursed his day and said, "Let the day perish when I was born, and the night in which it was said, A man-child is brought forth" (Job 3:1).

Let the day perish on which my father came to my mother and she said to him, "I am pregnant."

And how do we know that they answered not out of turn? "Then Job answered and said" (Job 3:2). "Then answered Eliphaz the Temanite and said" (Job 4:1). "Then answered Bildad the Shuhite and said" (Job 8:1). "Then answered Zophar the Naamathite and said" (Job 11:10). "Then Elihu the son of Barachel the Buzite answered and said" (Job 32:1).

Scripture arranged them one-by-one so as to let everyone in the world know that a sage does not speak before someone greater than he is wisdom. And he does not interrupt his fellow. And he does not answer hastily.

He asks a relevant question and answers properly:
This is exemplified by Judah, who said, "I will be surety for him" (Gen. 43:9).

Not asking a relevant question is exemplified by Reuben, as it is said, "And Reuben said to his father, You shall slay my two sons" (Gen. 42:37).

And he addresses each matter in its proper sequence, first, [then second]:
This is exemplified by Jacob.
And some say, this is exemplified by Sarah.
then second:
This is exemplified by the men of Haran. . . .

. . . And he concedes the truth:
This is exemplified by Moses: And the Lord said to me, They have said well that which they have spoken (Deut. 18:17).

It is further exemplified by the Holy One, blessed be he: "The Lord spoke to Moses, saying, The daughters of Zelophehad speak right" (Num. 27:6).

THE FATHERS ACCORDING TO RABBI NATHAN XXXVII:XI-XVII

Wives and Marriage

Sages placed the highest value upon marriage and the family, regarded women as the foundation of the virtuous life, and maintained that an unmarried man cannot achieve virtue.

Said R. Hanilai, "Any man who has no wife lives without joy, blessing, goodness:

"Joy: 'and you shall rejoice, you and your house' (Deut. 14:26).

"Blessing: 'to cause a blessing to rest on your house' (Ezek. 44:30).

"Goodness: 'it is not good that man should be alone' (Gen. 2:18)."

In the West they say: without Torah and without a wall of refuge.

without Torah: "Is it that I have no help in me and that sound wisdom is driven entirely out of me" (Job 6:13).

without a wall of refuge: "A woman shall form a wall about a man" (Jer. 31:22).

Raba bar Ulla said, "Without peace:

"'And you shall know that your tent is in peace, and you shall visit your habitation and shall miss nothing' (Job 5:24)."

Said R. Joshua b. Levi, "Every man who knows that his wife fears Heaven but does not 'visit' her sins: 'and you shall know that your tent is in peace' (Job 5:24)."

Our rabbis have taught on Tannaite authority:

He who loves his wife as he loves himself, he who honors her more than he honors himself, he who raises up his sons and daughters in the right path, and he who marries them off close to the time of their puberty—of such a one, Scripture says, "And you shall know that your tabernacle shall be in peace and you shall visit your habitation and you shall not sin" (Job 5:24).

Said R. Eleazar, "Any man who has no wife is no man: 'Male and female created he them and called their name Adam' (Gen. 5:2)."

And further said R. Eleazar, "Any man who has no land is no man: 'The Heavens are the Heavens of the Lord, but the earth he has given to the children of man' (Ps. 115:16)."

And further said R. Eleazar, "What is the meaning of this verse: 'I will make him a help meet' (Gen. 2:18)? If he enjoys divine favor, she is a help for him, if not, it she will be against him.'"

Others say, "R. Eleazar contrasted: 'It is written as though it could be read, "to strike him, but it is read as, "a help meet for him" If he enjoys favor, she is meet for him, if not, she is his punishment.'"

Yosé came upon Elijah. He said to him, "It is written, 'I will make him a help'—how does a woman help a man?"

He said to him, "If a man brings home wheat, does he chew it? If he brings home flax, does he wear flax? Doesn't she bring light to his eyes and set him on his feet?"

And further said R. Eleazar, "What is the meaning of the verse of Scripture: 'This is now bone of my bones and flesh of my flesh' (Gen. 2:23)? This teaches that Adam had sexual relations with every beast and wild animal and was left unsatisfied until he had sexual relations with Eve."

Rab was taking leave of R. Hiyya. He said to him, "May the All-Merciful shield you from something worse than death."

"And is there anything that is worth than death?"

He went out and found the verse: "And I find more bitter than death the woman" (Qoh. 7:26).

Rab was tormented by his wife. When he said to her, "Make me lentils," she made him small peas, "Small peas," she made him lentils. When his son, Hiyya, matured, he passed on his father's orders in reverse [so he asked for peas if the father wanted lentils].

He said to him, "Golly, your mother's coming up in the world."

He said to him, "I'm the one who passed on your orders in reverse."

He said to him, "That's what people say: 'Your own offspring will teach you right thinking.' But you shouldn't do that any more: 'They have taught their tongue to speak lies, they wear themselves' (Jer. 9:4)."

Hiyya was tormented by his wife. Still, when he found something nice, he wrapped it in his scarf and brought it to her. Said to him Rab, "Yeah, but she's always pecking away at you!"

He said to him, "It's enough for us that they raise our children and save us from sin."

Judah was reciting to his son R. Isaac the verse, "And I find more bitter than death the woman" (Qoh. 7:26).

He said to him, "Give me a for instance."

He said to him, "For instance, your very own momma-san."

But isn't it so that R. Judah repeated on Tannaite authority to his son, R. Isaac, "A man finds true serenity only with his first wife, as it is said, 'Let your fountain be blessed and have joy of the wife of your youth' (Prov. 5:18)."

He said to him, "Such as whom?"

He said to him, "Such as your mother."

She was easy to anger but easy to appease with a good word.

What is the definition of a bad wife?

Said Abbayye, "It is one who 'serves him a tray of food' when her 'mouth' is ready for him too."

Raba said, "It is one who 'serves him a tray of food' and then turns her back on him."

Said R. Hama bar Hanina, "When a man marries a wife, his sins are buried: 'Whoso finds a wife finds a great good and gets favor of the Lord' (Prov. 18:22)."

In the West, when somebody got married, they should say to him, "Is it 'finds' or 'find'? 'Who finds a wife finds a great good' (Prov. 18:22), or 'and I find more bitter than death the woman' (Qoh. 7:26)."

Said Raba, "As to a bad wife, it is a religious duty to divorce her: 'Cast out the scoffer and contention will go out, yes, strife and shame will cease' (Prov. 22:10)."

Raba further stated, "A bad wife with a weighty marriage-settlement—put a co-wife at her side: 'By her partner, not by a thorn.'"

Raba further stated, "A bad wife is as hard as a stormy day: 'A continual dropping in a very rainy day and a contentious woman are alike' (Prov. 27:15)."

Raba further stated, "Come and see how good is a good wife and how bad is a bad wife. How good is a good wife: 'Who finds a wife finds a great good' (Prov. 18:22). If Scripture speaks of the woman herself, then how good is a good wife whom Scripture praises! If Scripture speaks of the Torah, then how good is a good wife, with whom the Torah is to be compared.

"and how bad is a bad wife: 'And I find more bitter than death the woman' (Qoh. 7:26): If Scripture speaks of the woman herself, then how dreadful is a bad wife whom Scripture condemns! If Scripture speaks of Gehenna, then how bad is a bad wife, with whom Gehenna is to be compared!"

"Behold I will bring upon them evil, which they shall not be able to evade" (Jer. 11:11)—said R. Nahman said Rabbah bar Abbuha, "This refers to a bad wife with a weighty marriage settlement."

"The Lord has delivered me into their hands against whom I am not able to stand" (Lam. 1:14)—said R. Hisda said Mar Uqba bar Hiyya, "This refers to a bad wife with a weighty marriage settlement."

In the West they say, "This refers to one who completely depends upon his own cash to buy food [owning no land to provide his meals]."

"Your sons and daughters shall be given to another people" (Deut. 38:32)—said R. Hanan bar Raba said Rab, "This refers to the father's wife [stepmother to his children]."

"I will provoke them with a vile nation" (Deut. 32:21)—said R. Hanan bar Raba said Rab, "This refers to a bad wife with a weighty marriage-settlement."

Eliezer says, "This refers to the *minim*: 'The fool has said in his heart, there is no God' (Ps. 14:1)."

It is written in the book of Ben Sira:

"A good woman is a good gift, who will be put into the bosom of a God-fearing man. A bad woman is a plague for her husband. What is his remedy? Let him drive her from his house and be healed from what is plaguing him.

"A lovely wife—happy is her husband. The number of his days is doubled.

"Keep your eyes from a woman of charm, lest you be taken in her trap. Do not turn to her husband to drink wine with him, or strong drink, for through the looks of a beautiful woman many have been slain, and numerous are those who have been slain by her.

"Many are the blows with which a peddler is smitten [for dealing with women]. Those who make it a habit of committing fornication are like a spark that lights the ember. As a cage is full of birds, so are their houses full of deceit" (Jer. 5:27).

"Many are the wounds of a peddler, which lead him into temptation, like a spark that lights a coal.

"As a cage is full of birds, so whorehouses are full of deceit.

"'Do not worry about tomorrow's sorrow,' "For you do not know what a day may bring forth" (Prov. 27:1). Perhaps tomorrow you will no longer exist and it will turn out that you will worry about a world that is not yours.

"Keep large numbers of people away from your house, and do not let just anybody into your house.

"Let many people ask how you are, but reveal your secret to one out of a thousand."

Said R. Assi, "The son of David will come only after all of the souls in the body: 'For the spirit that wraps itself is from me, and the souls that I have made' (Isa. 57:16)."

It has been taught on Tannaite authority:

Eliezer says, "Anybody who does not get busy with being fruitful and multiplying is as though he shed blood: 'Whoever sheds man's blood by man shall his blood be shed' (Gen. 9:6) followed by, 'And you, be fruitful and multiply' (Gen. 9:7)."

Jacob says, "It is as though he diminished the divine form: 'For in the image of God made he man' (Gen. 9:6) followed by 'And you, be fruitful and multiply' (Gen. 9:7)."

Ben Azzai says, "It is as though he shed blood and diminished the divine form: 'And you, be fruitful and multiply' (Gen. 9:7)."

They said to Ben Azzai, "There are some talk a good game and play a good game, play a good game but don't talk a good game, but you talk a good game and don't play at all."

He said to him, "What am I supposed to do? For my soul lusts only after the Torah. So let the world be kept going by others."

Our rabbis have taught on Tannaite authority:

"And when it rested, he said, Return O Lord to the tens of thousands and thousands of Israel" (Num. 10:36)—this teaches you that the presence of God comes to rest on Israel only if there are two thousand and two tens of thousands. If they lacked one, and someone did not engaging in being fruitful and multiplying, will that one not turn out to cause the presence of God to remove from Israel?

Abba Hanan said in the name of R. Eliezer, "He is liable to the death penalty: 'And they [Nadab and Abihu] had no children' (Num. 3:4). So if they had children, they would not have died."

Others say, "He causes the presence of God to remove from Israel: 'To be a God to you and to your children after you' (Gen. 17:7)—where there is 'children after you' the presence of God comes to rest, but where there is no 'children after you,' among whom will it come to rest? Among trees or stones?"

BAVLI TO MISHNAH-TRACTATE YEBAMOT 6:6/62B-64A

Wives' Duties and Rights

Sages not only admired women and appreciated them, but they also assigned to them a variety of tasks in the maintenance of the household that would assure women a proper place in the economy of the home. Above all, they sought to give women tasks of dignity and importance.

These are the kinds of labor which a woman performs for her husband: she (1) grinds flour, (2) bakes bread, (3) does laundry, (4) prepares meals, (5) gives suck to her child, (6) makes the bed, (7) works in wool.

[If] she brought with her a single slave girl, she does not (1) grind, (2) bake bread, or (3) do laundry.

[If she brought] two, she does not (4) prepare meals and does not (5) feed her child.

[If she brought] three, she does not (6) make the bed for him and does not (7) work in wool.

If she brought four, she sits on a throne.

Eliezer says, "Even if she brought him a hundred slave girls, he forces her to work in wool,

"for idleness leads to unchastity."

Rabban Simeon b. Gamaliel says, "Also: He who prohibits his wife by a vow from performing any labor puts her away and pays off her marriage contract. For idleness leads to boredom."

He who takes a vow not to have sexual relations with his wife—

the House of Shammai say, "[He may allow this situation to continue] for two weeks."

And the House of Hillel say, "For one week."

Disciples go forth for Torah study without [the wife's] consent for thirty days.

Workers go out for one week.

"The sexual duty of which the Torah speaks (Exod. 21:10): (1) those without work [of independent means]—every day; (2) workers—twice a week; (3) ass-drivers—once a week; (4) camel-drivers—once in thirty days; (5) sailors—once in six months," the words of R. Eliezer.

She who rebels against her husband [declining to perform wifely services]—

they deduct from her marriage contract seven *denars* a week.

Judah says, "Seven *tropaics*."

How long does one continue to deduct?

Until her entire marriage contract [has been voided].

Yosé says, "He continues to deduct [even beyond the value of the marriage contract], for an inheritance may come [to her] from some other source, from which he will collect what is due him."

And so is the rule for the man who rebels against his wife [declining to do the husband's duties]—

they add three *denars* a week to her marriage contract.

Judah says, "Three *tropaics*. "

He who maintains his wife by a third party may not provide for her less than two *qabs* of wheat or four *qabs* of barley [per week]—

Said R. Yosé, "Only R. Ishmael ruled that barley may be given to her, for he was near Edom"—

And one pays over to her a half-*qab* of pulse, a half-*log* of oil, and a *qab* of dried figs or a *maneh* of fig cake.

And if he does not have it, he provides instead fruit of some other type.

And he gives her a bed, a cover, and a mat.

And he annually gives her a cap for her head, and a girdle for her loins, and shoes from one festival season to the next, and clothing worth fifty *zuz* from one year to the next.

And they do not give her either new ones in the sunny season or old ones in the rainy season.

But they provide for her clothing fifty *zuz* in the rainy season, and she clothes herself with the remnants in the sunny season.

And the rags remain hers.

He gives her in addition a silver *maah* [a sixth of a *denar*] for her needs [per week].

And she eats with him on the Sabbath by night.

And if he does not give her a silver *maah* for her needs, the fruit of her labor belongs to her.

And how much work does she do for him?

The weight of five *selas* of warp must she spin for him in Judea (which is ten *selas* weight in Galilee), or the weight of ten *selas* of woof in Judah (which are twenty *selas* in Galilee).

And if she was nursing a child, they take off [the required weight

of wool which she must spin as] the fruit of her labor, and they provide
more food for her.

Under what circumstances?

In the case of the most poverty-stricken man in Israel.

But in the case of a weightier person, all follows the extent of his
capacity [to support his wife].

MISHNAH-TRACTATE KETUBOT 5:5-9

Judah, son of R. Hiyya, son-in-law of R. Yannai, would go and
remain at the session of the household of the master, but every Friday
he would come home, and when he would come home, people saw a
pillar of light moving before him. But once, he was so distracted by his
subject that he didn't go home. Since that sign was not seen, said R.
Yannai to them, "Turn over his bed, for if Judah were alive, he would
not neglect his duty." It was like "an error that comes from the king"
(Qoh. 10:5), and he died.

Rabbi was involved in the marriage preparations for his son into
the household of R. Hiyya. When the time came to write the marriage
contract, the bride dropped dead. Said Rabbi, "God forbid, is there some
reason that the union was invalid?"

They went into session and examined the genealogy of Rabbi [and
found:] "Rabbi comes from Shephatiah [2 Sam. 3:4, son of David], son
of Abital, and R. Hiyya is from the family of Shimei, brother of David."
[Slotki: As the latter was not a descendant of the anointed king's family, it was not proper for his daughter to be united in marriage with one
who was.]

He went on to take up the marriage preparations for his son into
the household of R. Yosé b. Zimra. They contracted that the son would
spend twelve years at the schoolhouse. They brought the girl by him.
He said to them, "Let it be six years."

They brought the girl past him again. He said, "I'd rather marry her
now [no waiting], then I'll go." He was embarrassed before his father.

He said to him, "My son, you have the very mind of the one who
created you, for it is written first, 'You bring them in and plant them'
(Exod. 15:17), and then, 'and let them make me a sanctuary that I may
dwell among them' (Exod. 15:17)."

He went and remained at the session for two years in the schoolhouse, but by the time he came home, his wife went sterile. Said Rabbi,
"What should we do? Should he divorce her? People will say, 'This poor

woman waited for him for nothing.' Should he marry someone else? People will say, 'This one is his wife, that one is his whore.' So he prayed for mercy for her, and she was healed."

R. Hananiah b. Hakhinai was going to the schoolhouse at the end of R. Simeon b. Yohai's wedding celebration. The other said to him, "Wait for me, so I can come with you." He didn't wait for him. He went off and remained at the session for twelve years in the schoolhouse. By the time he got home, the streets of the town had changed, and he didn't know how to get to his house. He went and sat down at the river bank, and there he heard a girl being spoken to in this language: "Daughter of Hakhinai, daughter of Hakhinai, fill up your jug and let's go."
He thought, "It must follow that this girl is ours."
He followed her. His wife was sitting and sifting flour. She looked up and saw him, her heart was overwhelmed and she died. He said before him, "Lord of the world, is this to be the reward of this poor woman?" So he prayed for mercy for her, and she lived.

R. Hama bar Bisa went to the session for twelve years at the house of study. When he came home, he said, "I'm not going to act like Ben Hakhinai." He went into the session and sent word to his wife. His son [born after he left town], R. Oshayya, came along and went into session before him. He asked him a question on a tradition. He saw he was a sharp wit in his traditions. He became depressed. He said, "If I had been here, I could have produced children like this one."
He went home. His son came in. He rose before him, thinking he wanted to ask him some more questions. Said to him his wife, "Is there a father who rises before his son?"
R. Ammi bar Hama recited in his regard: "'And a threefold cord is not quickly broken' (Qoh. 4:12)—this refers to R. Oshayya son of R. Hama son of Bisa."

R. Aqiba was the shepherd of Ben Kalba Sabua. His daughter saw that he was chaste and noble. She said to him, "If we become betrothed to you, will you go to the schoolhouse?"
He said to her, "Yes."
She became betrothed to him secretly and sent him off.
Her father heard and drove her out of his house and forbade her by vow from enjoying his property.

He went and remained at the session for twelve years at the school-house. When he came back, he brought with him twelve thousand disciples. He heard a sage say to her, "How long are you going to lead the life of a lifelong widow?"

She said to him, "If he should pay attention to me, he will spend another twelve years in study."

He said, "So what I'm doing is with permission." He went back and stayed in session another twelve years at the schoolhouse.

When he came back, he brought with him twenty-four thousand disciples. His wife heard and went out to meet him. Her neighbors said to her, "Borrow some nice clothes and put them on."

She said to them, "'A righteous man will recognize the soul of his cattle' (Prov. 12:10)."

When she came to him, she fell on her face and kissed his feet. His attendants were going to push her away. He said to them, "Leave her alone! What is mine and what is yours is hers."

Her father heard that an eminent authority had come to town. He said, "I shall go to him. Maybe he'll release me from my vow." He came to him. He said to him, "Did you take your vow with an eminent authority in mind [as your son-in-law]?"

He said to him, "Even if he had known a single chapter, even if he had known a single law [I would never have taken that vow]!"

He said to him, "I am the man."

He fell on his face and kissed his feet and gave him half of his property.

The daughter of R. Aqiba did the same with Ben Azzai, and that is in line with what people say: "A ewe copies a ewe, a daughter's acts are like the mother's."

BAVLI TO MISHNAH-TRACTATE KETUBOT 5:6

The Youthful Sage

If sages deem Israel to possess resources of wisdom, they assign the richest treasures of sound insight to women and children. For them that was not a mark of sentimentality but a considered, weighty judgment.

There is the case of R. Joshua, who was walking on the way, and someone walking on the way saw him.

He said to him, "What are you doing?"

He said to him, "I am walking on the way."

He said to him, "Well said, for robbers like you have trodden it [stealing private property and making it public property through usufruct]."

He was walking along and found a child at a crossroad.

He said to him, "What is the nearest way to town?"

He said to him, "This way is near and far, and that is far and near."

R. Joshua went on the one that was near and far. But as he got near the wall, there were gardens and orchards surrounding it, so he could not get into town.

He went back to the child and said to him, "My child, did you not say to me that this way is near and far?"

He said to him, "My lord, you are a great sage in Israel. Did I not say to you that this is far and near, and that is near and far?"

At that moment said R. Joshua, "Happy are you O Israel, that all of you are sages, from your youngest to your oldest!"

He went further and came upon another child, who was holding a covered dish.

He said to him, "What is in that dish?"

He said to him, "If my mother wanted you to know what is in it, she would not have told me to cover it."

He went further and came upon another child, to whom he set the question, "What is the water of the city like?"

He said to him, "Don't worry, the garlic and onions are plentiful."

He went into the town and found a little girl standing and filling a pitcher of water from a cistern. He said to her, "Give me some water."

She said to him, "For you and for your ass."

After he had drunk and was turning away, he said to her, "My daughter, you have acted like Rebeccah."

She said to him, "I acted like Rebeccah, but you have not behaved like Eliezer [by giving me a gift, in line with Genesis 24]."

It has been taught on Tannaite authority: They leave over *peah* of a dish prepared in a boiling pot and it goes without saying, of one prepared in a tightly covered stew pot.

There is the following precedent:

R. Joshua b. Hananiah lodged with a widow, and she brought him a dish on the first day, and he ate it and did not leave *peah*; the second day and he did not leave *peah*; and as to the third day, what did she do? She oversalted a dish of pounded grain, and when he tasted it, he did not touch it.

She said to him, "Why did you leave aside the dish of pounded grain?"

He said to her, "I had already eaten during the day."

She said to him, "If you had already eaten during the day, why didn't you decline the bread in the way in which you declined the grain? Maybe you left it over as *peah*? And why did you not leave *peah* from the two dishes you ate as you left it from this pounded grain?"

Said R. Joshua, "No one ever got the better of me in an argument than those children and this widow and the little girl:

"so exemplifying the verse, 'she that was great among the nations.'"

LAMENTATIONS RABBATI XXXV:VII.4

Bibliography

The senior editor has translated all of the principal documents of the oral Torah and has provided introductions to each as well. Selections from these translations form the shank of the anthology. Exceptions are indicated by the name of another translator.

For a comprehensive introduction to the documents of the oral Torah, see the senior editor's *Introduction to Rabbinic Literature* (New York: Doubleday, 1994, The Doubleday Anchor Reference Library). Further bibliography for each document is provided there. A comprehensive bibliography of the Classical Literature of Judaism is given in H. L. Strack and G. Stemberger, *Introduction to the Talmud and Midrash*. Translated by Markus Bockmuehl. Foreword by Jacob Neusner. (Minneapolis: Fortress Press, 1992).

The translations of, and introductions to, the documents of the oral Torah are as follows:

Translations and Commentaries

A History of the Mishnaic Law of Purities. Leiden: Brill, 1974–1977. I-XXII.

I.	*Kelim. Chapters One through Eleven*. 1974.
II.	*Kelim. Chapters Twelve through Thirty*. 1974.
III.	*Kelim. Literary and Historical Problems*. 1974.
IV.	*Ohalot. Commentary*. 1975.
V.	*Ohalot. Literary and Historical Problems*. 1975.
VI.	*Negaim. Mishnah-Tosefta*. 1975.
VII.	*Negaim. Sifra*. 1975.
VIII.	*Negaim. Literary and Historical Problems*. 1975.
IX.	*Parah. Commentary*. 1976.
X.	*Parah. Literary and Historical Problems*. 1976.
XI.	*Tohorot. Commentary*, 1976.
XII.	*Tohorot. Literary and Historical Problems*. 1976.
XIII.	*Miqvaot. Commentary*. 1976.
XIV.	*Miqvaot. Literary and Historical Problems*. 1976.
XV.	*Niddah. Commentary*. 1976.
XVI.	*Niddah. Literary and Historical Problems*. 1976.
XVII.	*Makhshirin*. 1977.
XVIII.	*Zabim*. 1977.
XIX.	*Tebul Yom. Yadayim*. 1977.
XX.	*Uqsin. Cumulative Index, Parts I-XX*. 1977.

The Judaic Law of Baptism. Tractate Miqvaot in the Mishnah and the Tosefta. A Form-Analytical Translation and Commentary, and a Legal and Religious History.

Atlanta: Scholars Press for South Florida Studies in the History of Judaism, 1995. Second Printing of *A History of the Mishnaic Law of Purities*. Volumes XIII and XIV.

The Tosefta. Translated from the Hebrew. New York: Ktav, 1977–1980. II–VI.

    II. *The Tosefta. Translated from the Hebrew. Second Division. Moed.*
    III. *The Tosefta. Translated from the Hebrew. Third Division. Nashim.*
    IV. *The Tosefta. Translated from the Hebrew. Fourth Division. Neziqin.*
    V. *The Tosefta. Translated from the Hebrew. Fifth Division. Qodoshim.* Second printing: Atlanta: Scholars Press for USF Academic Commentary Series, 1995.
    VI. *The Tosefta. Translated from the Hebrew. Sixth Division. Tohorot.* Second printing: Atlanta: Scholars Press for *South Florida Studies in the History of Judaism,* 1990. With a new preface.

Edited: *The Tosefta. Translated from the Hebrew. I. The First Division (Zeraim).* New York: Ktav, 1985.

The Tosefta: Its Structure and its Sources. Atlanta: Scholars Press for Brown Judaic Studies, 1986. Reprise of pertinent results in *Purities* I–XXI.

A History of the Mishnaic Law of Holy Things. Leiden: Brill, 1979. I–VI.

    I. *Zebahim. Translation and Explanation.*
    II. *Menahot. Translation and Explanation.*
    III. *Hullin, Bekhorot. Translation and Explanation.*
    IV. *Arakhin, Temurah. Translation and Explanation.*
    V. *Keritot, Meilah, Tamid, Middot, Qinnim. Translation and Explanation.*

Form Analysis and Exegesis: A Fresh Approach to the Interpretation of Mishnah. Minneapolis: University of Minnesota Press, 1980.

A History of the Mishnaic Law of Women. Leiden: Brill, 1979–1980. I–V.

    I. *Yebamot. Translation and Explanation.*
    II. *Ketubot. Translation and Explanation.*
    III. *Nedarim, Nazir. Translation and Explanation.*
    IV. *Sotah, Gittin, Qiddushin. Translation and Explanation.*

A History of the Mishnaic Law of Appointed Times. Leiden: Brill, 1981–1983. I–V.

    I. *Shabbat. Translation and Explanation.*
    II. *Erubin, Pesahim. Translation and Explanation.*
    III. *Sheqalim, Yoma, Sukkah. Translation and Explanation.*
    IV. *Besah, Rosh Hashshanah, Taanit, Megillah, Moed Qatan, Hagigah. Translation and Explanation.*

A History of the Mishnaic Law of Damages. Leiden: Brill, 1983–1985. I–V.

    I. *Baba Qamma. Translation and Explanation.*
    II. *Baba Mesia. Translation and Explanation.*
    III. *Baba Batra, Sanhedrin, Makkot. Translation and Explanation.*
    IV. *Shebuot, Eduyyot, Abodah Zarah, Abot, Horayyot. Translation and Explanation.*

The Mishnah. A New Translation. New Haven and London: Yale University Press, 1987. *Choice* Outstanding Academic Book List, 1989. Second printing: 1990. Paperbound edition: 1991.

Underway: Translation into Finnish by Kari Kelho, Helsinki.

The Talmud of the Land of Israel. A Preliminary Translation and Explanation. Chicago: The University of Chicago Press, 1982–1993. IX-XII, XIV-XV, XVII-XXXV.

IX.	*Hallah.* 1991
X.	*Orlah. Bikkurim.* 1991.
XI.	*Shabbat.* 1991.
XII.	*Erubin.* 1990.
XIV.	*Yoma.* 1990.
XV.	*Sheqalim.* 1990.
XVII.	*Sukkah.* 1988.
XVIII.	*Besah. Taanit.* 1987.
XIX.	*Megillah.* 1987.
XX.	*Hagigah. Moed Qatan.* 1986.
XXI.	*Yebamot.* 1986.
XXII.	*Ketubot.* 1985.
XXIII.	*Nedarim* 1985.
XXIV.	*Nazir.* 1985.
XXV.	*Gittin.* 1985
XXVI.	*Qiddushin.* 1984.
XXVII.	*Sotah.* 1984.
XXVIII.	*Baba Qamma.* 1984.
XXIX.	*Baba Mesia.* 1984.
XXX.	*Baba Batra.* 1984.
XXXI.	*Sanhedrin. Makkot.* 1984.
XXXII.	*Shebuot.* 1983.
XXXIII.	*Abodah Zarah.* 1982.
XXXIV.	*Horayot. Niddah.* 1982.

Edited: *In the Margins of the Yerushalmi. Notes on the English Translation.* Chico: Scholars Press for Brown Judaic Studies, 1983.

Torah from Our Sages: Pirke Avot. A New American Translation and Explanation. Chappaqua: Rossel, 1983. Paperback edition: 1987.

Law as Literature. Chico: Scholars Press, 1983. = *Semeia. An Experimental Journal for Biblical Criticism* Volume 27. Co-edited with William Scott Green.

The Talmud of Babylonia. An American Translation. Chico, then Atlanta: 1984-1995: Scholars Press for Brown Judaic Studies.

I.	*Tractate Berakhot*
II.A.	*Tractate Shabbat. Chapters One and Two.*
II.B.	*Tractate Shabbat Chapters Three through Six*
II.C	*Tractate Shabbat Chapters Seven through Ten*
II.D	*Tractate Shabbat Chapters Eleven through Seventeen*
II.E	*Tractate Shabbat Chapters Eighteen through Twenty-Four*
III.A.	*Tractate Erubin. Chapters One and Two*
III.B.	*Tractate Erubin, Chapters Three and Four*
III.C.	*Tractate Erubin, Chapters Five and Six*
III.D.	*Tractate Erubin, Chapters Seven through Ten*
IV.A	*Tractate Pesahim. Chapter One*
IV.B	*Tractate Pesahim. Chapters Two and Three*
IV.C	*Tractate Pesahim. Chapters Four through Six*
IV.D	*Tractate Pesahim. Chapters Seven and Eight*

IV.E	*Tractate Pesahim. Chapters Nine and Ten*
V.A	*Tractate Yoma. Chapters One and Two*
V.B	*Tractate Yoma. Chapters Three through Five*
V.C	*Tractate Yoma. Chapters Six through Eight*
VI.	*Tractate Sukkah*
XI.	*Tractate Moed Qatan*
XII.	*Tractate Hagigah*
XIII.A.	*Tractate Yebamot. Chapters One through Three*
XIII.B.	*Tractate Yebamot. Chapters Four through Six*
XIII.C.	*Tractate Yebamot. Chapters Seven through Nine*
XIII.D	*Tractate Yebamot. Chapters Ten through Sixteen*
XIV.A.	*Tractate Ketubot. Chapters One through Three*
XIV.B.	*Tractate Ketubot. Chapters Four through Seven*
XIV.C.	*Tractate Ketubot. Chapters Eight through Thirteen*
XV.A.	*Tractate Nedarim. Chapters One through Four*
XV.B.	*Tractate Nedarim. Chapters Five through Eleven*
XVII.	*Tractate Sotah*
XVIII.A.	*Tractate Gittin. Chapters One through Three*
XVIII.B.	*Tractate Gittin. Chapters Four and Five*
XVIII.C.	*Tractate Gittin. Chapters Six through Nine*
XIX.A.	*Tractate Qiddushin. Chapter One*
XIX.B.	*Tractate Qiddushin. Chapters Two through Four*
XX.A.	*Tractate Baba Qamma. Chapters One through Three*
XX.B.	*Tractate Baba Qamma. Chapters Four through Seven*
XX.C	*Tractate Baba Qamma. Chapters Eight through Ten*
XXI.A.	*Tractate Baba Mesia. Introduction. Chapters One and Two*
XXI.B.	*Tractate Baba Mesia. Chapters Three and Four*
XXI.C.	*Tractate Baba Mesia. Chapters Five and Six*
XXI.D.	*Tractate Bava Mesia. Chapters Seven through Ten*
XXII.A.	*Tractate Baba Batra. Chapters One and Two*
XXII.B.	*Tractate Baba Batra. Chapter Three*
XXII.C.	*Tractate Baba Batra. Chapters Four through Six*
XXII.D.	*Tractate Baba Batra. Chapters Seven and Eight*
XXII.E.	*Tractate Baba Batra. Chapters Nine and Ten*
XXIII.A	*Tractate Sanhedrin. Chapters One through Three*
XXIII.B	*Tractate Sanhedrin Chapters Four through Eight*
XXIII.C	*Tractate Sanhedrin Chapters Nine through Eleven*
XXIV.	*Tractate Makkot*
XXV.A.	*Tractate Abodah Zarah. Chapters One and Two*
XXV.B.	*Tractate Abodah Zarah. Chapters Three, Four, and Five*
XXVII..A	*Tractate Shebuot. Chapters One through Three*
XXVII.B	*Tractate Shebuot. Chapters Four through Eight*
XXVIII.A.	*Tractate Zebahim. Chapters One through Three*
XXVIII.B.	*Tractate Zebahim. Chapters Four through Eight*
XXVIII.C.	*Tractate Zebahim. Chapters Nine through Fourteen*
XXIX.A.	*Tractate Menahot. Chapters One through Three*
XXIX.B.	*Tractate Menahot. Chapters Four through Seven*
XXIX.C.	*Tractate Menahot. Chapters Eight through Thirteen*
XXXI.A.	*Tractate Bekhorot. Chapters One through Four*
XXXI.B.	*Tractate Bekhorot. Chapters Five through Nine*
XXXII.	*Tractate Arakhin*

XXXIII.   *Tractate Temurah*
XXXIV.   *Tractate Keritot*
XXXVI.A   *Tractate Niddah. Chapters One through Three*
XXXVI.B   *Tractate Niddah. Chapters Four through Ten*

For Leviticus Rabbah, see below, *Judaism and Scripture: The Evidence of Leviticus Rabbah*

Genesis Rabbah. The Judaic Commentary on Genesis. A New American Translation. Atlanta: Scholars Press for Brown Judaic Studies, 1985. I. *Genesis Rabbah. The Judaic Commentary on Genesis. A New American Translation. Parashiyyot One through Thirty-Three. Genesis 1:1-8:14.*

Genesis Rabbah. The Judaic Commentary on Genesis. A New American Translation. Atlanta: Scholars Press for Brown Judaic Studies, 1985. II. *Genesis Rabbah. The Judaic Commentary on Genesis. A New American Translation. Parashiyyot Thirty-Four through Sixty-Seven. Genesis 8:15-28:9.*

Genesis Rabbah. The Judaic Commentary on Genesis. A New American Translation. Atlanta: Scholars Press for Brown Judaic Studies, 1985. III. *Genesis Rabbah. The Judaic Commentary on Genesis. A New American Translation. Parashiyyot Sixty-Eight through One Hundred. Genesis 28:10-50:26.*

Sifra. The Judaic Commentary on Leviticus. A New Translation. The Leper. Leviticus 13:1-14:57. Chico: Scholars Press for Brown Judaic Studies, 1985. [With a section by Roger Brooks.] Based on *A History of the Mishnaic Law of Purities. VI. Negaim. Sifra.*

Sifré to Numbers. An American Translation. I. 1-58. Atlanta: Scholars Press for Brown Judaic Studies, 1986.

Sifré to Numbers. An American Translation. II. 59-115. Atlanta: Scholars Press for Brown Judaic Studies, 1986. [III. *116-161:* William Scott Green].

The Fathers According to Rabbi Nathan. An Analytical Translation and Explanation. Atlanta: Scholars Press for Brown Judaic Studies, 1986.

Pesiqta deRab Kahana. An Analytical Translation and Explanation. I. 1-14. Atlanta: Scholars Press for Brown Judaic Studies, 1987.

Pesiqta deRab Kahana. An Analytical Translation and Explanation. II. 15-28. With an Introduction to Pesiqta deRab Kahana. Atlanta: Scholars Press for Brown Judaic Studies, 1987.

For Pesiqta Rabbati, see below, *From Tradition to Imitation. The Plan and Program of Pesiqta deRab Kahana and Pesiqta Rabbati.*

Sifré to Deuteronomy. An Analytical Translation. Atlanta: Scholars Press for Brown Judaic Studies, 1987. I. *Pisqaot One through One Hundred Forty-Three. Debarim, Waethanan, Eqeb, Re'eh.*

Sifré to Deuteronomy. An Analytical Translation. Atlanta: Scholars Press for Brown Judaic Studies, 1987. II. *Pisqaot One Hundred Forty-Four through Three Hundred Fifty-Seven. Shofetim, Ki Tese, Ki Tabo, Nesabim, Ha'azinu, Zot Habberakhah.*

Sifra. An Analytical Translation. Atlanta: Scholars Press for Brown Judaic Studies, 1988. I. *Introduction* and *Vayyiqra Dibura Denedabah* and *Vayiqqra Dibura Dehobah.*

Sifra. An Analytical Translation. Atlanta: Scholars Press for Brown Judaic Studies, 1988. II. *Sav, Shemini, Tazria, Negaim, Mesora,* and *Zabim.*

Sifra. An Analytical Translation. Atlanta: Scholars Press for Brown Judaic Studies, 1988. III. *Aharé Mot, Qedoshim, Emor, Behar,* and *Behuqotai.*

Mekhilta Attributed to R. Ishmael. An Analytical Translation. Atlanta: Scholars Press for Brown Judaic Studies, 1988. I. *Pisha, Beshallah, Shirata, and Vayassa.*

Mekhilta Attributed to R. Ishmael. An Analytical Translation. Atlanta: Scholars Press for Brown Judaic Studies, 1988. II. *Amalek, Bahodesh, Neziqin, Kaspa and Shabbata*

Translating the Classics of Judaism. In Theory and in Practice. Atlanta: Scholars Press for Brown Judaic Studies, 1989.

Lamentations Rabbah. An Analytical Translation. Atlanta: Scholars Press for Brown Judaic Studies, 1989.

Esther Rabbah I. An Analytical Translation. Atlanta: Scholars Press for Brown Judaic Studies, 1989.

Ruth Rabbah. An Analytical Translation. Atlanta: Scholars Press for Brown Judaic Studies, 1989.

Song of Songs Rabbah. An Analytical Translation. Volume One. *Song of Songs Rabbah to Song Chapters One through Three.* Atlanta: Scholars Press for Brown Judaic Studies, 1990.

Song of Songs Rabbah. An Analytical Translation. Volume Two. *Song of Songs Rabbah to Song Chapters Four through Eight.* Atlanta: Scholars Press for Brown Judaic Studies, 1990.

Introductions and Studies

A History of the Mishnaic Law of Purities. Leiden: Brill, 1977. XXI. *The Redaction and Formulation of the Order of Purities in the Mishnah and Tosefta.*

A History of the Mishnaic Law of Purities. Leiden: Brill, 1977. XXII. *The Mishnaic System of Uncleanness. Its Context and History.*

The Mishnah before 70. Atlanta: Scholars Press for Brown Judaic Studies, 1987. [Reprise of pertinent results of *A History of the Mishnah Law of Purities* Vols. III, V, VIII, X, XII, XIV, XVI, XVII, and XVIII.]

A History of the Mishnaic Law of Holy Things. Leiden: Brill, 1979. VI. *The Mishnaic System of Sacrifice and Sanctuary.*

A History of the Mishnaic Law of Women. Leiden: Brill, 1980. V. *The Mishnaic System of Women.*

A History of the Mishnaic Law of Appointed Times. Leiden: Brill, 1981. V. *The Mishnaic System of Appointed Times.*

A History of the Mishnaic Law of Damages. Leiden: Brill, 1985. V. *The Mishnaic System of Damages*

The Talmud of the Land of Israel. A Preliminary Translation and Explanation. Chicago: The University of Chicago Press, 1983. XXXV. *Introduction. Taxonomy.*

The Integrity of Leviticus Rabbah. The Problem of the Autonomy of a Rabbinic Document. Chico: Scholars Press for Brown Judaic Studies, 1985.

Comparative Midrash: The Plan and Program of Genesis Rabbah and Leviticus Rabbah. Atlanta: Scholars Press for Brown Judaic Studies, 1986.

From Tradition to Imitation. The Plan and Program of Pesiqta deRab Kahana and Pesiqta Rabbati. Atlanta: Scholars Press for Brown Judaic Studies, 1987. [With a fresh translation of Pesiqta Rabbati *Pisqaot 1-5, 15.*]

Canon and Connection: Intertextuality in Judaism. Lanham: University Press of America. *Studies in Judaism* Series, 1986.

Midrash as Literature: The Primacy of Documentary Discourse. Lanham: University Press of America *Studies in Judaism* series, 1987.

The Bavli and its Sources: The Question of Tradition in the Case of Tractate Sukkah. Atlanta: Scholars Press for Brown Judaic Studies, 1987.

Invitation to Midrash: The Working of Rabbinic Bible Interpretation. A Teaching Book. San Francisco: Harper & Row, 1988.

Russian translation: Moscow, 1997: University of Moscow Judaic Studies Department.

What Is Midrash? Philadelphia: Fortress Press, 1987. Second printing: Atlanta: Scholars Press, 1994.

Dutch translation: Hilversum: Gooi & Sticht, 1994.
Japanese translation: Tokyo: Kyo Bun Kwan, 1995.

Sifré to Deuteronomy. An Introduction to the Rhetorical, Logical, and Topical Program. Atlanta: Scholars Press for Brown Judaic Studies, 1987.

Uniting the Dual Torah: Sifra and the Problem of the Mishnah. Cambridge and New York: Cambridge University Press, 1989.

Sifra in Perspective: The Documentary Comparison of the Midrashim of Ancient Judaism Atlanta: Scholars Press for Brown Judaic Studies, 1988.

Mekhilta Attributed to R. Ishmael. An Introduction to Judaism's First Scriptural Encyclopaedia. Atlanta: Scholars Press for Brown Judaic Studies, 1988.

The Midrash Compilations of the Sixth and Seventh Centuries. An Introduction to the Rhetorical Logical, and Topical Program. I. *Lamentations Rabbah.* Atlanta: Scholars Press for Brown Judaic Studies, 1990.

The Midrash Compilations of the Sixth and Seventh Centuries: An Introduction to the Rhetorical Logical, and Topical Program. II. *Esther Rabbah I.* Atlanta: Scholars Press for Brown Judaic Studies, 1990.

The Midrash Compilations of the Sixth and Seventh Centuries: An Introduction to the Rhetorical Logical, and Topical Program. III. *Ruth Rabbah.* Atlanta: Scholars Press for Brown Judaic Studies, 1990.

The Midrash Compilations of the Sixth and Seventh Centuries: An Introduction to the Rhetorical Logical, and Topical Program. IV. *Song of Songs Rabbah.* Atlanta: Scholars Press for Brown Judaic Studies, 1990.

A Midrash Reader Minneapolis, 1990: Augsburg-Fortress. Second printing: Atlanta: Scholars Press, 1994.

Making the Classics in Judaism: The Three Stages of Literary Formation. Atlanta: Scholars Press for Brown Judaic Studies, 1990.

The Mishnah. An Introduction. Northvale, N.J.: Jason Aronson, Inc., 1989. Paperback edition: 1994.

The Midrash. An Introduction. Northvale: Jason Aronson, Inc., 1990. Paperback edition: 1994.

The Yerushalmi. The Talmud of the Land of Israel. An Introduction. Northvale: Jason Aronson, Inc, 1992.

The Tosefta. An Introduction. Atlanta: Scholars Press for South Florida Studies in the History of Judaism, 1992.

The Bavli. The Talmud of Babylonia. An Introduction. Atlanta: Scholars Press for South Florida Studies in the History of Judaism, 1992.

The Canonical History of Ideas. The Place of the So-called Tannaite Midrashim, Mekhilta Attributed to R. Ishmael, Sifra, Sifré to Numbers, and Sifré to Deuteronomy. Atlanta: Scholars Press for South Florida Studies in the History of Judaism, 1990.

The Talmud: Close Encounters. Minneapolis: Fortress Press, 1991.

Tradition as Selectivity: Scripture, Mishnah, Tosefta, and Midrash in the Talmud of Babylonia. The Case of Tractate Arakhin. Atlanta: Scholars Press for South Florida Studies in the History of Judaism, 1990.

Language as Taxonomy. The Rules for Using Hebrew and Aramaic in the Babylonian Talmud. Atlanta: Scholars Press for South Florida Studies in the History of Judaism, 1990.

The Bavli That Might Have Been: The Tosefta's Theory of Mishnah-Commentary Compared with That of the Babylonian Talmud. Atlanta: Scholars Press for South Florida Studies in the History of Judaism, 1990.

The Rules of Composition of the Talmud of Babylonia. The Cogency of the Bavli's Composite. Atlanta: Scholars Press for South Florida Studies in the History of Judaism, 1991.

The Bavli's One Voice: Types and Forms of Analytical Discourse and Their Fixed Order of Appearance. Atlanta: Scholars Press for South Florida Studies in the History of Judaism, 1991.

The Bavli's One Statement. The Metapropositional Program of Babylonian Talmud Tractate Zebahim Chapters One and Five. Atlanta: Scholars Press for South Florida Studies in the History of Judaism, 1991.

How the Bavli Shaped Rabbinic Discourse. Atlanta: Scholars Press for South Florida Studies in the History of Judaism, 1991.

The Bavli's Massive Miscellanies. The Problem of Agglutinative Discourse in the Talmud of Babylonia. Atlanta: Scholars Press for South Florida Studies in the History of Judaism, 1992.

Sources and Traditions. Types of Composition in the Talmud of Babylonia. Atlanta: Scholars Press for South Florida Studies in the History of Judaism, 1992.

The Law Behind the Laws. The Bavli's Essential Discourse. Atlanta: Scholars Press for South Florida Studies in the History of Judaism, 1992.

The Bavli's Primary Discourse. Mishnah Commentary, Its Rhetorical Paradigms and Their Theological Implications in the Talmud of Babylonia Tractate Moed Qatan. Atlanta: Scholars Press for South Florida Studies in the History of Judaism, 1992.

The Discourse of the Bavli: Language, Literature, and Symbolism. Five Recent Findings. Atlanta: Scholars Press for South Florida Studies in the History of Judaism, 1991.

How to Study the Bavli: The Languages, Literatures, and Lessons of the Talmud of Babylonia. Atlanta: Scholars Press for South Florida Studies in the History of Judaism, 1992.

Form-Analytical Comparison in Rabbinic Judaism. Structure and Form in The Fathers *and* The Fathers According to Rabbi Nathan. Atlanta: Scholars Press for South Florida Studies in the History of Judaism, 1992.

The Bavli's Intellectual Character. The Generative Problematic in Bavli Baba Qamma Chapter One and Bavli Shabbat Chapter One. Atlanta: Scholars Press for South Florida Studies in the History of Judaism, 1992.

Decoding the Talmud's Exegetical Program: From Detail to Principle in the Bavli's Quest for Generalization. Tractate Shabbat. Atlanta: Scholars Press for South Florida Studies in the History of Judaism, 1992.

The Principal Parts of the Bavli's Discourse: A Final Taxonomy. Mishnah-Commentary, Sources, Traditions, and Agglutinative Miscellanies. Atlanta: Scholars Press for South Florida Studies in the History of Judaism, 1992.

The Torah in the Talmud. A Taxonomy of the Uses of Scripture in the Talmuds. Tractate Qiddushin in the Talmud of Babylonia and the Talmud of the Land of Israel. I. Bavli Qiddushin Chapter One. Atlanta: Scholars Press for South Florida Studies in the History of Judaism, 1993.

The Torah in the Talmud. A Taxonomy of the Uses of Scripture in the Talmuds. Tractate Qiddushin in the Talmud of Babylonia and the Talmud of the Land of Israel. II. Yerushalmi Qiddushin Chapter One. And a Comparison of the Uses of Scripture by the Two Talmuds. Atlanta: Scholars Press for South Florida Studies in the History of Judaism, 1993.

The Bavli's Unique Voice. A Systematic Comparison of the Talmud of Babylonia and the Talmud of the Land of Israel. Volume One. *Bavli and Yerushalmi Qiddushin Chapter One Compared and Contrasted.* Atlanta: Scholars Press for South Florida Studies in the History of Judaism, 1993.

The Bavli's Unique Voice. A Systematic Comparison of the Talmud of Babylonia and the Talmud of the Land of Israel. Volume Two. *Yerushalmi's, Bavli's, and Other Canonical Documents' Treatment of the Program of Mishnah-Tractate Sukkah Chapters One, Two, and Four Compared and Contrasted. A Reprise and Revision of* The Bavli and its Sources. Atlanta: Scholars Press for South Florida Studies in the History of Judaism, 1993.

The Bavli's Unique Voice. A Systematic Comparison of the Talmud of Babylonia and the Talmud of the Land of Israel. Volume Three. *Bavli and Yerushalmi to Selected Mishnah-Chapters in the Division of Moed. Erubin Chapter One, and Moed Qatan Chapter Three.* Atlanta: Scholars Press for South Florida Studies in the History of Judaism, 1993.

The Bavli's Unique Voice. A Systematic Comparison of the Talmud of Babylonia and the Talmud of the Land of Israel. Volume Four. *Bavli and Yerushalmi to Selected Mishnah-Chapters in the Division of Nashim. Gittin Chapter Five and Nedarim Chapter One. And Niddah Chapter One.* Atlanta: Scholars Press for South Florida Studies in the History of Judaism, 1993.

The Bavli's Unique Voice. A Systematic Comparison of the Talmud of Babylonia and the Talmud of the Land of Israel. Volume Five. *Bavli and Yerushalmi to Selected*

Mishnah-Chapters in the Division of Neziqin. Baba Mesia Chapter One and Makkot Chapters One and Two. Atlanta: Scholars Press for South Florida Studies in the History of Judaism, 1993.

The Bavli's Unique Voice. A Systematic Comparison of the Talmud of Babylonia and the Talmud of the Land of Israel. Volume Six. *Bavli and Yerushalmi to a Miscellany of Mishnah-Chapters. Gittin Chapter One, Qiddushin Chapter Two, and Hagigah Chapter Three.* Atlanta: Scholars Press for South Florida Studies in the History of Judaism, 1993.

The Bavli's Unique Voice. Volume Seven. *What Is Unique about the Bavli in Context? An Answer Based on Inductive Description, Analysis, and Comparison.* Atlanta: Scholars Press for South Florida Studies in the History of Judaism, 1993.

From Text to Historical Context in Rabbinic Judaism: Historical Facts in Systemic Documents. I. *The Mishnah, Tosefta, Abot, Sifra, Sifré to Numbers, and Sifré to Deuteronomy.* Atlanta: Scholars Press for South Florida Studies in the History of Judaism, 1993.

From Text to Historical Context in Rabbinic Judaism: Historical Facts in Systemic Documents. II. *The Later Midrash-Compilations: Genesis Rabbah, Leviticus Rabbah, Pesiqta deRab Kahana.* Atlanta: Scholars Press for South Florida Studies in the History of Judaism, 1994.

From Text to Historical Context in Rabbinic Judaism: Historical Facts in Systemic Documents. III. *The Latest Midrash-Compilations: Song of Songs Rabbah, Ruth Rabbah, Esther Rabbah I, and Lamentations Rabbah.* Atlanta: Scholars Press for South Florida Studies in the History of Judaism, 1994.

Introduction to Rabbinic Literature. New York: Doubleday. The Doubleday Anchor Reference Library, 1994. Religious Book Club Selection, 1994.

Italian: Bologna, 1996: Edizioni Piemme

Where the Talmud Comes From: A Talmudic Phenomenology. Identifying the Free-Standing Building Blocks of Talmudic Discourse. Atlanta: Scholars Press for South Florida Studies in the History of Judaism, 1995.

The Initial Phases of the Talmud's Judaism. Atlanta: Scholars Press for South Florida Studies in the History of Judaism, 1995. I. *Exegesis of Scripture.*

The Initial Phases of the Talmud's Judaism. Atlanta: Scholars Press for South Florida Studies in the History of Judaism, 1995. II. *Exemplary Virtue.*

The Initial Phases of the Talmud's Judaism. Atlanta: Scholars Press for South Florida Studies in the History of Judaism, 1995. III. *Social Ethicse.*

The Initial Phases of the Talmud's Judaism. Atlanta: Scholars Press for South Florida Studies in the History of Judaism, 1995. IV. *Theology.*

Talmudic Dialectics: Types and Forms. Atlanta: Scholars Press for South Florida Studies in the History of Judaism, 1995. I. *Introduction. Tractate Berakhot and the Divisions of Appointed Times and Women.*

Talmudic Dialectics: Types and Forms. Atlanta: Scholars Press for South Florida Studies in the History of Judaism, 1995. II. *The Divisions of Damages and Holy Things and Tractate Niddah.*

Are the Talmuds Interchangeable? Christine Hayes's Blunder. Atlanta: Scholars Press for South Florida Studies on the History of Judaism, 1996.

Index

Index of Scriptural References